THE ZODIAC ORACLE

WHAT THE STARS TELL YOU ABOUT YOUR PERSONALITY AND FUTURE

ALICE EKREK

This edition published in 2018 by Arcturus Publishing Limited
26/27 Bickels Yard, 151–153 Bermondsey Street,
London SE1 3HA

AD006194UK

Printed in the UK

Contents

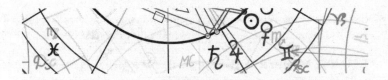

Introduction

What is Astrology?

Most of us have a basic knowledge of what astrology is – we encounter it daily in the form of newspaper, magazine and Internet horoscope columns. These simplified forms of astrology have enjoyed mass appeal over the last century, but did you know that these are merely the tip of an enormous astrological iceberg?

So much more than a mere coffee-break activity, astrology is a group of systems, traditions and beliefs for studying the heavens in order to find out something about life here on Earth. Some dictionaries refer to it as a 'pseudoscience' but this term undermines the power of something that has been practised and perfected over millennia, and is central to the development of science as we know it today. Put in the simplest of terms, astrologers look to the planets and their positions in the zodiac, as well as their positions in relation to one another, to divine the future and tell us about an individual, an animal, a decision or an event – anything that begins at a particular point in time and space.

In the same way that people interpret the symbolism of dreams to gain insight into the workings of the psyche, so astrologers interpret the movements of the planets as symbolic of developments on Earth.

How Does it Work?

We often say that a particular event, or union, was 'written in the stars'. But was it? Many critics of astrology say that they can't see how the transit of the planets could possibly influence our lives here on Earth. Here are two scenarios showing how they can, and do:

EXAMPLE NUMBER 1: THE WEEK YOU'D RATHER FORGET

Have you ever experienced one of those weeks when everything goes wrong and the universe seems to be turned against you? First, you miss your train to work because you failed to properly read and memorize the new timetable, and then, when you (finally) arrive at work, you ignore the sign that clearly reads 'wet floor' and stumble, spraining an ankle and denting your pride. Not only that, but your email account won't receive messages properly, your annual appraisal goes badly (despite the fact that you've worked unusually hard all year), you row with your partner and your kids… the list of mishaps and miscommunication goes on and on!

The truth is we've all had weeks like that, and we've all wondered why on earth nothing is going right for us. The answer may be that Mercury, the planet of communication, is in retrograde (appearing to travel backwards in the sky) making relationships terse and scuppering even the best-laid plans. Wouldn't you like to know when a week like that is coming up, so you could prepare for it a little better?

EXAMPLE NUMBER 2: THE MID-LIFE CRISIS

It may be a stereotype, but it's also a scene we often encounter in real life, as well as in movies: the middle-aged man who suddenly gives up a high-powered job in the city to follow a long-held passion for llama farming, gets himself a younger girlfriend or buys himself a cherry red sports car. We've seen it all before, but did you know that Uranus, a planet of revolutionary change, reaches its first opposition at around the age of 42, and can bring with it the excitement of new experiences and the urge to break free from what feels like the confines of everything we have built so far? It feels somehow comforting to think that there is a higher force at work here, doesn't it?

There are many books, studies and theories about exactly how astrology works, but at heart it remains a mystery.

We live in a scientific age, where science is valued above all other disciplines. This approach has led to enormous benefits worldwide, but the human mind is capable of imaginative and intuitive thinking as well, and these are essential in developing wisdom and providing insight into our lives. Both are central to the practice of astrology.

In this book we will be looking at the astronomical facts and the symbolic traditions of astrology. These two approaches sit alongside each other comfortably for astrologers, and the more we study and use astrology, the more we are astounded by how well the system works.

Where Does it Come From?

Studying astrology and the meanings behind the astrological symbols will open the door to a different kind of knowledge that has been passed down from generation to generation for thousands of years, and even pre-dates some of the world's major religions.

Since ancient times, stories about the Earth and heavens, planets and stars, and the characters that populated them, have grown out of human imagination and experience. Today we continue to tell these stories in films, plays, novels and songs, and observe them all around

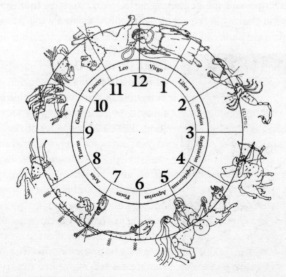

The zodiac constellations form the numbers on a huge clock around the ecliptic circle.

us. The meanings of the astrological symbols are connected with these mythical tales. Clusters of stars captured the imagination of ancient peoples, who joined them up to form the images of the epic characters that populated their myths. Early prototypes of constellations we use today can be traced back to the Mesopotamian regions during the Bronze Age – more than 3,000 years ago. The twelve constellations that astrologers refer to today have been in use, in their current form, at least since the 1st century BCE.

We can see from the images of the constellations as they appear in the sky that they overlap each other and take up different amounts of space. It was the Babylonian astrologer-astronomer priests who divided the constellations into twelve equal parts of 30°, forming the horoscopic circle. This system was much more practical to use, and simplified their jobs considerably. This symbolic representation of the zodiac belt has been used by astrologers ever since.

As the horoscopic chart was evolving alongside the calendar system, the year was divided into twelve months and each month was associated with one of the constellations. The vernal equinox, around 20 March, marked the beginning of the year. Since, at that time, the Sun rose in the sky in the constellation of Aries, Aries was associated with the first month, and so on through the zodiac.

Carl Gustav Jung (26 July 1875 – 6 June 1961).

CARL JUNG AND SYNCHRONICITY

In the 1930s, the Swiss psychiatrist and founder of analytical psychology, Carl Jung, published his paper on the theory of synchronicity – a term he coined to describe the meaningful coincidences all of us experience in everyday life. Jung wrote about his own experiences, and those of his patients, of the guiding power of coincidences and the ability they have to change a person's outlook and therefore, his/her future. He conducted statistical experiments using astrological data to demonstrate his findings.

Many people find that the coincidences that are smattered throughout our everyday existence – the chance meetings, the missed trains, the symbols that recur again and again in seemingly unconnected places – give us a sense that there is some pattern at work in the universe. Astrology is about noticing these meaningful coincidences, becoming aware of the patterns that exist all around us, and thinking about what they might mean for us.

Jung himself practised astrology, and found it an invaluable tool for gaining insight into his own experiences as well as those of his patients. He explored the ancient philosophies and alchemical texts from which astrology developed to inform his psychological theories. In turn, his theories have been incorporated into the astrology we practise today, including his theory of synchronicity, the collective unconscious, archetypes, and the path of the individual towards meaningful development, or individuation.

WHO ELSE HAS USED ASTROLOGY?

Throughout history, a surprising number of influential men and women have used astrology to help achieve their aims. In fact the world's first billionaire, J.P. Morgan, is known to have said 'millionaires don't use astrology, billionaires do'. He clearly thought he owed at least some of his success to its principles, and he wasn't the only one.

Before modern times, astrologers were used by royal courts around the world, and the early birth charts were drawn up for kings and queens, as representatives of the society they ruled. In 1556, the Italian princess Catherine De Medici summoned the French astrologer Nostrodamus to draw up her children's horoscopes. She was so convinced of the power of astrology that she consulted Nostradamus right up until his death in 1566. Queen Elizabeth I's close relationship with her renowned astrologer, John Dee, is well documented. Dee was one of her most trusted advisors during her turbulent time as Queen of England.

In the preface to his famous work, *Poor Richard's Almanac*, Benjamin Franklin refers to astrology as a 'divine' and 'noble art'. This has led many to believe that he too was a follower.

During the Second World War, Winston Churchill consulted an astrologer. Not because he was a believer in astrology himself, but because intelligence suggested that Adolf Hitler consulted an astrologer, and he wanted to try and second-guess his actions. The British intelligence services hired a Hungarian astrologer named Ludwig von Whol and accommodated him at an exclusive hotel in Park Lane, London, where he made his predictions. They also reputedly sent him to the US to help persuade the Americans to enter the war.

Following the 1981 assassination attempt on Ronald Reagan, Nancy Reagan is said to have consulted an astrologer on all matters to do with his schedule. The positions of the planets were used to determine when the time was right to sign a document, fly abroad or attend a state dinner. The media may have derided her, but to all intents and purposes her method was found to work.

Other notables who have nurtured an interest in astrology include Johannes Kepler, Isaac Newton, D.H. Lawrence, Ted Hughes, W.B. Yeats, and Princess Diana. So, merely by picking up this book, you have found yourself in great company.

How Does This Book Work?

The first section of this book is called Understanding Your Birth Chart. Its aim is to introduce you to the building blocks of a birth chart, including the twelve signs of the zodiac, the ten planets and luminaries, the twelve houses, and the various aspects and angles that make up your horoscope. You can use it to find out exactly what a birth chart is, where you can acquire one and what information (or birth data) you will need. Use this section to familiarize yourself with the various elements of the birth chart, so that you can begin to apply the information to your own chart.

The second section, The Power of the Planets, goes into further detail regarding each of the ten planets and luminaries, and explains how they may be acting upon your chart. Which planet is your chart ruler, and how does its position in your chart affect your life and determine your future? What does the position of Venus in your chart say about your relationships and the kinds of partners you attract? And where have all these ideas come from, anyway? The answers to these questions can be found in this section of the book.

The third section, The Signs and Their Planetary Rulers, follows on from the previous section to examine each of the twelve signs of the zodiac and their planetary rulers. Most of us know a little about our Sun (otherwise known as our 'star') sign, but did you also know that the sign on the Ascendant (your rising sign), and the position of the Moon at the time of your birth, are almost as important to your personality as the position of the Sun? Are you as familiar with your Sun sign as you think you are? This section will tell you everything you need to know.

The fourth and final section of this book is called the Day-by-Day Oracle. Use it to look up your birth date for added insight and advice. Each reading provides you with a daily affirmation specifically designed to invite the planets to work for you, to strengthen relationships and take that next step on the path towards your ultimate goal in life.

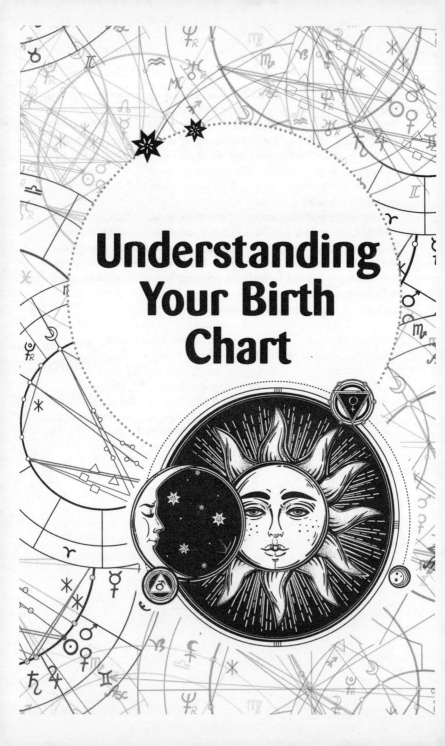

Understanding Your Birth Chart

What is a Birth Chart and How is it Used?

A birth chart takes information about the date, time and location of your birth, and the corresponding location of each planet within the zodiac, and displays that information in the form of a map. An astrologer – and by that I mean anyone who has studied astrology and understands the meanings associated with the planets – is able to read the chart in order to tell us something about your personality and experiences, and foretell what the future may hold for you.

Birth charts don't just apply to individual humans, but can also be cast for anything which is born, or begins, at a particular point in time – including animals, countries, companies, weddings, funerals, births and other events.

The meaning of each component of the birth chart follows basic guidelines and traditional associations that have developed over many millennia. However, the language of symbols is not an exact science, and other factors are involved, such as intuition, understanding, imagination and the psyche. It is useful to remember that methods of interpretation vary depending on the person reading the chart, and which form of astrology they have studied.

You may find that learning about the basic building blocks of a chart, and the meanings assigned to them, often feels like you are remembering something that you already knew, tapping into knowledge that was already inside you, waiting to be awakened.

In this section we will take a closer look at the components of a birth chart, explain what each one means and what you can learn from it.

Calculating Your Birth Chart

There are numerous books and websites that can help you to obtain a diagram of your own birth chart. Many of these will explain how to calculate your chart from scratch, and you will need a collection of tables of astrological data – called an Ephemeris – for the year in which you were born. Calculating a birth chart and drawing it by hand is extremely rewarding, but will take many hours to complete.

These days many astrologers use computer software to calculate charts in an instant. Many websites provide chart calculation software free of charge – one such website is www.astro.com. Birth charts can also be purchased from various Internet sites as well as from astrology shops.

You should request that the chart is drawn using the Placidus house system – the reason for this will be explained later in this section, when we come to talk about the astrological houses (see page 29).

Your Birth Data

In order to be able to calculate your chart – either by hand or using a computer – you will need to know your birth date, the location and the precise time at which you were born, to the minute, if possible.

You may not know the exact time of your birth, and if you can't find out this information don't worry – it is still possible to draw up your chart and interpret it, but less information will be gleaned from it. For example, certain factors of your chart, such as your Ascendant, angles and houses, can't be taken into consideration; also, you won't know the precise location of your inner planets, particularly the Moon, which is the fastest moving planetary body and can travel through half a sign and move between signs over the course of a day. For this reason it is worth asking parents and relatives, checking birth certificates and hospital records to find out the time of your birth so you can cast the most accurate possible chart.

If you have no way of finding out exactly when you were born, some astrologers will try to work out the correct time from your character, appearance and life experiences (a technique known as rectification). It is also quite common for astrologers to draw up a chart for noon on the day of your birth when the actual time is not available.

If you don't know the time of your birth to the minute, but have a pretty good general idea – for example, you know you were born around lunchtime – you may want to pick a precise time and stick to that. In astrology there are many guidelines for plotting, drawing and interpreting birth charts, but there is also a magical element that depends on a person's intention and intuition – if you have a sense of the correctness of a particular time, then go ahead and experiment with it to see how it works.

The Building Blocks of the Birth Chart

The Horoscopic Circle

The astrological birth chart, or horoscope, is a circular diagram representing the horizon and skyscape at the moment of birth from a

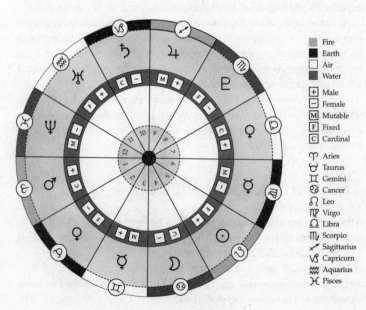

	Fire
	Earth
	Air
	Water

⊞	Male
⊟	Female
M	Mutable
F	Fixed
C	Cardinal

♈	Aries
♉	Taurus
♊	Gemini
♋	Cancer
♌	Leo
♍	Virgo
♎	Libra
♏	Scorpio
♐	Sagittarius
♑	Capricorn
♒	Aquarius
♓	Pisces

particular point on Earth, with the individual placed at an imaginary point at the centre. It is from this position that the surrounding horoscope is calculated.

The main components of the birth chart are the planets, the signs of the zodiac, angles, houses, and aspects, and all of these components are plotted within the horoscopic circle.

Although today's birth chart is most commonly in the shape of a circle, in medieval times it was popularly displayed in the form of a square, and the square is still popular in Vedic (also known as Hindu or Jyotish) astrology, which is used in India. Many other shapes and styles have been used by various astrological traditions around the world, and at different times. Whichever shape is used, the horoscope is a symbolic representation of the position of the planets and other components of the chart, for a particular date, time and place. Here we will focus on the circular version because it is the form you are most likely to encounter.

In esoteric symbolism, the circle represents wholeness, unity, heaven, sacred space, and the female principle, while the cross represents matter, incarnation, the four elements of earth, air, fire and water, and the male principle. Put simply, the circle with a cross symbolizes the joining of heaven and Earth. In astrology today, these shapes are joined to form the basic structure of the birth chart, and can be understood to represent the divine incarnation of the individual, object or event being born into the world.

The circle also reflects the cyclical movement of the planets in the solar system which are integral to astrology – astrologers believe that through the cycles of the heavens we learn to explore the unseen cycles in our own lives.

The Astrological Planets

Most of today's astrologers recognize ten planets and use them to plot the birth chart. They are: The Sun, Moon, Mercury, Venus, Mars, Jupiter, Saturn, Uranus, Neptune and Pluto.

The Sun and Moon are not strictly planets, but in astrology they are often referred to as such for the sake of simplicity. They are also traditionally known as the *luminaries*.

The first seven planets and luminaries – the Sun, Moon, Mercury, Venus, Mars, Jupiter and Saturn – were known to the ancients as they were visible in the sky and could be seen with the naked eye. These have become known as the *inner* or *personal* planets (Sun, Moon, Mercury, Venus and Mars) and the *social* planets (Jupiter and Saturn).

The development of telescopes led to the discovery of the *outer* or *transpersonal* planets – Uranus in 1781, Neptune in 1846 and Pluto in 1930. Those responsible for naming the planets kept to the theme of gods of Greek and Roman mythology.

Astrologers interpreted the meanings of the outer planets according to the mythology of their names, the pace of their cycles and their physical characteristics, along with what was happening in the world at the time of their discovery. These meanings were then applied to the planets' positions in a specific birth chart to see how they might be working in the life of the individual in question.

Through these methods, astrologers have tended to conclude that the outer planets of Uranus, Neptune and Pluto are 'collective' planets, which have more to do with the generation you are born into and the society in which you live than with your personal life, although the two are, of course, intertwined – particularly when the outer planets are in contact with personal planets in the birth chart.

A NOTE ABOUT PLUTO

Planetary bodies, dwarf planets and planetoids are still being discovered, and will probably go on being discovered for as long as the technology is available. Some of the most recent major discoveries were Chiron in 1977, Sedna in 2003 and Eris in 2006.

Many of these new planetary bodies are used, to a greater or lesser extent, in astrology today, although they tend to be assigned minor significance when compared to the ten traditional and outer planets, which have made up the tried and tested building blocks of astrology for some time.

The reclassification of Pluto by the IAU in 2004 captured the imaginations of a generation. Widespread protests ensued when the IAU released a revised definition of what constitutes a planet and Pluto was found to be outside the new definition. Whatever its astronomical classification, Pluto continues to be used in astrology as if it were one of the planets in the solar system and, for the purpose of this book, we will look at the traditional inner and contemporary outer planets up to, and including, Pluto.

PLANETARY RULERSHIPS

Each of the ten astrological planets have been assigned rulership of specific signs of the zodiac. In the birth chart, the qualities associated with a planet are most evident when the planet is in the sign ruled by it. For example, Mars rules the sign of Aries, and is associated with characteristics like forcefulness and passion. So if you were born with Mars in Aries, you will feel the effects of Mars most strongly – you may be a dynamic and competitive person, who is quick to express excitement or anger.

Before the outer planets were discovered, Scorpio was ruled by Mars, Aquarius was ruled by Saturn, and Pisces' ruler was Jupiter. However, since the discovery of the outer planets, Pluto has been assigned as the ruler of Scorpio, Uranus is the ruler of Aquarius and Neptune is the ruler of Pisces. These days both the old and new rulers tend to be taken into consideration for these signs.

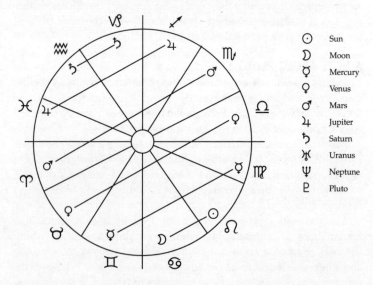

The horoscopic circle showing traditional planetary rulerships.

The Signs of the Zodiac

The zodiac is an imaginary belt that runs along the Sun's apparent pathway around the Earth – known as the ecliptic.

The word 'zodiac' is Greek in origin and means 'circle of animals'. The zodiac belt is made up of patterns of stars which form the twelve signs of the zodiac, many of which (though not all) are represented by animals. They are: Aries the Ram, Taurus the Bull, Gemini the Twins, Cancer the Crab, Leo the Lion, Virgo the Maiden, Libra the Scales, Scorpio the Scorpion, Sagittarius the Archer, Capricorn the Goat, Aquarius the Water Bearer and Pisces the Fish. The Sun, Moon and planets all appear to travel along the ecliptic against the backdrop of the constellations that form the zodiac belt.

The constellations only appear to form these patterns from Earth, as in reality the stars in each constellation are at vastly differing distances from each other, and if viewed from another part of space they would not appear to be in the same vicinity at

TABLE OF PLANETS AND RULERSHIPS

SIGN	TRADITIONAL RULER	NEW RULER
Aries	Mars	
Taurus	Venus	
Gemini	Mercury	
Cancer	Moon	
Leo	Sun	
Virgo	Mercury	
Libra	Venus	
Scorpio	Mars	Pluto
Sagittarius	Jupiter	
Capricorn	Saturn	
Aquarius	Saturn	Uranus
Pisces	Jupiter	Neptune

all – yet another example of the value of the imagination as well as the meaningful coincidences that are scattered throughout the astrological tradition.

Although the actual constellations for each sign of the zodiac are of varying sizes in the sky, and often overlap each other, astrologers since the ancient Greeks have taken a symbolic approach and divide the signs into twelve equally-sized 30° segments along the ecliptic and in the birth chart.

Each planet travels through the ecliptic at varying speeds, and their positions in the zodiac are constantly changing, as are their positions in relation to each other. The birth chart provides a snapshot of the position of the planets at a particular moment, from a particular location on Earth.

When a planet is travelling through a sign of the zodiac, we say it is 'in' that sign. For example, in the tropical zodiac, the Sun is in the sign of Pisces from around 20 February to 20 March, so, if you were born during that period, you will have your Sun in Pisces.

In the birth chart, the symbols of the twelve signs of the zodiac are drawn around the outer rim of the horoscopic circle in an anti-clockwise direction. The symbols of the planets are normally drawn within this rim, next to the degree of the zodiac in which the planet is placed.

You may wish to practise drawing the symbols for the planets and signs of the zodiac to help you become familiar with them.

The signs of the zodiac have inspired artists and storytellers for millennia, and can be seen in the buildings and landscapes all around us. Some famous examples are the stained glass images of the zodiac at Chartres Cathedral in France, the astronomical clock in Prague, Czech Republic, and the Glastonbury zodiac, which is a series of pathways, signs, landmarks and natural features that mark out the symbols of the zodiac across the landscape around Glastonbury in Somerset, England.

A NOTE ABOUT THE PRECESSION OF THE EQUINOXES

The precession of the equinoxes is an astronomical phenomenon that refers to slight shifts in the Earth's axial rotation, which means that over the years it has become out of sync with the position of the Sun and the constellations as they appeared in the sky in the first millennium BCE.

Due to this phenomenon, the Sun no longer rises in the constellation of Aries at the vernal equinox around 20 March, and the Sun's journey through the other signs of the zodiac no longer aligns with the same months of the year as it used to – in Aries and Libra at the spring and autumn equinoxes, or Cancer and Capricorn at the winter and summer solstices.

Western astrology tends not to take the precession of the equinoxes into account, and the tropical zodiac, as it has become known, continues to use the original division of the zodiac signs – beginning with 0° Aries at the vernal equinox around 20 March. This is mainly because Greek philosophers, such as Ptolemy, shaped the way we practise astrology today, and modern Western astrologers appreciate the practical simplicity as well as the enduring symbolic value of the original system.

Vedic astrology tends to use the sidereal zodiac, which takes the precession of the equinoxes into consideration and uses the actual positions of the signs as they appear in the sky.

At the moment there is about 24° difference between the tropical and the sidereal zodiacs, so that 0° Aries in the tropical zodiac is actually around 6° Pisces in the sidereal zodiac. In real terms this means that a Western (tropical) birth chart for a person born on, or around, 20 March would show the Sun in Aries, but a Vedic (sidereal) birth chart would show the Sun in Pisces, and the whole chart would be moved back by 24°.

Many critics of astrology find this to be one of the shortcomings of astrological theory – how can both tropical and sidereal zodiacs be correct? However, this is just one of the many differences between the various branches of astrology, and even though each system uses different criteria, they are thought to have their own integrity, and each system is found to work. For the purpose of this book, we will be using the tropical zodiac, as is common in Western astrology.

The Elements and Polarities

The four elements – fire, earth, air and water – form the bedrock of astrological theory and practice. Each of the signs belong to a particular element – Aries is a fire sign, Taurus an earth sign, Gemini an air sign, Cancer a water sign, and so on around the zodiac.

The four elements are traditionally known as the triplicities, because there are three signs of the zodiac in each element. The elements are further divided into polarities – earth and water are considered to be negative, feminine or yin principles, while air and fire are considered to be positive, masculine or yang principles.

To work out your element balance, you first need to look at the planets in your birth chart and find out which signs of the zodiac they occupy. The planets (particularly the inner planets, and especially the Sun and Moon) bring those signs and elements to life, and help to make you who you are.

You can check the general element balance of your birth chart to find out:

- if you have planets in all the elements;
- if there is an emphasis in one or two elements;
- if any elements are missing.

A balance between all the elements is favoured in the birth chart, while a predominance of fire and air signs can suggest an extroverted, active nature, and a predominance of earth and water signs indicates an introverted, passive nature (although obviously this depends on the other factors at work in the chart).

If you do have an emphasis in some elements, they will have a more powerful effect for you, and the description for those elements (detailed below) will fit your personality much better.

Similarly, if one or two elements are missing in your birth chart (such as a lack of air or water) those qualities can either be underdeveloped or in some cases overdeveloped, because you are overcompensating for the missing elements.

FIRE – ARIES, LEO, SAGITTARIUS

The fire signs are confident, enthusiastic, lively and full of energy. They like to stay active in mind and body, and tend to be curious and full of new ideas. They are dreamers and aim high, whether or not it is realistic to do so. Fire signs are competitive and like a challenge, as long as they win! Quick to anger, but just as quick to forget what it was they were angry about in the first place, they can be honest to the point of tactlessness. They are pioneering travellers and explorers who initiate and get things moving, whether out in the world or through their imaginations.

EARTH – TAURUS, VIRGO, CAPRICORN

The earth signs are in tune with nature and their own physical bodies. They tend to be realistic and practical, stable and grounded. They can make solid and dependable friends and partners. They are reliable and take responsibilities seriously. Earth signs are hardworking and take time to master a skill and use it to its full potential. Having a natural tendency to craft words and language to optimum effect, they have a strong wit and a good sense of comic timing. They are good at working with their hands and take pleasure in working with natural materials such as cotton, wool, wood and stone. They enjoy physical comforts and make excellent cooks and artisans.

AIR – GEMINI, LIBRA, AQUARIUS

The air signs have strong rational abilities and need a lot of space to think! They like to stay objective and keep a clear sense of perspective. Having a natural concern for society, human rights and environmentalism, they have strong ideals and work on formulating ideas about how systems and organizations could be improved. They can often be seen fighting for causes and protesting against injustice. Air signs tend to be sociable and like to share ideas and argue about fundamental issues with anyone who is willing to listen. They value freedom and don't like to be tied down. They make excellent scientists, mathematicians and social reformers.

WATER – CANCER, SCORPIO, PISCES

The water signs are naturally creative and imaginative, have a dreamy quality, and can be very gentle in their demeanour. Water is associated with the emotions as well as the unconscious. They are in touch with a vast well of feeling within that inspires them to imagine and create. They can be visionaries, and sometimes have psychic abilities. Water signs are sensitive to their environment and tend to have natural empathy for everyone and everything around them. They like to help others and put others first, often at the expense of their own needs. They can be found in the caring professions as well as the creative and the performing arts.

The Modes

Each sign of the zodiac falls into one of three modes – cardinal, fixed or mutable. These are sometimes referred to as the quadruplicities, because there are four signs in each mode. The modes combine with the elements to further characterize each sign.

CARDINAL – ARIES, CANCER, LIBRA, CAPRICORN

The Sun's entry into the cardinal signs corresponds with the equinox and solstice points, with its entry into Aries at the spring equinox around 20 March, into Cancer at the summer solstice around 21 June, into Libra at the autumn equinox around 21 September, and into Capricorn at the winter solstice around 21 December. These points in the annual calendar mark the changing of the seasons, and represent the gateway to new beginnings.

Cardinal signs are active, energetic and pioneering. They like to initiate new projects, but are not always good at maintaining their enthusiasm for long, or following things through to their conclusion. They are always looking for challenges to occupy them and new ground to tread.

FIXED – TAURUS, LEO, SCORPIO, AQUARIUS

The fixed signs correspond with the height of the seasons, spring (Taurus), summer (Leo), autumn (Scorpio) and winter (Aquarius), and mark the time when the seasons are in full swing.

Fixed signs have stability and staying power, but they find change difficult and resist any attempt to change their minds or make them step out of their comfort zones. They are able to turn the ideas initiated by the cardinal signs into concrete reality and bring them to fruition.

MUTABLE – GEMINI, VIRGO, SAGITTARIUS, PISCES

The mutable signs correspond to the waning of the seasons, and mark the time of preparation for change, when spring blossoms disappear (Gemini), crops are past their full bloom (Virgo), the leaves have disappeared from the trees as the days get darker and colder (Sagittarius) and the winter starts to thaw and give way to the first buds of renewal (Pisces).

Mutable signs are able to change and adapt easily, but they are not good at initiating new projects or sticking to plans. They are able to think outside the box and bring new ideas to improve on what was started by the cardinal signs and carried out by the fixed signs. They can bring projects to a close and reap the rewards.

The Angles

The angles in astrology form the cross in the birth chart diagram. Named the Ascendant, Descendant, Midheaven and Imum Coeli, they orientate your birth chart by placing it within the compass points of north (Imum Coeli for locations in the northern hemisphere), south (Midheaven for locations in the northern hemisphere), east (Ascendant) and west (Descendant).

The angles are considered to be the most powerful points in the chart, with the Ascendant – the point rising in the east – having the greatest significance.

The time and location of your birth are needed in order to be able to calculate your angles, as well as the houses which are based around them. If you don't know the correct time, you can use noon as the time but bear in mind that the angles and houses can't be taken into consideration when interpreting your chart.

THE ASCENDANT-DESCENDANT AXIS
The Ascendant (ASC) is the point on the eastern horizon where the planets and signs rise in the sky, and the Descendant (DSC) is the point on the western horizon where the planets and signs set. Together they form the horizontal axis, and represent the Earth's horizon at the moment of birth. Their axis divides the chart into northern and southern hemispheres.

THE ASCENDANT
The sign of the zodiac that is on your Ascendant – also known as your rising sign – was rising in the east at the moment of your birth. The Ascendant is the doorway into your birth chart and is key to your perception of the world around you. It indicates the way you interact with other people and the world around you, and colours

the way you view life as well as how you appear to others and the first impressions you make. The zodiac sign and any planets on the Ascendant and in the first house describe the characteristics people will perceive when they first meet and interact with you, and can also describe your physical appearance and mannerisms.

For example, if you have an Ascendant in Aries, you may appear to be lively and energetic, with a strong jaw line and muscular body. You approach the world assertively and with confidence, and can be very competitive. You look for challenges, or challenges seem to find you wherever you go. This description will also apply to you if the sign's ruling planet, Mars, is on the Ascendant, or in the first house.

See the section on the signs of the zodiac later in this book to read up on the sign on your Ascendant and find out how it can manifest in your appearance and interaction with the world.

THE CHART RULER

The chart ruler is the planet that 'rules' the sign on your Ascendant (see the table of planetary rulers on page 19). For example, if Aries is your Ascendant, then Mars is your chart ruler, as Mars rules the sign of Aries. If Leo is your Ascendant, then the Sun is your chart ruler. In the case of a Scorpio Ascendant, both Pluto and Mars are co-rulers of your chart, as they both rule the sign of Scorpio; and so on.

Your chart ruler and its position in your birth chart is one of the primary factors to take into consideration when exploring your chart. Along with the sign on the Ascendant, the sign and house in which the chart ruler is placed, and the aspects it makes to other planets, will indicate how you express yourself to others and how you experience the world.

THE DESCENDANT

While the Ascendant describes the 'self', the sign on the Descendant of your birth chart describes the 'other', or the people you come into contact with in the world, your partners in both romantic and business relationships, and what you look for in long-term partnerships. For example, if you have Libra on the Descendant, you may seek partners who are attractive, charming, peace-loving, idealistic and indecisive.

Along with the sign on the Descendant, you can also look to the planet which rules the sign and its position in your chart (and the

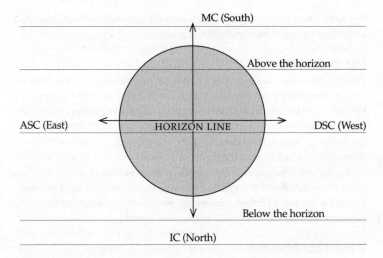

The chart circle and axis points for a location in the northern hemisphere.
(For the southern hemisphere, the MC is due north and the IC is due south,
although the MC remains the highest point above the horizon.)

aspects it makes to other planets) to give further indication of your
approach to relationships and the sort of people you attract.

Once you know which sign is on the Descendant of your chart, you
can find out more about the sign and its ruler, as well as any planets
on the Descendant (or in the 7th house) of your chart, to see how they
may apply to you and your relationships.

THE MIDHEAVEN-IMUM COELI AXIS

The Midheaven (MC) and Imum Coeli (IC) form the vertical axis
which divides your chart into eastern and western hemispheres.
When the chart is drawn for a location in the northern hemisphere
(such as the UK), the Midheaven points to the south and the Imum
Coeli points to the north; when drawn for a location in the southern
hemisphere (such as Australia), these compass points are reversed.

In both northern and southern hemispheres, the top half of the
chart shows all that is in the visible sky above the horizon, with the
Midheaven at the highest culminating point in the visible skyscape
(also called the zenith). The bottom half of the chart shows all that is

below the horizon, under the earth beneath us, with the Imum Coeli at the lowest point (also called the nadir).

THE MIDHEAVEN

The Midheaven indicates your goals, aims and aspirations in the world, and describes your career and social standing. For example, if you have Capricorn on the Midheaven, it can suggest strong ambition and a desire to achieve public recognition for the work that you do. You may do well in the banking or legal sectors, in politics or similar long-standing establishments.

Along with the sign on the Midheaven, you can also look to the planet which rules the sign and its position in your chart (and the aspects it makes to other planets) to give further indication of your goals in life and the type of career you are likely to pursue. For example, with Capricorn on the Midheaven, the ruler will be Saturn, and its position in the birth chart will have a bearing on the way the Midheaven functions in your life.

Once you know which sign is on the Midheaven of your chart, you can find out more about the sign and its ruler, as well as any planets on the Midheaven (or in the 10th house) of your chart, to see how they may apply to you and your aims, goals and career.

THE IMUM COELI

The Imum Coeli, or IC, represents your home and family background. For example, Cancer on the IC can mean that you had a nurturing upbringing, and have a strong urge to build a safe and secure home for your own family. Gemini here may indicate a sociable home life, the need to move house often and a reluctance to be tied down to one place.

Once you know which sign is on the Imum Coeli of your chart, you can find out more about the sign and its ruler, as well as any planets on the Imum Coeli (or in the 4th house) of your chart, to see how they may apply to your home life and family background.

The Astrological Houses

In addition to the twelve signs, the horoscopic circle is further divided into twelve houses. The planets are the key players in the birth chart, like the pieces in a chess set, and the signs of the zodiac in which the planets are placed represent 'how' the planetary principles express themselves, while the astrological houses describe 'where' and in which sphere of life the planets operate.

For example, if your Sun is in the sign of Virgo, then you will tend to be naturally hardworking, practical and happy to be of service to others. If the Virgo Sun is in the 10th house, you will apply these qualities to the work you do in the world, and even though Virgo is a shy sign, the Virgo Sun will want to shine and be recognized in public for its skills and handiwork.

The houses govern the following general areas of life:

1ST HOUSE
Corresponds to: Aries, Cardinal, Fire, Positive
The self, our body, appearance, persona, mannerisms, sunrise, first spark, incarnation, beginnings, initiation, independence, inspiration.

2ND HOUSE
Corresponds to: Taurus, Fixed, Earth, Negative
House, property, possessions, money, earnings, savings, personal resources, security (material and psychological), values.

3RD HOUSE
Corresponds to: Gemini, Mutable, Air, Positive
School, education, learning, teaching, knowledge, early environment, siblings, relatives, neighbours, travel (short distances), walking, cycling, accidents.

4TH HOUSE
Corresponds to: Cancer, Cardinal, Water, Negative
Home, roots, childhood, past, family, background, nationality, origins, land, foundations, father (or mother).

5TH HOUSE
Corresponds to: Leo, Fixed, Fire, Positive
Recreation, fun, games, children, playground, park, parties, creative pursuits, theatre, acting, pleasure, love affairs, risks, gambling, stock market.

6TH HOUSE
Corresponds to: Virgo, Mutable, Earth, Negative
Daily activity, routine, rituals, habits, hobbies, workplace, employees, health, hygiene, nutrition, small animals.

7TH HOUSE
Corresponds to: Libra, Cardinal, Air, Positive
Partners, relationships with others, marriage, business partners, enemies.

8TH HOUSE
Corresponds to: Scorpio, Fixed, Water, Negative
Crisis, transformation, birth, death, regeneration, wills, family inheritance, legacies, shared resources, other people's money, intimate relationships, personal unconscious, fate.

9TH HOUSE
Corresponds to: Sagittarius, Mutable, Fire, Positive
Religion, philosophy, culture, higher education, knowledge, meaning, teaching, travel (long distances), exploration, adventure, expansion.

10TH HOUSE
Corresponds to: Capricorn, Cardinal, Earth, Negative
Job, career, vocation, talent, calling, achievement, ambition, social status, public role, contribution to society, mother (or father).

11TH HOUSE
Corresponds to: Aquarius, Fixed, Air, Positive
Friends, acquaintances, social groups and networks, clubs, societies, communities, ideals, hopes and dreams, group consciousness.

12TH HOUSE

Corresponds to: Pisces, Mutable, Water, Negative

Institutions, hospitals, prisons, monasteries, retreats, hidden enemies, mysticism, self-transcendence, collective unconscious, endings.

THE POSITIONS OF THE HOUSES IN THE BIRTH CHART

The positions of the houses in your horoscope are linked to your Ascendant, and run in an anticlockwise direction from your ascending point, which marks the start (known as the 'cusp') of the 1st house. The Descendant marks the cusp of the 7th house. Depending on the house system used, the IC may also correspond with the 4th house cusp, and the MC with the 10th house cusp.

Do remember that, as with the angles, the time and place of your birth are needed in order to calculate the houses. If the time is not known, then the angles and houses cannot be used in chart interpretation.

A NOTE ON HOUSE SYSTEMS

There are a number of house systems in popular use, and an even larger number in existence. They each use a different method of dividing space and time, and were developed in different cultures and periods in history.

The two main house systems in Western astrology today, which we normally encounter when we first learn about astrology, are the Equal House and Placidus systems.

The Equal House system of house division is the easiest to calculate without a computer, as the houses are divided into twelve equal parts of 30° each, starting from the ASC. However, Equal House is not a quadrant system, which means that the MC and IC do not form the 10th and 4th house cusps, nor do they necessarily fall in the 10th and 4th houses, although the meanings of the MC and 10th house, and the IC and 4th house, do overlap.

The Placidus system of house division is a quadrant system, which means that the MC-IC axis corresponds with the 10th and 4th house cusps. This is the recommended house system we will be using throughout this book, but as you become more experienced with practising astrology, you can pick the house system that you prefer.

PACKED HOUSES

If you have planets in a house, the particular sphere of life which that house represents is highlighted. Any houses which contain two or more planets have an increased emphasis in your life.

Planets near the end of a house and within a few degrees of the next house cusp are often interpreted as belonging to the next house. For example, if a planet falls at the end of the 7th house and near the 8th house cusp, the planet is considered to be in the 8th house. Similarly, if a planet is a few degrees behind an angle, it is considered to be on the angle.

Aspects

The aspects in astrology refer to the angular distances in degrees (°) that connect the planets to each other, and to other significant points in the chart, such as the angles (see page 25).

For example, if planets are next to each other in your birth chart, they are said to be 'conjunct' each other. If they are on opposite sides of your birth chart, they are 180° apart and are thought to be in opposition to each other. The aspects are based on the idea that numbers have sacred and symbolic meaning – for example, one represents unity and wholeness, two represents duality, and so on. This idea can be traced at least as far back as Ancient Greece, and the 'father of mathematics', Pythagoras of Samos.

In astrology, the meanings of the aspects are based on the numerological qualities of the numbers they represent. When the circle of the horoscope is divided by one, we get the conjunction, which contains the quality of 'oneness'. When it is divided by two, we get the opposition, which is understood in terms of its dual nature, and so on.

The major aspects which are used today are known as the Ptolemaic aspects, because they were those used by Ptolemy – these are the

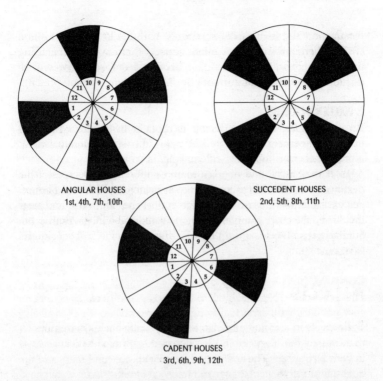

ANGULAR HOUSES
1st, 4th, 7th, 10th

SUCCEDENT HOUSES
2nd, 5th, 8th, 11th

CADENT HOUSES
3rd, 6th, 9th, 12th

TABLE OF ASPECTS			
Symbol	**Aspect**	**Degree**	**Maximum Orb**
☌	Conjunction	0°	8°
✶	Sextile	60°	4°
□	Square	90°	8°
△	Trine	120°	8°
⚻	Inconjunct/ Quincunx	150°	3°
☍	Opposition	180°	8°

conjunction (0°), sextile (60°), square (90°), trine (120°) and opposition (180°). There are numerous minor aspects that are used, including the inconjunction (also called the quincunx, 150°), which we will be including here due to its current popular use.

A NOTE ON ORBS

An exact aspect between planets is thought to be strongest – for example, if planets are exactly 120° apart, this is considered a 'tight' aspect. However, they are still considered to be in trine with each other if they are a few degrees more or less than 120° apart. This distance from the exact aspect is known as an orb, and the maximum orb varies depending on the aspect in question, and on the planets involved – the inner planets are generally allowed wider orbs than the outer planets. The maximum orbs are detailed in the table of aspects (see page 33).

CONJUNCTION – 0° (ORB 8°)

The conjunction (page 36, top left) tends to be considered as neither an easy nor a difficult aspect, although this depends on the planets and signs involved and any other aspects they make. Planets are conjunct each other when they are in the same degree or next to one another in your birth chart. The energies of the planets are combined, and the qualities of the particular sign and house are intensified.

A cluster of more than two planets that are conjunct each other are referred to as a stellium. Even if the planets are not within an 8° orb of each other, but are clustered together within a sign or house, they will still indicate a greater emphasis on the qualities of that particular sign and house in your chart.

SEXTILE – 60° (ORB 4°)

The sextile (page 36, top right) is considered to be an 'easy' aspect between planets, as they are thought to be in a harmonious relationship with one another. This is because the signs in a sextile are compatible (either air and fire signs or earth and water signs). Sextiles are passive aspects that feel like a pleasant bond between the planets in question, and can be very creative. They can indicate talents and resources which may lie dormant for years, but usually bear fruit with time.

SQUARE – 90° (ORB 8°)

The square (page 36, centre left) is considered to be one of the most 'difficult' aspects between planets, and they take a lot of strain in the birth chart. The signs involved in the square belong to the same mode, but the elements are incompatible (either fire and earth, earth and air, air and water or water and fire). The squares are highly energetic, forcing a struggle between the planetary energies which leads to great creative development and achievement in the world. Although it can feel quite stressful at times, the squares force you to act and become master of your own fate. Squares challenge you to feel the fear and do it anyway!

TRINE – 120° (ORB 8°)

The trine (page 36, centre right) is considered to be the 'easiest' and most harmonious aspect between planets, even more so than the sextile. It connects planets that are in the same element together (earth, air, fire or water), and the planets form an alliance which emphasizes a particular element in the chart. Like the sextile, trines also describe your innate talents, and they can be a very beneficial aspect to have in your birth chart. However, they can also allow you to be complacent and take your talents for granted. You may even allow them to remain dormant for too long.

INCONJUNCT/QUINCUNX – 150° (ORB 3°)

The inconjunct (page 36, bottom left) is considered to be a 'difficult' but highly creative aspect between planets. The signs in question are not connected by element or mode, and so feel quite alien to each other. This makes the connection exciting as well as deeply ambivalent. The two planets want to connect but can't quite seem to manage it – this can make for very erotic and creative situations.

OPPOSITION – 180° (ORB 8°)

The opposition (page 36, bottom right) is considered to be a 'difficult' aspect, although because the planets are opposite each other, and they are both in the same mode as well as along the same axis, they can balance each other's qualities in a way that the squares can't. Oppositions are, by nature, two very different qualities connected

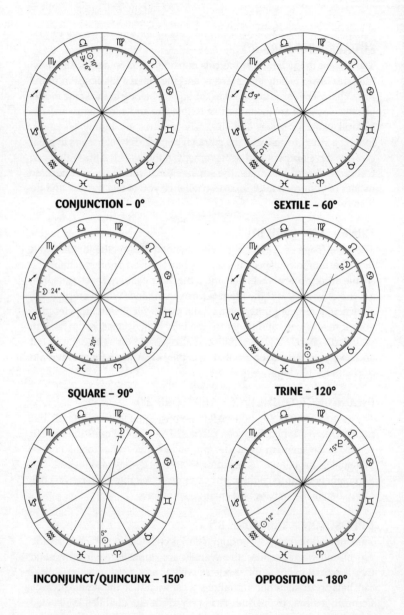

CONJUNCTION – 0°

SEXTILE – 60°

SQUARE – 90°

TRINE – 120°

INCONJUNCT/QUINCUNX – 150°

OPPOSITION – 180°

together, and there can be a tendency to side with one end of the opposition or the other. This can create a lot of stress, but your challenge is to learn how to balance both sides and find a middle way. It is possible to reconcile the two ends, particularly as you get older.

Grand Aspect Patterns

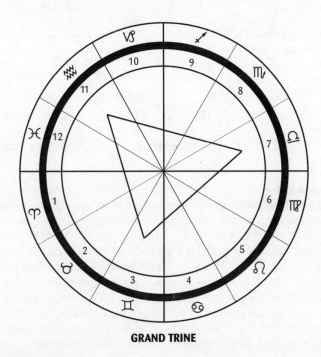

GRAND TRINE

GRAND TRINE

The grand trine is made up of three trines joined together to make an equilateral triangle in your birth chart. Like the trines, the grand trine is a benevolent and harmonious aspect pattern that brings great strength and easy expression to a particular element.

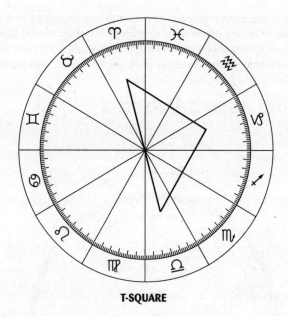

T-SQUARE

T-SQUARE

The T-square is made up of two squares and an opposition. It is a common aspect pattern that can be highly challenging, like the squares and oppositions that make up the pattern. If you have them in your chart, you will have to work hard to overcome obstacles and achieve your goals. In turn, it tends to be a very productive combination. It is less stable than the grand cross, but it has more room to manoeuvre. If you have T-squares in your chart, you may find that the 'empty leg' (the opposition to the square, which would have made a grand cross had a planet been there) is a significant point for you, and you attract relationships with people who have planets on the missing leg.

GRAND CROSS

The grand cross consists of exactly what it describes – two oppositions forming a cross, and joined together by four square aspects. It forms a highly stable and powerful structure, and can produce enormous energy, which you should use to your advantage. If you have this pattern in your chart, you can be quite unshakeable and firm in your decisions. This aspect pattern can also be set in its ways and create a lot of stress if it is not used wisely. Your challenge is to harness the energy inherent in this aspect pattern and channel it into something worthwhile and beneficial.

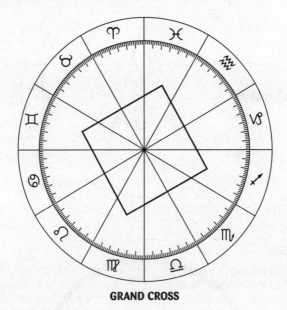

GRAND CROSS

YOD

The yod, also known as a 'finger of God', joins two inconjunctions and a sextile together. It is a highly creative combination, which is intent on forging new ground and finding creative solutions to old problems. The planet at the apex (where the two inconjuncts meet) is the focal point of the yod, and takes on the creative strain of the aspect pattern. Therefore, the function of this focal planet may be highly developed for you, and will play a central role in your birth chart.

KITE

The kite is formed by a grand trine, an opposition and two sextiles. It contains the tension of the opposition but with many opportunities for its creative expression. This combination can encourage you to make good use of your talents and creative gifts, and be a high-flyer!

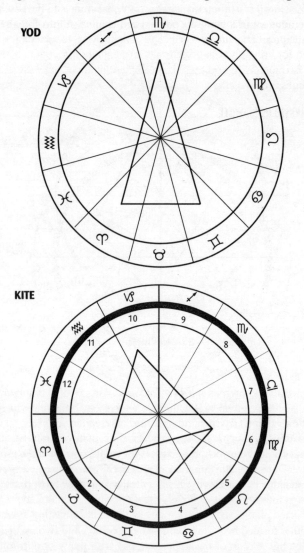

MYSTIC RECTANGLE

This pattern is quite rare and consists of two trines, two sextiles and an opposition. Like the kite, there is a combination of stressful and harmonious aspects here. It also contains combinations of the same polarities (air and fire or earth and water). This aspect pattern is known for bringing about dilemmas, but equally it seems to resolve them harmoniously, and there is an element of good luck inherent in this configuration.

MYSTIC RECTANGLE

UNASPECTED PLANETS

Planets that do not make any aspects at all operate alone in your birth chart. They may seem disconnected from your life and difficult to access. Conversely, as with missing elements, you may find one unaspected planet overcompensates and becomes the most powerful planet in the chart. It is definitely worth finding out more about any unaspected planets in your chart and working out how they function for you.

Learning to Read Your Birth Chart

When learning to read your birth chart it is important to look at the whole picture rather than draw conclusions from any one part of it. Often, important themes will be repeated in different areas of your birth chart, and the more times they are repeated, the more prevalent they will tend to be in your life. One birth chart that perfectly illustrates this point is that of Diana, Princess of Wales. Princess Diana was very interested in astrology and consulted astrologers throughout her adult life. Because the details of her life are so widely documented, by studying her chart, you can start to apply your knowledge of astrology to what you know about Diana's character and experiences, enabling you to begin to form ideas about what your chart says about you.

DIANA'S SUN

Diana Spencer was born on 1 July, 1961 at 14.00 hrs in Sandringham, England. The Sun was in the sign of Cancer, which is ruled by the Moon, the great mothering sign of the zodiac. As the wife of Prince Charles, the future king of England, Diana had the responsibility of bearing children who would be heirs to the throne. She embraced this responsibility wholeheartedly, and was a devoted mother to her two sons, William and Harry.

In Diana's chart, Mercury is conjunct the Sun in Cancer. This indicates someone whose mind and sense of identity and purpose were closely aligned, and served to enhance her Cancerian qualities. Diana epitomized the caring and nurturing qualities that are associated with Cancer – she was particularly well-known for her charity work, and while this formed part of her duties as a member of the royal family, she had been working with children and charity groups since her teens, and seemed to have a special connection with people who were sick or vulnerable.

The Sun and Mercury are in the 7th house of Diana's birth chart. This area of the chart is associated with our relationships, and in this position the Sun and Mercury in Cancer suggest that relationships were extremely important to Diana's sense of personal identity. It also suggests that she expected to receive emotional warmth and nurturing from those she was close to.

Alongside Diana's personal relationships, perhaps another manifestation of this 7th house chart placement was her relationship with the media. Like the crab that symbolizes the sign, Cancerians have a soft and vulnerable centre and a hard shell, which they use to protect themselves. While drawn to the glare of the spotlight, this inclination would have conflicted with Diana's shyness and innate desire to protect her privacy.

DIANA'S MOON
The Moon in Diana's chart forms a T-square with Uranus and Mars and Venus. This aspect indicates that her emotional life and matters of the heart were likely to be unusual, unpredictable and turbulent. It suggests she would have found it very difficult to feel she was receiving the necessary emotional security, support and sustenance from her relationships.

Diana's moon is in Aquarius, which means that she needed a lot of freedom, independence and time to think. These qualities are also shared by Diana's Ascendant; Sagittarius, and this would have created conflict with the Cancerian side of her personality. When conflicting qualities such as these appear in the chart, we are challenged to find creative ways to make them work in our lives. In the attempt we often meet with painful lessons, which help us to develop and, in the long run, fulfil our highest potential. Diana's Moon is in the 2nd house of material wealth, comfort and security. When the Moon is in this position, the subject needs to value his or herself and feel valued by others in order to feel comfortable and secure. As we have seen, the Moon makes difficult aspects to Uranus and Mars (oppositions), and to Venus (square), suggesting that these needs were not always met. Diana's experiences would have forced her to find a way to come to terms with this, and develop her own sense of inner security.

DIANA'S ASCENDANT/CHART RULER
Diana's chart ruler (the planetary ruler of her Sagittarian Ascendant) is Jupiter. This planet represents how she expressed herself in the

world. Jupiter is in Aquarius, along with the Moon (although they are not conjunct because the orb is too wide). Aquarius is associated with progressive thinking and humanitarian causes. Diana was able to express this side of her character through the work she did with AIDS charities, as well as with numerous other worthwhile causes. This work would have been deeply satisfying to her.

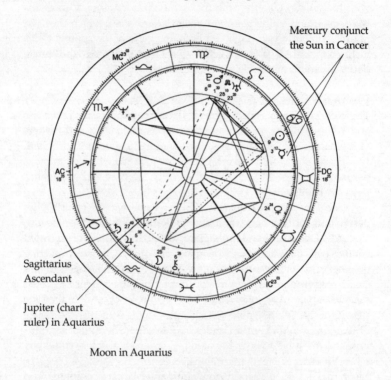

Mercury conjunct
the Sun in Cancer

Sagittarius
Ascendant

Jupiter (chart
ruler) in Aquarius

Moon in Aquarius

PRINCESS DIANA'S BIRTH CHART

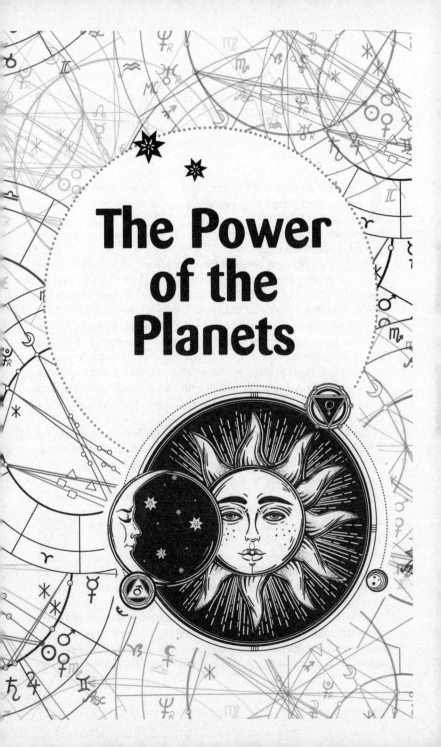

The Power
of the
Planets

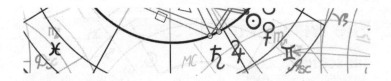

Like members of many other esoteric and scientific traditions, astrologers believe that everything in the universe is connected. This idea is often visualized as some kind of invisible thread or resonance between everything, from physical objects, to people's thoughts and feelings.

Most of us have experienced this connection for ourselves at one point or another. For example, have you ever felt rejuvenated or insightful while sitting on a beach watching waves crash against the shore, or enjoyed a sense of reverie and empowerment when looking at sunlight streaming through a stained-glass window? Both of these familiar scenarios demonstrate the intangible connection between our environments and our lives. If you have a special place you go to when you need to think, or have filled your home with wood or stone because you feel a connection with these natural materials, then somewhere deep down you are already aware of this link, and have integrated it into your life.

Certain principles, objects and characteristics are connected by the same thread or vibration resonating between them. This is one of the main reasons for the apparent correspondence between the planets and our lives on Earth. As well as our thoughts, feelings and actions, planetary principles are also known to correspond with stones, colours, plants, foods and all sorts of other objects around us.

There are ten significant planetary bodies in astrology: The Sun, The Moon, Mercury, Venus, Mars, Jupiter, Saturn, Uranus, Neptune and Pluto. Each of these have come to represent a set of principles and characteristics based on the planet's physical attributes and behaviour in the sky, as well as its mythological background and the symbolism that has evolved over centuries.

This section explores the meanings associated with each of the ten planetary bodies in astrology, and seeks to explain how, depending on their position in the zodiac at the precise time of your birth, they may apply to your personality and to events in your life.

The Wisdom of the Sun

THE SCIENCE

Although astrologers think of the sun as a planet, it is actually an average-sized star formed of dust and gas clouds. Its role in our lives is crucial; it is the central, and by far the largest, thing in our solar system, the main object we see in the sky and the source of all our energy in the form of heat and light. It is the Earth's movement in relation to the Sun that determines the length of our days and nights. Together with the Moon, the Sun governs our seasons, calendars, agriculture and festivals, and influences our lives in countless other ways, many of which we take for granted.

The Sun is about four and a half billion years old and around halfway through its lifespan. It is approximately one million times the size of Earth, and about 150 million kilometres (93 million miles) away from us. At its core the sun converts hydrogen to helium, a gas which derives its name from Helios, the Ancient Greek god of the Sun.

THE MYTH

The Sun is central to many of the stories we tell about who we are and where we come from. Throughout history, many cultures from around the world have created myths and rituals that recognize our dependence on the Sun and its rhythms. Many of these take the form of creation stories, in which the Sun is responsible for creating the Earth, Moon and stars. In some cultures the Sun is represented as female, but in the vast majority of cases it is associated with masculine energy.

The Celts were among many who saw the Sun's annual cycle through the seasons as symbolic of the journey of life – from its birth in the spring to its youth in the summer, maturity in autumn and its death in the winter, followed by its rebirth in spring. Many of the religious and cultural festivals we celebrate today are based on the seasons created by the Sun. For example, many people mark midsummer's day in some way, whether by visiting a sacred site such as Stonehenge, as the druids do, or simply toasting the summer ahead with a glass of wine.

CYCLE: The Sun moves around the birth chart and returns back to its original position approximately every 365.25 days (one year), and spends around one month in each sign

SIGNS: The Sun rules Leo (23 July–23 August)

COLOURS: Yellow, orange, gold

STONES: Ruby, carbuncle, chrysolite, peridot, sunstone, tiger's eye

METALS: Gold

PLANTS: Sunflower, marigold, mistletoe, juniper, bay, cedar, chamomile, cinnamon, rosemary

PARTS OF THE BODY: Heart, back, spine, immune system

KEYWORDS: Light, heroism, hope, potential, joy, consciousness, ego, expression, vitality, power, freedom, talent, truth, growth

CHARACTERISTICS: Warm, creative, playful, confident, egotistical, purposeful, courageous, generous, insightful, nourishing

ROLES: Hero, king, father, child, performer

The Sun god in Ancient Rome was Apollo, and in the earlier Greek myth he was known as Helios. Apollo was known for riding his chariot of fire across the heavens from east to west, pulled by four horses. At night he sailed eastwards again in a golden bowl, only to repeat the cycle the next day. Apollo was thus credited with bringing heat and light to the world.

The Sun also represents the idea of the hero in myth, from Hercules and Jason and the Argonauts, to Harry Potter in the present day. In each of these stories, the hero embarks on a journey and faces a series of dangers and pitfalls, which must be overcome through some form of sacrifice. At the very end, the hero's efforts bring victory, recognition and reward. His success has implications for the whole community, who benefit from the peace and prosperity brought by his victory. In return, they offer him a position of responsibility, and their adulation.

THE MEANING

Inscribed in the Temple of Apollo at Delphi is the age-old adage 'know thyself'. It is a phrase that has resonated in Western thought for centuries. We ask ourselves 'who am I?' and 'why am I here?' because we have a sense that our lives have purpose, that we are born with a mission to perform, and we want to find out what that might be.

One of the main purposes of astrology is to help us answer these questions and, like the Oracle at Delphi, we look at our birth charts to find out about our character and our destiny. As we learn about our birth charts and gain greater insight into who we are, we can make more conscious choices and participate more actively in our own future, rather than leave it to fate.

We look to the whole birth chart for answers, and the person we are is represented by a combination of all our planets and chart factors, and the way they all work together. But, in particular, the Sun represents its heart, and points to our sole purpose in life.

It is useful to note that this has not always been the case, and in ancient and medieval times the planet ruling the sign on the Ascendant and the Moon received greater attention in astrology.

These days the Sun is considered to be the main focal point of the horoscope, and it has been likened to an orchestra conductor who conducts the other planets and chart factors, bringing them together to create our own personal theme tune!

We all tend to know the sign of the zodiac in which our Sun was placed at birth before we become familiar with the rest of our birth chart, and the 'Sun sign' horoscope columns in newspapers and magazines are testament to the Sun's central importance in astrology today. We learn through these horoscope columns that our Sun sign describes something about the essence of our personality and the characteristics with which many of us identify.

Occasionally we don't identify with our Sun signs, however, and this may be for a variety of reasons – often it is because we have another strong planet or aspect which influences or overrides the power of the Sun in our awareness. But it is our job to discover our Sun sign qualities and find ways to apply them in our lives. This may mean engaging in activities or wearing the colours or stones associated with the Sun and the sign of the zodiac it is placed in. This may help to awaken us and integrate the planet more consciously into our lives. In doing so we find greater satisfaction in the process.

SYMBOL

The symbol of the Sun ⊙ is a circle with a dot in the centre. The circle signifies the spirit, or unity, and the dot in the centre suggests the consciousness of the human being at our centre, or the seed of potential that lies at our core. The Sun's path describes our journey toward self discovery. Like Apollo riding in his chariot across the heavens, the Sun represents our own heroic journey through life. Its position is an indication of our divine calling, or vocation. Thus it can be linked to the work we do, or are 'meant' to do, in the world. This is the activity which gives us the greatest pleasure and satisfaction, or our 'talent', and through this work we can shine our light and radiate joy to ourselves and others.

Above all else the Sun just spreads its rays and shines brightly. It represents our inner light and source of our energy, health and vitality.

The Sun is our conscious ego and the core of who we are as individuals. It likes to feel special, like the hero or the divine child in us all, and we love to be praised and admired for being who we are.

As we get to know our Sun, we find out what we are creatively meant to do in the world. However, the Sun's journey does not tend to be a straightforward one and, as the heroic myths suggest, there are many pitfalls and lessons to learn along the way. It is through these struggles that we are tested to our limits, face loss and sacrifice, and are forced to become our highest potential selves.

The Sun (along with Saturn, see page 77) represents the father principle. The sign in which our Sun is placed describes our experience of our father figure and his expectations of us. As children, our first hero tends to be our father, and we want him to be proud of us. We also look to our teachers and other authority figures who fulfil the father principle in the outside world, and their validation helps us grow in confidence and self-assurance. We also tend to struggle with these figures and rebel against the rules and restraints they impose upon us, and this is part of discovering our own authority as individuals.

LEO

The Sun is the ruling planet for the sign of Leo, and its symbol of the lion represents royalty and nobility. It also symbolizes the primal instinct towards 'individuation' – a term coined by psychologist Carl Jung referring to meaningful development by integrating all the various layers and conflicts we each contain. Over time we learn to integrate all the differing elements of our personalities, and become who we always were, but more consciously and with greater mastery over our lives.

Which sign of the zodiac is your Sun placed in? This sign represents the characteristics of your core self, your sense of purpose, and where your greatest gifts and talents lie. For example, the Sun in Aries, a cardinal fire sign, will shine brightly by being energetic and outgoing. Its core purpose will be connected with its pioneering and courageous nature, and its need to assert its will in the world. In the mutable airy sign of Gemini, the Sun may be happiest, having many different outlets for its varied interests, and its core purpose will be connected with learning and exploring new ideas.

The Emotional Moon

THE SCIENCE

The Moon is known for changing appearance over the course of its 28-day long cycle around the Earth. It ranges from being nearly invisible

CYCLE: The moon makes one revolution around the Earth every 28 days, spending around 2.5 days in each sign of the zodiac

SIGNS: The Moon rules Cancer (22 June–22 July)

COLOURS: White, silver, grey

STONES: Moonstone, pearl, selenite, abalone, opal, coral, aquamarine

METALS: Silver

PLANTS: Palm, cypress, linden, amaranth, moonwort, daisy, poppy, water lily, seaweed, lemon, cauliflower, cabbage, lettuce, mushroom

PARTS OF THE BODY: Breasts and mammary glands, oesophagus, stomach, intestines, pancreas, liver, gall bladder, bodily fluids

KEYWORDS: Darkness, subconscious, reflection, retreat, childbirth, nature, connections, cycles, commitment, relationships, habits, routines, memory

CHARACTERISTICS: Nurturing, sensitive, emotional, sustaining, moody, protective

ROLES: Mother, heroine, witch

in the night sky, to a silver crescent, increasing in increments until it is a full shining circle, and then gradually diminishing until it is nearly invisible again. Like the planets, the Moon has no light of its own but reflects the light of the Sun, hence its silvery shine. As the Moon revolves around the Earth, its position in relation to the Sun changes and the part that is visible to us is illuminated at a different angle, and this is what creates its differing shapes. The phases of the Moon are detailed in the diagram overleaf (on page 56).

The Moon is around a quarter of the size of the Earth, and while the Sun and the Moon appear to be around the same size in the sky, this is an illusion. In truth they are vastly different in size. The Sun's diameter is around 400 times that of the Moon, but because the Moon is also 400 times closer to us, they appear to be of similar size from Earth. It is possible to view total eclipses of the Sun by the Moon, from our vantage point on Earth.

The Moon spins around us like the Earth's cosmic dance partner, and yet, no matter what phase it is in, we always see the same face. The other side – the side we often refer to as 'the dark side of the moon' – is always hidden from view.

THE MYTH

We tell many stories about the Moon and the way it affects our lives. Who hasn't heard the tale of the man in the Moon, or the rabbit that appears to be having a snooze inside it, and what child hasn't wondered, at one time or another, whether the Moon is in fact made out of Swiss cheese?

We associate the full moon, in particular, with supernatural creatures of the night, such as werewolves, vampires, ghosts and ghouls and with stories of madness and lunacy (a word derived from 'Luna', the Latin word for moon). Many people also believe that violent crime increases around the time of a full moon, although the phenomenon is not proven.

WHEN IN ROME:

In Ancient Greece, the Moon was associated with the mother principle, and the Sun with father, and this idea has filtered, via the Romans, into our own culture. The Roman Moon goddess, Diana, was identified with the Greek goddess Artemis, the twin sister of Apollo (the Sun). Like Diana, Artemis was a virgin goddess associated with woodland and hunting. She was a fierce protector of children and all that is innocent and vulnerable. Other Ancient Greek Moon goddesses include Selene and Hecate. In pagan myth, the Moon is represented as a 'triple goddess', with the three phases of waxing, full and waning moons associated with the three ages of womanhood – the maiden, the mother and the crone.

THE MEANING

The Moon rules our moods and needs, which shift and change like its phases. It is concerned with our memories of the past and nostalgia for the things that have come and gone. It represents our emotional nature, and how we experience the world on an internal, subjective level.

It is associated with the feelings and emotions as well as with the body, where the emotions are thought to be stored. Sometimes our emotions can affect our physical health, and physical symptoms often indicate emotional pain which has been left unresolved or unexpressed. A lot of this process occurs on an unconscious level, so we might not always be aware of what we are feeling, and need to find the time and space to get in touch with our Moon's realm. The Moon tends to process our experiences, checking them against our comfort zones. Sometimes when we have a 'bad feeling' about something, this can be our Moon's receptors gauging how we feel, and testing whether something is safe or not. We have a sense that we should trust our instincts and it is advisable that we listen to our Moon and use it to help us navigate through life.

Our Moon needs to feel part of a group, and finds comfort in emotional attachment. It is naturally inclined to nurture the self as well as others, and is concerned with food, nutrition and sustenance.

Our lunar nature seeks a sense of safety and security, and naturally inclines us to retreat into the home where we can look after ourselves as well as take care of the family. At home we can relax and be surrounded by all our treasured people and possessions, and with all the comforts we need. It is a private place where we can be intimate with others and allow our vulnerable side to show.

The Moon's monthly cycle is naturally linked to the menstruation cycle in women, hence its age-old associations with fertility and childbirth. Its sign and position in the chart is sometimes an indicator of the kind of mothering we had, or the way we experienced our mothers. It can also describe the kind of mothering we offer to others, including our friends and partners, as well as our children.

The Moon's cycle also represents our daily habits and routines, including household chores such as cooking and cleaning – no sooner are they finished, they must be repeated again! When we repeat something often enough and for long enough, it has an affect on our bodies and every aspect of our lives. For example, if we slouch every time we sit in front of the computer it will affect our posture, and if we drink lots of water we see the effect on our skin!

The Moon's position in the birth chart can suggest the types of patterns we perpetuate, which are visible in our physical health as well as our general lifestyle. It describes what we are like to live with and in close personal relationships, where we let our vulnerable side show. It can describe our family background, as well as our current home and family life.

In which sign of the zodiac is your Moon placed? Find out what it says about your emotional world by looking up the sign of your Moon in the next section. For example, if your natal Moon is placed in the sign it rules – cardinal and watery Cancer – then its natural tendencies described here will be very strong. If it is in an air sign, such as fixed Aquarius, then your Moon will be less expressive of its emotions and moods, and may need space and time alone to think, rather than being too closely attached to family.

Phases of the Moon

In astrology, the relationship between the Sun and Moon is an important one, and each of the Moon's phases has its own symbolic meaning. We can observe the position of the Moon over the course of the month and use its energies in our daily lives. We can also look at our birth chart to find out which phase our Moon was in at birth, and use our understanding of the phase alongside the sign in which our Moon is placed to find out what this might indicate about our lunar tendencies.

PHASES OF THE MOON

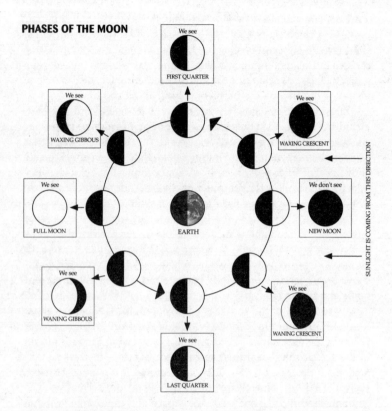

NEW MOON (SUN AND MOON 0°– 8° APART)

The New Moon appears as a barely visible black disc in the sky. This means that the Sun and Moon are in the same area in the heavens, and appear to be conjunct (next to each other) in the horoscope.

The New Moon is considered the beginning of the lunar cycle, when things lie dormant in their potential, like a seed, awaiting expression in life. This is a good time to sow seeds as well as lay down plans for a new project or endeavour, apply for new jobs or courses, do some background research and formulate ideas. It is also a good time to break old habits and patterns that are no longer required.

People born with the Sun and Moon conjunct in the birth chart like to retreat from the world and spend more time in their own company.

They tend to be sensitive to their own needs as well as those of others, and need a lot of 'me' time to relax and recharge. If the Sun and Moon are conjunct in the same house and sign of the zodiac, they will tend to display the qualities of the house and sign more strongly. In astrology this is known as a 'double Aries' or 'double Pisces'.

WAXING MOON (SUN AND MOON 1°–179° APART, MOON IS AHEAD OF THE SUN IN THE ZODIAC)

As the Moon starts to become visible as a crescent in the sky and increases into a half circle followed by a gibbous (three-quarter waxing) Moon, the time is ripe to realize our ideas in the world, embark on new projects, build new structures and get things started.

It is a good time for new beginnings such as moving house, starting a course or new job, making friends, starting relationships, and other projects that require momentum to get going.

During this phase the space betweeen the Sun and Moon is increasing and each is forced to develop and grow independently. People born during the waxing Moon strive hard to get what they want in life, and can overcome any obstacle to achieve their goals. They can be very single-minded and tenacious about everything they do, whether work or play. They tend to see things through to completion, and once they have started something they tend not to give up, no matter how many obstacles need to be overcome.

FULL MOON (SUN AND MOON 172°–188° APART)

The Moon is 'full' when the Earth is located between the Sun and the Moon, and the Sun's rays are shining over the largest surface of the Moon visible from the Earth, to create a shining silver disc in the sky.

In the planting season, this is when flowers are in full bloom, or when fruits are ripe and ready to be picked. The Moon is at the height of its power, and the time is ripe to enjoy the fruits of a project, showcase achievements and hold a celebration. Relationships can blossom at this time, and passions are heightened for romance! Tensions may also be heightened, and a good argument may be needed to clear the air, although care is advised!

During a full moon, the Sun and Moon are in opposite signs in the zodiac. For individuals with this configuration in their birth chart, this indicates that the qualities of the Sun and Moon may sometimes be in conflict and sometimes in balance. This can contribute to an open, outgoing and extroverted nature, which needs to be active and in the limelight as much as possible. These individuals tend to live life to the full, but can burn themselves out because it can be difficult for them to take time to rest and recharge. Relationships with others are very important to people born during the full Moon, as they tend to see themselves most clearly when reflected back by others. They may look for a partner who can take care of them and provide a lot of comfort and nurturing, as they are not always able to do it for themselves.

WANING MOON (SUN AND MOON 181°–359° APART, SUN IS AHEAD OF THE MOON IN THE ZODIAC)

After reaching its full potential, the Moon starts to wind down again through the disseminating, last quarter and balsamic Moon phases (when the Moon is less than 45° behind the Sun). This is a time when energies are waning and getting ready to return to a new Moon phase, and we start to retreat from the world and look within for new ideas and inspiration.

Now the Moon is on its way to reunite with the Sun, and is concerned with tearing down the old structures that were developed in the first half of the phase, and getting ready to replace them with new ones. It is a good time to take what we have learned during the previous period and review how things have gone so we can tie up any loose ends and go back to the drawing board, ready to start again. People born with the Sun and Moon in the waning phase tend to have the ability to be quite imaginative and inward-looking, and generate a lot of ideas. They are good at taking stock, assessing situations, solving problems, making necessary changes, taking what is useful from the past and planning how to use it in the future.

Mercury the Messenger

THE SCIENCE

Mercury is the closest planet to the Sun and has the most eccentric (elliptical) orbit of all the planets. All the inner planets are made of rock and metal, and Mercury is the smallest of them all – it is two and a half times smaller than the Earth. Despite its size, it has the second highest mass, next to the Earth.

As viewed from Earth, Mercury never travels more than 28° from the Sun. Because of its proximity to the Sun, it is difficult to observe in the sky and, along with Venus, can best be seen around sunrise and sunset.

THE MYTH

Mercury was one of the most important gods in ancient Greece and Rome, and ruled over such diverse areas as language, writing, storytelling, music, agriculture, merchants, business and commerce, wealth, peace and prosperity, roads, travel, games, gambling, tricks and magic. He was also known as the protector of animals and the patron of thieves.

The Roman god Mercury was largely based on the Greek god Hermes. He was known as the messenger of the gods, and wore a winged cap and sandals to help him move more quickly across land and water. Hermes was able to travel anywhere, even to the underworld and back, a privilege that most of the other gods did not possess.

Hermes had a reputation for being fast and athletic. He was also known for being clever and mischievous from the moment he was born, and was said to have crawled away from his sleeping mother after his birth, and created the first musical instrument, the lyre. He then stole his half-brother Apollo's cattle, by cleverly making them walk backwards, so that their footprints appeared to go in the opposite direction and anyone looking for them would look in the wrong place!

Apollo was furious when he found out about the cattle, but Hermes offered him a gift of the lyre by way of apology, which he accepted. Apollo became associated with the lyre and the gift of music thereafter, and he has Hermes' ingenuity to thank for it!

THE SYMBOL

In return for the gift of music, Apollo gave Hermes a staff intertwined with ribbons, which later became associated with snakes. This was known as the caduceus, and is one of Mercury's enduring symbols. The astronomical symbol used for the planet Mercury ☿ is thought

CYCLE: Mercury orbits the Sun in 88 days, but due to its apparent retrograde motion takes approximately a year to make one revolution around the birth chart

SIGNS: Mercury rules Gemini (22 May–21 June) and Virgo (24 August–23 September)

COLOURS: Light blue, white

STONES: Emerald, fire stone, citrine

METALS: Mercury

PLANTS: Lily of the valley, marjoram, valerian, fern, lavender, fennel, anise, bergamot, peppermint, thyme, dill, lemongrass

PARTS OF THE BODY: Brain, lungs and respiratory system, nervous system

KEYWORDS: Business, travel, catalysts, networks, communication, language, humour, mischief, magic, change, understanding, trade

CHARACTERISTICS: Quick, curious, agile, intelligent, witty, expressive, adaptable

ROLES: Sibling, youth, thief, inventor, businessperson, journalist, teacher

to be based on the symbol of the caduceus. The caduceus itself has also become the emblem of the medical profession and organizations connected with healing around the world.

THE MEANING

Mercury rules the mental and communication faculties, and describes how our mind works, the way we receive and process information, as well as how we express and articulate ourselves. The planet represents our sense of curiosity and interest in exploring the world, and the position of Mercury in the birth chart describes where our particular areas of interest lie.

In myth, Mercury had unlimited access, even to the underworld. This ability to enter any realm suggests that Mercury is able to cross boundaries and unite opposites – also indicated by the two winding snakes on his staff. The ability to travel to the underworld indicates that Mercury is able to delve and probe into the depths of a matter to help get to the heart of it if need be.

In the birth chart, Mercury and the Sun are never more than 28° apart from each other. This means Mercury is either conjunct (next to) the Sun, or in the same sign as the Sun, or in the previous or following sign of the zodiac to the Sun. As Apollo's half brother in mythology, and creator of the Sun god's lyre, Mercury in astrology is the Sun's facilitator or personal assistant, helping the Sun express itself, develop its talents and achieve its purpose and potential in the world. It is one of the Sun's most trusty companions and one of the most useful tools in its toolbox! A well-oiled Mercury helps the whole chart connect and work together.

Social situations are ideal environments to network with others, and Mercury enjoys being a social butterfly at business or social gatherings and even virtual chat rooms – anywhere that can provide a forum to exchange ideas and information. This information provides fuel for Mercury's inventive mind, which likes to understand ideas, gain mastery over processes, and solve problems. It uses the information gathered to connect people and coordinate things so that they work more smoothly and with greater efficiency in the world around us. Mercury is interested in using the mental faculties to make connections and aid progress so that we can advance and grow.

MERCURY THE TRICKSTER

Like the Joker in a pack of cards, Mercury the trickster is often thought to behave like a wildcard in astrology, and wherever there are problems with communications technology, such as computers or microphones playing up, then Mercury tends to be blamed for playing tricks!

The trickster Mercury is also excellent at getting out of tricky situations, either by being creative with the truth, or by working out the best way to wriggle out of a fix. In this way, Mercury has been associated with lying, thievery and the criminal mind!

Mercury also represents youth and siblings, and our relationships with our own brothers and sisters, and with our peer group. As we grow up, we learn from our siblings and peers as much as from the adults and teachers around us. We learn how to explore and play, and sometimes how to get up to mischief! Our early experiences of education and learning with our peers can tell us a lot about how Mercury functions in our lives.

GEMINI AND VIRGO

Mercury rules the signs of Gemini and Virgo, and Mercury's qualities tend to be at home and strongest in these signs. Gemini is an air sign and Virgo is an earth sign. Both are mutable, which naturally lends them to the easily changeable and elusive qualities of Mercury. Both signs are also seen as having strong mental agility, language and communication skills, and are associated with research, teaching and learning. Virgo is known particularly for its organizational abilities, and Gemini is identified with Mercury's trickster qualities!

In which sign is Mercury placed in your birth chart? You can apply the meaning of Mercury to the sign it is placed in to find out how your mind tends to work, how you learn, the kind of things you are interested in and how you express yourself.

For example, Mercury in Virgo, the sign which it rules, can be very strong and authoritative, wanting to gain understanding and mastery over any task it applies itself to. Particular interests may include craftwork, health and nutrition, reading and writing. It can be very well organized and have excellent written and communication skills. Mercury in Libra may be more of a dreamer, and apply its mind to more abstract and hypothetical thinking, such as pure mathematics, or to beauty and form, such as design or architecture. It will idealize situations, concepts and individuals.

MERCURY RETROGRADE

When observed from the Earth, Mercury appears to be moving retrograde (backwards to its normal orbit direction in the sky) for a couple of weeks, three or four times each year. When Mercury is retrograde (symbolized within the horoscope), normal business practice, communications and travel plans tend to be disrupted. Astrologers advise against signing contracts and closing deals at this time, as it can lead to obstacles for the project in the future. It is an ideal time to undertake background research, avoid tight schedules, leave extra time to catch trains and other forms of transport and plan for delays!

Depending on the situation, a retrograde Mercury can indicate a change in course will be taken, or that something is returning, being re-evaluated or prolonged, or an unexpected change can occur. The main message is to try and go with the flow at these times, and wait for normal service to be resumed after it returns to direct motion again.

People born with Mercury retrograde in the birth chart tend to be shy and reserved in expressing themselves, taking time to think things through carefully, and are more reflective in their communication with others. But, as usual, the extent of this tendency will depend on other factors in the birth chart, and if there are strong indicators of quick and direct communication elsewhere in the chart (such as Mars in Gemini on the Midheaven), then the effect of a retrograde Mercury may be counteracted.

Stellar Venus

THE SCIENCE

The planet Venus is about the same size as the Earth, but unlike the Earth it has a dense, hot and uninviting atmosphere full of sulphuric acid. It is also known for having the most circular orbit around the Sun out of all the planets (orbits tend to be elliptical rather than circular). Because of its size and proximity to us, it is the brightest object in the sky other than the Sun and the Moon. Like Mercury, Venus travels closely with the Sun, and can best be seen in the sky alongside the Sun and Mercury during sunrise and sunset hours.

THE MYTH

Venus was the goddess of love, beauty, sexuality and fertility in ancient Rome, and was influenced by the Greek goddess Aphrodite, who had similar attributes. As with all the characters in mythology, Aphrodite herself was based on earlier goddesses from nearby cultures, including Ishtar, Astarte and Inanna from Mesopotamia and Babylonia.

These earlier deities were beautiful as well as fierce and independent warriors, and chose their own consorts. Sexuality was a large part of their power, and each of these goddesses were known for their cult of sacred prostitutes in these earlier cultures, where women worked as courtesans, or *hetaerae* as they were known in ancient Greek society, and took lovers as part of their devotional rituals to the goddess.

Aphrodite had a magical start in life, as many versions of the story describe how she was born from the phallus of a castrated Ouranos (Uranus), which fell into a foamy sea, from which she emerged. She floated to shore on a scallop shell, and became associated with pearls – hence the famous image of her rising out of the sea by the Italian Renaissance painter Botticelli.

According to the myth, Aphrodite's beauty caused so much fighting between the gods that, as their king, Zeus (Jupiter) had to take action, and married her off to Hephaistos, a dull and unattractive god, to keep the peace. However, Hephaistos was no match for Aphrodite, and she took lovers and bore children by numerous other gods, including Dionysus, Ares (Mars) and Adonis.

In many of the stories, Aphrodite wants nothing more than to be desired by all men and recognized as the most beautiful goddess in all eternity, and in her desperation to receive this recognition her actions inadvertently spark off the Trojan wars, the most devastating conflict in Greek mythology.

THE MEANING

Venus is the image of feminine beauty and charm. She is the drop-dead gorgeous woman who exudes confidence and sex appeal, making heads turn wherever she goes. We all love her, want to be her, or are filled with envy at the sight of her, or all of these at once! Those

CYCLE: Venus makes one revolution around the Sun approximately every 225 days but, like Mercury, due to its apparent periodic retrograde motion, it takes about a year to travel around the horoscope, spending about a month in each sign

SIGNS: Venus rules Taurus (21 April–21 May) and Libra (24 September–23 October)

COLOURS: White, pink, green

STONES: Diamond, white sapphire, rose quartz, carnelian, red and white coral, alabaster, lapis lazuli, azurite

METALS: Copper, brass

PLANTS: Birch, walnut, almond, myrtle, violet, daffodil, geranium, elderflower, laudanum, burdock, passion flower, mint, coriander, fig, peach, apricot, olive

PARTS OF THE BODY: Throat, kidney, lumbar region

KEYWORDS: Beauty, symmetry, balance, harmony, attraction, devotion, desire, sex, pleasure, fertility, luxury, money

CHARACTERISTICS: Feminine, passionate, idealist, charming, alluring, sensual, vain, lazy, envious

ROLES: Lover, muse, gardener, artist, beautician, model, opera singer

born with a strong emphasis on Venus in their birth chart are known for their captivating beauty, and Venus can be about the heights and depths of love and desire, and all that comes with it.

Men have Venus in their charts too – they are not only from Mars! – and the inclination to be attractive along with the rest of the Venusian attributes are as relevant to men as to women. The planets are not literally about gender or sexual orientation, but about the principles and drives in us all.

Venus represents our methods of seduction. The planet seeks to attract attention and devotion from the objects of her desire. She was usually portrayed naked in the myths, and had no sense of shame about it – she took pleasure in her appearance and sexuality and used it to her advantage. These days, Venus represents the inclination to enhance our beauty with the right clothes, hairstyle and make-up, and our tendency to keep glancing in the mirror!

Venus may be prone to focus on appearances to the point of vanity. We all want to emulate an ideal of beauty and may go to great lengths to do this, from anti-aging facial creams to plastic surgery to wearing impossibly high heels. There is sometimes the idea that we must suffer for our beauty, and we might go to great lengths to achieve our idea of physical perfection.

Venus inherited her idealism from Uranus, from whose castrated loins she was created. She is concerned with the ideals of beauty, harmony and perfect proportion in the physical as well as the abstract sense. It has been found that symmetrical facial features are one of the main indicators of beauty, and we strive for beauty, balance and proportion in all areas of our lives.

THE SYMBOL
The symbol for Venus ♀ combines the circle above the cross, which is symbolic of the superiority of the spiritual over the material. This

suggests that Venus is more concerned with high ideals than with physical reality, or that it brings her ideals down to earth.

Venus is the harmonising principle, it seeks to find common ground between two people, and ways for them to complement (and preferably compliment!) each other in order to make the relationship work. The planet uses charm to preserve the peace, and can have excellent cooperative skills when it wants to, making it an accomplished diplomat.

We should remember that despite the planet's associations with peace and harmony, Venus remains a warrior at heart, and can be self-serving to the point of disaster, even sparking off wars in the extreme example of the myth, just to get what it wants!

Not the most practical planet, Venus is more concerned with lounging around and satisfying its own desires than living in the real world and working hard for a living. It has a reputation, perhaps fairly, of being lazy, and Venus tends to expect a comfortable and pampered lifestyle handed to it on a plate.

Venus is concerned with money, however – she needs it to pay for her perfume and manicures! The planet is traditionally one of the significators of money in the birth chart. This is partly down to her powers of attraction, which draw valuable gifts to her like a magnet. She also has no trouble finding highly paid employment if she wants to, since beauty and attractiveness are keys to success and promotion in the workplace, as shown by numerous studies. We know that beauty sells as well as sex, and is the driving force behind the cosmetics, fashion and beauty industries.

Money is connected with our sense of value, which is another area which belongs to Venus. We value the things we love and desire, and we use the term 'value' to indicate how much money something is worth. Venus is also about appreciation, another term associated with money and investments.

The planet's primary inclination is to be loved and valued through relationships with others. Ultimately, our sense of self-worth cannot be based on others' opinions. We need to learn how to value ourselves, and Venus is about this process.

Venus is our sense of personal taste. This can cover everything from food, to scent or to our preferred airline. What sort of music we listen to, how we decorate our homes, what we enjoy in the world around us; Venus values the things that satisfy our tastes and bring us pleasure.

Being the planet second closest to the Sun, Venus is never more than 48° away from it when viewed from the Earth. This means that Venus will always appear to be within 48° of the Sun in the horoscope, and is often conjunct (next to) the Sun or in the same sign, and never more than two zodiac signs away. Along with Mercury, Venus works with the Sun to help achieve its aims, through attracting other people and experiences, helping the Sun to relate with others, while gaining enjoyment and pleasure from life.

TAURUS AND LIBRA

Venus rules the zodiac signs of Taurus and Libra. Both of these signs are expressions of Venusian values, Taurus in a materialistic way and Libra in a mental and idealistic way.

In which sign is Venus in your birth chart? This will indicate how we want to be loved and valued, and the way in which we use our charm to attract the things we desire. For example, Venus in Leo, the Sun's sign, will shine brightly, and can play queen (or king) to her heart's content, giving orders to all around her and ensuring she is the centre of everyone's attention. Venus can gain a lot of enjoyment and pleasure in Leo, and will tend to have confidence and value herself highly. In Capricorn, Venus will have high expectations and may measure her value in terms of her career and how much she earns. She may be very good at charming her colleagues, managers and business contacts. She may even find romance in the workplace!

Warriors of Mars

THE SCIENCE

Mars is known as the 'red planet' because it appears reddish in colour, due to the iron-rich minerals in its soil. It is about half the size of the Earth, and it is cool and dry with a thin atmosphere. Recent experiments on Mars have shown that there is water on the surface, currently in the form of frozen ice, and there may once have been life on Mars.

THE MYTH

In ancient Rome, the deity Mars governed war, as well as fertility and agriculture, and was protector of cattle and crops – associations which held him in high esteem among the Romans. Rome was thought to have been founded by Romulus, one of Mars' twin sons (the other twin being Remus), and it was believed that all Romans were descended from Mars.

According to Roman mythology, Mars' mother, Juno, was impregnated by a magical plant, hence his association with agriculture. It also meant that Mars did not have a father as such (in the same way that Venus did not have a mother). Known as Ares in ancient Greece, where he was a much more brutish and bloodthirsty character, the god was not so widely revered and did not have a major role in the Greek pantheon. The Greeks attributed Ares with being the cause behind every war. His parents, Zeus and Hera, rejected him because of his brutality. In some accounts, Hera had Ares alone, as in the Roman version of his conception.

Although known as a warmonger, Ares was also responsible for defending cities and protecting the defenceless. In one instance he murdered Halirrhothius, son of Poseidon, for raping his daughter Alcippe, and was tried and acquitted for doing so.

He had numerous children with Aphrodite (Venus), including the twins Phobos (Panic) and Deimos (Fear), who accompanied him on the battlefield (and more recently became the names of Mars' two moons after their discovery in 1877). Ares also had numerous violent, warmongering siblings who accompanied him, and he was killed on the battlefield by his sister, Athene, while fighting in the Trojan Wars.

THE MEANING

Mars in mythology is a formidable character! These days we tend to be against wars and aggression and, while we support our soldiers and recognize their bravery, we are more like the civilized ancient Greeks in our attitude than the militaristic Romans. We would prefer to live in perpetual peace, but tend to accept the need for warfare in special circumstances, such as defence, and this is where we recognize the Mars principle as being at its most honourable and courageous.

However, in astrology, Mars is about a lot more than war and bloodshed! It represents the active principle, the energy we need to spark into action. It gets us out of bed every morning and helps us to achieve our goals throughout the day. It is the red blood that runs through our veins and our life force. It is also our image of masculinity, in the way that Venus is the image of femininity. Both men and women need a well-functioning Mars, so that we feel potent and in charge of our lives.

Mars needs challenges, not only in battle or conflict, but also in physical activities such as competitive games and sports, or any area in which it can flex its muscles and compete with others for victory. Sports and exercise are an ideal way to channel Martian energy, as are all forms of activity that help to get our hearts pumping and build up our strength in the process. In this way we keep in touch with our physical strength and life force and feel alive and empowered.

Like Venus, sexuality and the sexual act are associated with Mars, and both planets are descriptive of our approach to sexuality and courtship. Mars, however, particularly enjoys the chase and the conquest. Unlike Venus, it is not naturally relationship-oriented, and can lose interest quickly after it has won the object of its passions, unless there is more competition involved! This tension gives rise to the games we play to keep things fresh and alive in romantic relationships.

The position of Mars in the birth chart describes the way we pursue (Mars) the objects of our desire (Venus). Sometimes Mars is used as an indicator specifically of the types of men, and Venus of the types of women, we become romantically involved with, although a combination of both (along with the entire chart) have a bearing on our love relationships.

Mars can be active in a verbal as well as in a physical way, and it is useful in persuading others of our point of view through argument. Of course, Mars is known for its desire to dominate, and it can go too far and try to force its will on other people. But we soon learn that others have an opinionated Mars as well. Things can get nasty very quickly if we don't take care to maintain respect for others' opinions as well!

Mars represents our primal passions, including anger. In the Roman myth of his origins, the suggestion that Mars did not have a father indicates that the father principle is missing in some way, and

CYCLE: Mars is the fourth planet from the Sun (after the Earth), and makes one revolution in the sky approximately every two years (687 days)

SIGNS: Mars rules Aries (21 March–20 April) and Scorpio (24 October–22 November)

COLOURS: Red

STONES: Ruby, carnelian, red coral, bloodstone, brimstone, pyrite, jasper, garnet

METALS: Iron

PLANTS: Pine, pepper, chilli, arsenic, belladonna, nettle, radish, horseradish, onion, chives, garlic, ginger, rhubarb, tobacco

PARTS OF THE BODY: Head, muscles, adrenal glands, sexual organs

KEYWORDS: Energy, strength, power, expression, courage, competition, conquest, aggression, domination, victory

CHARACTERISTICS: Brave, honourable, strong, defensive, stubborn, explosive, active, driven, primal

ROLES: Warrior, leader, hunter, sportsman

there is no parental restraint to curb his hot-headed tantrums. Mars will naturally play up at times, and can get us into sticky situations.

However, Mars reminds us that his qualities are part of our nature, and we do need to release our anger as it arises, as well as assert our opinions, defend ourselves, redress wrongs and maintain our honour when necessary. This is extremely important to our health, as we can become quite ill if we suppress these energies, and the repression of anger is linked to ailments such as stress and depression. We need to get to know our Mars, honour and express it with confidence, for it to serve us well.

Mars drives the Sun toward achieving its aims and helps us thrive, realize our talents and achieve our purpose and ambition in life. Being able to assert our will and make what we want happen in the world is itself a talent that we need to learn and, after trial and error, we usually tend to become more adept at utilizing Mars to its best potential in our thirties and forties.

THE SYMBOL
Mars' symbol of the arrow above the circle ♂ is an indication of the active will (arrow) of the spirit (circle). Some describe it as the shield and arrow or sword of Ares. The symbol used to consist of a cross (signifying matter) above the circle (signifying spirit), but has evolved into an arrow in recent centuries.

ARIES AND SCORPIO
Mars rules the zodiac signs of Aries, which is a cardinal fire sign, and Scorpio (traditional ruler), which is a fixed water sign. In Aries, Mars is particularly strong, spontaneous and quick to act on its will. It can also be spontaneous with its temper, and can have explosive moments followed by calm, and it doesn't tend to hold on to angry feelings for long. The will is also strong with Mars in Scorpio, but its action tends to be planned and executed in a controlled fashion so that it is more precise and effective, like a laser beam. Mars in Scorpio tends to express itself with words and feelings rather than through fighting. Sexual expression is important to both signs, and Mars in Scorpio tends to make love with greater emotional intensity, and in Aries with greater focus on physical enjoyment and release.

In which sign of the zodiac is Mars in your birth chart? You can apply the active and assertive qualities of Mars to its sign to find out how it works in your life. For example, if your Mars is in mutable watery Pisces, it will be quite gentle and passive, and find it hard to express itself assertively. It may tend to hold back its anger for fear of upsetting others, and may act in less direct ways, including through behaving like a martyr so others feel guilty and let us have our own way! Mars in an earth sign, such as fixed Taurus, tends to be very calm and slow to react, but takes slow and patient steps towards getting what it wants. Like a bull, it can pack tremendous power, and can charge at its assailant when it gets angry or feels threatened. Mars can also be very passionate and lusty in Taurus, making an excellent lover with tremendous stamina!

Jupiter the Adventurer

THE SCIENCE

Jupiter is the largest and densest planet of all, being more than ten times bigger than the Earth, and twice the mass of all the other planets put together! It also has the largest number of known moons – sixty-four have been discovered so far.

Being the largest planet, Jupiter is easily visible in the night sky. It is one of the most magnificent planets to look at by telescope, with bright orangey-pink stratification in its atmosphere. Like the other gas giants (Saturn, Uranus and Neptune), Jupiter has a thick layer of dense gas, which transforms into liquid and then into solid, rocky matter as it gets closer to its core.

THE MYTH

The Roman god Jupiter, also known as Jove, was Zeus to the ancient Greeks. He was known as the king of the gods and had a central function to play in both Greek and Roman mythology, and we still associate many of his attributes with the idea of an all-seeing, all-powerful god today.

Zeus was a sky god, and governed thunder, using thunderbolts as a punishment for those who misbehaved. He was seen as a father figure and the highest authority among the gods. He acted as a judge in trials and intervened to mediate conflicts, and oaths were sworn in his name. This power did not corrupt him, and he was seen as just and fair. He was also attributed with starting the Great Deluge, a flood which was intended to destroy all of humanity so that the world could be started anew.

As his father, Cronus (Saturn), had done before him, Zeus repeated a family pattern by overthrowing his father and becoming king of the gods in his place. Although he did not swallow all his children, as his father did, he instead swallowed his consort, the goddess Metis, after impregnating her, because it was prophesied that she would bear him powerful children who would overthrow him. Metis and their children did eventually escape, but Zeus is never overthrown, and this family pattern ends with him.

Also like his father, Zeus' consort was one of his sisters, Hera, and he sired numerous children with her as well as other goddesses and humans. One of his favourite sons was the hero Heracles (Roman Hercules), conceived with the mortal woman Alcmene. Among Zeus' other siblings were Demeter (Ceres), Poseidon (Neptune) and Hades (Pluto). After his father Cronus was slain, he drew lots with his brothers to decide which realm each would rule; Zeus picked the sky, while Poseidon picked the sea and Hades the underworld.

The Roman Jupiter was the father of Mars (although the connection is tenuous, as his wife Juno was impregnated by a plant in some versions of the story), and thus it was believed he was related to every Roman citizen through Mars' son, Romulus, the founder of Rome. In any case, Jupiter was thought to be the great protector and benefactor of Rome, and was believed to have blessed the Romans with good fortune in their military campaigns. Consequently members of the Roman Empire worshipped him above all other gods.

THE MEANING

Jupiter's qualities in astrology are connected with its enormous size, and are based on ideas about growth and expansion. The planet represents a positive attitude and belief in limitless opportunities, resisting any attempt to be restricted or controlled. It signifies the freedom to explore new ideas and experiences,

CYCLE: Jupiter makes one full revolution in the sky and in our birth charts in just under twelve years, and spends around a year in each sign

SIGNS: Jupiter rules Sagittarius (23 November– 21 December) and Pisces (20 February–20 March)

COLOURS: Purple, deep blue

STONES: Amethyst, sapphire, serpentine, turquoise, aventurine

METALS: Tin

PLANTS & TREES: Oak, hazel, pine, maple, birch, willow, cherry, mulberry, pear, liquorice, cherry, birch, liverwort, wheat, mace, saffron, clover

PARTS OF THE BODY: Thighs, liver

KEYWORDS: Growth, expansion, development, improvement, celebration, freedom, adventure, journeys, judgement, justice, wisdom, omnipotence

CHARACTERISTICS: Hopeful, intrepid, positive, exuberant, enthusiastic, generous, fair, greedy, indulgent, humorous, philosophical

ROLES: Judge, father, king, teacher, priest, guru, lord

and is connected with our sense of meaning, religious and philosophical beliefs and perspective.

Jupiter likes to enjoy life to the full, and can do so to the point of excess. It is known for representing qualities of generosity and goodwill, for throwing lavish parties and making sure that everyone has a full glass and is having a good time. The planet is often associated with addictions and weight problems, along with the Moon and Neptune – especially when these planets are in aspect to each other, or are strongly placed in the birth chart.

Cronus (Saturn), his father and authority figure in mythology and voice of reason and moderation, is thought to function as a containing principle to Zeus' (Jupiter's) expansive qualities. However, Zeus deposed his father and replaced him as king, rendering him powerless, and in astrology this suggests that Saturn's efforts are not very effective when it comes to Jupiter's determination to be free to act as it pleases!

Although Zeus does repeat the family pattern by castrating his father and usurping his role as king, and swallows Metis to prevent the same thing happening to him, when Metis is set free his children do not usurp him as prophesied, and the pattern ends with him. This may suggest that Jupiter works with negative family patterns in a new way, adopting a positive attitude that can break the curse. Certainly Jupiter is not a fearful planet, and in many ways can behave as if he were invincible! In this way, problems seem to slide off Jupiter's back, or bounce off him, usually without his even noticing.

The structures and routines of our daily lives are hard for Jupiter to bear. As a result, the planet finds any form of commitment difficult, from jobs to relationships and people with a strong Jupiter in their birth chart tend to find these areas of life quite difficult.

Jupiter transits can bring good fortune with them, sometimes on the scale of lottery wins! But the meaning of Jupiter can't always be guaranteed, and he can occasionally surprise us with a less desirable outcome. We have to keep an open mind with regard to Jupiter, and consider how his position might apply in a particular case. For example, transiting Jupiter conjunct Venus in the birth chart may indicate that we will receive large sums of money, but it could equally show that we will spend money on a grander scale than we can earn it, and thus it could be an indicator of large debts!

THE SYMBOL

The symbol of Jupiter ♃ is composed of the cross of matter beneath the crescent, which represents the soul, indicating the importance of meaning and enriching the soul over the material world.

SAGITTARIUS AND PISCES

Jupiter rules the mutable fire sign of Sagittarius and the mutable water sign of Pisces (traditional ruler; see table on page 19). In both cases they are mutable signs, in the same way that the remaining two mutable signs (Gemini and Virgo) have the same ruler, Mercury. These mutable and easy-going signs lend themselves to the adaptable and malleable qualities of Jupiter, allowing it the flexibility it requires to expand, grow and explore limitless possibilities. Jupiter in Sagittarius can be fascinated with world religions and will explore every culture and tradition to find meaning. In Pisces, Jupiter tends to have a mystical approach and can find meaning through more esoteric religious beliefs and practices.

In which sign is Jupiter in your birth chart? You can apply the qualities of Jupiter to the characteristics of the sign, and see how you think it functions in your life. For example, if your Jupiter is in airy Libra, it can be fair-minded and can make an excellent mediator. It will also be concerned with finding meaning through partnership, and may attract lots of relationships into its life. Jupiter in earthy Capricorn can hold very strong religious convictions, or can be strongly atheistic – the god image tends to be quite strict and austere, or possibly absent, so that we have to build our own sense of meaning. With these placements, opportunities are not expected to come knocking at our door, but we expect to create our own luck in the world.

The Genius of Saturn

THE SCIENCE

Saturn is the second largest planet in the solar system next to Jupiter, and is about nine times bigger than the Earth. It also has a high mass – around 95 times higher than the Earth's. It is the furthest planet in our solar system that is clearly visible with the naked eye.

Saturn is known as a 'gas giant', along with Jupiter, Uranus and Neptune. Like them, it is a gaseous planet with a number of satellite moons – sixty-two have been discovered to date. The moons are named after the Titans in Greek mythology, and the largest moon, Trident, is even larger than Mercury. The second largest moon, Rhea, has been found to have a ring system of its own. Saturn is also known for having the most impressive ring system of all the planets.

THE MYTH

The Roman Saturn was the equivalent of the Greek god Cronus, son of Ouranos the sky god and Gaia the earth mother. The name Cronus means 'time', and he ruled things associated with time and the passing of the seasons, such as planting and agriculture.

Cronus was one of the Titan children of Ouranos (Uranus) who had been buried by their father in Gaia's (the Earth's) womb. With Gaia's assistance, Cronus escaped and castrated his father with a sickle, throwing his genitals into the sea. Cronus then took his father's place as king of the gods. Ouranos was furious and cursed his children, prophesying that Cronus would one day be overthrown by one of his children in the same way as he had overthrown his father.

Cronus married one of his sisters, Rhea, but was so terrified that one of his children would depose him that he repeated history, this time by swallowing his children. After the birth of his son, Zeus (Jupiter), Rhea tricked Cronus by hiding the child on the island of Crete, and gave Cronus a stone wrapped in a baby's swaddling clothes in his son's place. Cronus swallowed the stone and thought nothing more about it. When Zeus had grown up, he returned to confront his father and forced him to regurgitate all the children and relatives he had swallowed. Zeus then became king and deposed his father, as predicted. He tied his father in chains and sent him into the underworld.

Both Cronus and the Roman Saturn were affiliated with the myth of a Golden Age, which is an idea that at one time in the distant past, society worked in perfect balance and nobody wanted for anything. During this perfect age, Saturn/Cronus was king, and there was peace and prosperity throughout the land.

Like Mars, Saturn was more highly revered by the Romans than Cronus was by the Greeks, and the Romans celebrated the winter

CYCLE: Saturn takes around 29 years to make one revolution around the Sun, and the birth chart

SIGNS: Saturn rules Capricorn (22 December–20 January) and Aquarius (21 January–19 February)

COLOURS: Black, brown, grey

STONES: Sapphire, jet, malachite, sardonyx, marble, flint

METALS: Lead

PLANTS: Cypress, yew, hemp, tamarisk, wolfbane, hemlock, nightshade, ivy, moss, sage, parsnip, comfrey, cumin

PARTS OF THE BODY: Bones, teeth, skin, knees, gall bladder, spleen

KEYWORDS: Time, boundaries, independence, self-sufficiency, structure, restriction, transformation, old age, authority, rules

CHARACTERISTICS: Independent, self-sufficient, structured, restricting, responsible, serious, traditional, harsh, melancholic, ritualistic, ambitious, enduring

ROLES: Priest, judge, banker, politician, king, father, grandfather, time-keeper

solstice with the great feast of Saturnalia, when it was traditional to reverse roles of master and slave, and suspend normal codes of social conduct, in remembrance of Saturn's Golden Age.

THE MEANING

Saturn is the Lord of Time, to which we are all held in allegiance. It rules the process of aging and the restrictions we experience as we get older, as well as an awareness of our own mortality. It governs the calendar and the cycle of the seasons, as well as the religious traditions and festivals that have developed around them which we celebrate as a community. Saturn is also known as the Lord of Karma, and sees to it that we are rewarded with the fruits of our actions – that we reap what we sow.

Saturn represents the structures that contain us, the social traditions we live by, and our political, economic and religious institutions. It is the authorities that maintain them, such as the priest, judge, police officer, banker or politician.

Saturn marks a boundary to the known universe, and represents boundaries in general. Where Jupiter expands, Saturn contracts and holds back. It rules the skin, and marks our clear boundaries between ourselves and the rest of the world. We need strong boundaries to develop a sense of ourselves as separate to everyone else, and Saturn helps our Sun to develop as a unique and separate individual. Through growing up and gaining independence we become self-sufficient adults.

Saturn is concerned with duty and discipline – by working hard, over long periods, we accomplish our goals in the world and achieve things we can be proud of, and in the process are transformed. We need Saturn's discipline in every area of our lives, from doing the dishes to earning a living. A well-functioning Saturn helps us to be effective in the world and to fulfil our social functions and responsibilities to others as well as ourselves.

The planet is known for being realistic and practical but has the propensity to be overly harsh. Its expectations can be too high. A strong Saturn in a chart may indicate that we need to be in control of everything in our lives to the extent that we feel like a failure if we do not achieve the goals that we have set for ourselves. If we fall short of these expectations, and we can't help but do so, it can strip away the confidence we have in ourselves and our abilities. However, Saturn provides the urge to develop the areas in which we feel less able, and its perceived weaknesses can become our greatest strengths because of this. It is important to utilize Saturn's drive and ambition to improve ourselves while being realistic about our goals, respecting our limits and keeping things in perspective.

Saturn has endurance and staying power. It is the glue which binds us together, and is usually prominent in our long-term relationships. A strong Saturn contact between the two charts in a relationship (especially if one person's Saturn is in aspect with the other person's Sun or Moon) can show serious long-term commitment that may last forever (whether we want it to or not!).

Conversely, Saturn also rules endings, and can equally bring a partnership to an end. Sometimes the thing that binds us in the first place to another person may fizzle out after a relationship has run its course, and Saturn contacts can involve the experience of rejection.

Saturn was known as the 'Great Malefic' in medieval astrology, and was generally thought to bring about misfortune, although (like Jupiter) this depended on the particular question and context, and in some cases Saturn could bring about a favourable result as much as an undesirable one. The planet was traditionally associated with a melancholic disposition. Depending on its position, it can indicate sadness and depression, where we hold back our feelings and feel cut off from others. Saturn believes in facing harsh realities head on, and recognizes that we are all ultimately alone. It can be quite hard on itself and others, and can sometimes bring the cold harshness of reality into painful view.

THE SYMBOL

The symbol of Saturn ♄ is composed of the cross of matter above the crescent of the soul, indicating the importance of practical considerations over personal meaning.

CAPRICORN AND AQUARIUS

Saturn rules the earth sign Capricorn and the air sign Aquarius (traditional ruler). In Capricorn the planet is concerned with practical reality and common sense, as well as developing careers, goals and responsibilities. In Aquarius it tends to be more focused on realism and rational thinking, as well as the social structures and traditions which we are part of.

In which sign is Saturn in your birth chart? This will indicate the characteristics you need to develop to help you succeed in the world and gain a sense of achievement. For example, Saturn in Gemini may be concerned with developing writing and communication skills and may work well in areas involved with language and education. A person with Saturn in Gemini may feel challenged or under-skilled in these areas, but the drive to develop them brings enormous satisfaction.

THE SATURN RETURN

The Saturn cycle and its return has become the most popular of all the planetary returns. All the planets have 'returns' – this is the amount of time they take to make one complete revolution around the Sun, and the amount of time increases with each planet as we move further out from the Sun.

The Saturn return takes place approximately every 29 years, and is considered to have great bearing on our lives at around the age of 29, and then again at 58 and 87 (if we are lucky enough to live to a ripe old age). As with the other chart cycles, the squares (around age 7, 21, 36, 51, etc.) and oppositions (at around age 14, 44, 73, etc.) are also considered significant times in the planet's cycle. The Saturn return can be a time of crisis, when old structures no longer serve us, and we are ready to grow up and take the next step towards maturity. Saturn helps us to take stock of what we have achieved so far, and prepares us for the next level.

Existing relationships can sometimes break down at the Saturn return points, as we find we have grown in a different direction to our partner and have contrasting goals in life, or we might have a child for the first time (29 is currently the average age at which we become parents in Western cultures). Relationships formed around this time will take us in a new direction in life, particularly with regard to our work and taking on new responsibilities.

Whatever the case, our experiences around these ages are accompanied with the realization that we are not as young as we once were, and they tend to be marked by crises and changes that give us a sense of being initiated into the next level of maturity and independence.

Uranus the Revolutionary

THE SCIENCE

Uranus is pale blue in colour, and one of the family of gas giants in the solar system, along with Jupiter, Saturn and Neptune. Like the other gas giants it has a ring system and numerous moons – twenty-seven moons have been discovered so far. It is sometimes classed as an 'ice giant' with Neptune, given both planets' high proportion of icy materials.

The planet is known for its eccentric axial tilt – it is lying on its side in comparison with most other planets, and its poles are placed where others normally have their equators!

The planets up to Saturn have been known since ancient times and can be seen without the aid of a telescope. Even though Uranus can also be seen very faintly with the naked eye, it has such a slow orbit that it was not recognized as a planet until the 18th century. However, with the development of telescopes, new planetary bodies began to be discovered, and Uranus was the first of these. Its discovery in 1781 was attributed to William Herschel, who observed the planet through a telescope at his home in Bath, UK.

THE MYTH

Uranus was named after the Greek sky god Ouranos. In Roman mythology, his equivalent was Caelus (from *caelum*, meaning 'sky' in Latin).

Ouranos was the father of Cronus (Saturn), Rhea and the Titans (the earlier order of gods, before Zeus and the Olympians), and grandfather of Zeus (Jupiter), among many other descendents. He was one of the primordial beings alongside Gaia, the mother of all creation, and together they created the Greek pantheon of gods.

According to the myth, Ouranos hated the children he produced with Gaia, and imprisoned them back in her womb, deep within the Earth. Gaia helped her children escape and gave her sons a sickle with which to castrate their father, so he would not be able to father any

CYCLE: Uranus takes approximately 84 years to make one revolution around the Sun

SIGNS: Uranus rules Aquarius (21 January– 19 February) (with Saturn)

COLOURS: Silver, electric blue, neon colours

STONES: Fluorite, meteorite, moldavite

METALS: Platinum, uranium

PLANTS: Orchid

PARTS OF THE BODY: Ankles, circulatory system

KEYWORDS: Community, change, transformation, freedom, liberation, revolution, progress, society, new technology

CHARACTERISTICS: Unconventional, eccentric, genius, aware, quirky, fair, idealist, radical, community minded

ROLES: Environmentalist, electrician, technologist, scientist, human/animal rights advocate, brother, rebel

more children. Cronus (Saturn) took up the challenge – he castrated his father and usurped his position as king of the gods. Ouranos cursed Cronus, saying that one day one of Cronus' sons would do the same to him. Ouranos then returned to the sky, bringing stability to the heavens.

Cronus did, indeed, repeat history after hearing Ouranos' prophesy, and swallowed his children in case they overthrew him in the way he had overthrown his father. The family pattern continued with his son (Ouranos' grandson), Zeus, but Zeus was never overthrown, and the pattern ended there.

The transformational energy of the planet Uranus in astrology is also often linked to the myth of Prometheus, a Titan god who was known as the 'Awakener', because he stole fire from Zeus by hiding it in a fennel stalk, and brought it to humans. This gift brought intelligence to the mortal humans, empowering and transforming them forever. This idea of the theft of fire which brings progress to humanity is one that reappears in myths from around the world.

According to the Greek myth, Zeus was furious with Prometheus, and decreed that as his punishment he should be tied to a rock, where every day an eagle would come and peck out his liver, and each night a new one would grow in its place, to be eaten by the eagle again. Because he was an immortal god, Prometheus could not die, but he could feel pain, and would have been left to suffer like this for all eternity. Years later, Zeus' son and hero Heracles finally shot the eagle and set Prometheus free.

In his rage, Zeus also sent Pandora and her famous box of horrors to humanity, so that any benefits they received from the fire were counteracted by the evil and misfortune that they unleashed on the world. In some versions of the story, Hope was also in the box!

THE MEANING

Uranus represents progress and the idealization of human potential. It is associated with the revolutionary and freedom fighter, who has a vision of a fairer and better society for all. It is also linked to the image of the mad scientist and genius inventor, who dares to think outside the box. Uranus also represents the Eureka moment, like a flash of lightning in our brains, bringing with it a new discovery or vision.

As with all the newly discovered planets, the signs of the times around Uranus' discovery are found to correspond with the meaning of the planet. Uranus was discovered during a period of revolutions in technology, thought, government and society, including the first wave of the Industrial Revolution, the Age of Enlightenment in Europe, and the French and American political revolutions, among others.

Like Prometheus' fire, the vision of progress was taking hold of humanity and new ideas started to develop from these. Many major scientific discoveries, including electricity, and the components of air (nitrogen, oxygen, carbon dioxide, and hydrogen) were also made in this period.

Our own particular ideals and vision of perfection depend on where Uranus is placed in our birth charts. Wherever it falls, it sets to work to revolutionize the sign, house and any planets or angles that it comes into contact with, and in this way we each develop our own ideals and theories about how to improve society and make a difference in the world.

Like Saturn, Uranus has high expectations which are often not realized, and it can have a difficult time in the real world. People with a strong Uranus in their birth charts tend to live with their head in the clouds – Ouranos' domain – and find reality as disappointing and difficult to bear as the god Ouranos felt about the children he produced with Gaia.

Also like Saturn, Uranus is concerned with the rational mind, and in the name of social or scientific progress can often lose sight of the effect of its ideals on the individual. Concerned with what is objectively right and true, the subjective feelings and experience of the individual can be forgotten, and those with a strong Uranian emphasis in their charts can easily fall out of touch with what makes us human – our emotions. Indeed, emotions to Uranus can be like electricity to water – an enormous shock!

Uranian energy is lively and active. This may be useful when there is a revolution or some kind of upheaval. However, it can be disruptive and difficult in everyday life. People with a prominent Uranus in their charts can hold very strong beliefs and convictions and take every opportunity to discuss the issues which they see as vital, but are tiresome to others around them. Also, being uncomfortable around other people's feelings, those with strong Uranian personalities can feel out of place in social gatherings, and tend to be treated like outsiders wherever they go.

Uranus makes one full revolution around the birth chart and returns to its original position approximately every 84 years. It is square to its original position at around the ages of 21 and 63 years old, and opposite to its birth position at around 42 years old, around the time we tend to experience what is known as the 'mid-life crisis'. Each of these ages marks a time in our lives when we experience the urge to break free from the lifestyles and structures that bind us, and bring change and new thinking to our attitude and approach to life. (The Saturn and Neptune cycles also correspond with some of the key points in the Uranus cycle, including the mid-life crisis).

Uranus spends a generation – about seven years – in each sign, and while it has significance in our own lives and characters, it is also a reflection of our wider generation group, describing the particular attitude and zeitgeist of that group. Its significance in our own life depends on how prominent Uranus is in the birth chart, and how connected it is to the personal planets (from the Sun to Saturn).

THE SYMBOL

The symbol for Uranus ♅ is thought to be based on earlier symbols for Mars and the Sun, as Ouranos is thought to be related to the principles of both planets. It is also thought to have an H at the top for Herschel, who discovered the planet.

AQUARIUS

In the years since its discovery, Uranus has become associated with the zodiac sign of Aquarius, and many astrologers use it as the sign's new ruler. The sign's traditional ruler, Saturn, is still considered its co-ruler. Uranus is thought to be strongest in Aquarius, and was transiting through the sign from 1996 to 2003, a period of great technological advance – including the development of the Internet and the mobile phone – that have revolutionized society.

Uranus was also in Aquarius from 1912 to 1919, at the time of the First World War, a period which also led to great technological advances and massive social changes. It can be useful to trace the periods in which Uranus travels through the signs, and observe its correspondence with related areas of transformation in society as well as in our own lives.

In which sign was Uranus when you were born? How does the sign it was placed in correspond to changes in society around that time, your own strongly held convictions about how society can progress and your vision for a better world?

The Poetry of Neptune

THE SCIENCE

Neptune is four times the size of the Earth, and the smallest of the gas giants (the others being Jupiter, Saturn and Uranus). Its deep blue atmosphere is made up of gases – mainly hydrogen and helium. It is also classed as an 'ice giant' with Uranus because it contains a high proportion of icy material. It has thirteen known moons, the largest of which is Triton.

Neptune was discovered in 1846, after a gravitational disturbance on Uranus' orbit was observed, and another planet's presence was suspected before it was actually spotted in the heavens. Given the planet's great distance from us and its cloudy surface, much remains obscure about Neptune, such as the reason for its unusually high temperature of around 480°C.

THE MYTH

The Roman Neptune was Poseidon in Greek myth, the god of the sea who was also associated with floods and earthquakes. There were many other gods of the seas and rivers, but they all came under the jurisdiction of Poseidon, who was the supreme god of the waters.

Poseidon's father was Cronus (Saturn), the king of the gods, and his mother was Rhea. Along with his other brothers and sisters, Poseidon was swallowed at birth by his father. After Zeus castrated his father and saved his siblings, he succeeded him as king of the gods, and drew lots with his brothers to divide up the world between them. Poseidon took the sea while Zeus took the sky and Hades (Pluto) took the underworld.

Poseidon married Amphitrite, with whom he had a son, Triton, who was a merman, with the upper body of a man and the tail of

CYCLE: Neptune takes approximately 165 years to make one revolution around the Sun

SIGNS: Neptune rules Pisces (20 February– 20 March) (with Jupiter)

COLOURS: Purple, lilac, sea green, blue

STONES & MINERALS: Amethyst, sodalite

METALS: Neptunium

PLANTS: Water lily, mushroom

PARTS OF THE BODY: Nervous system

KEYWORDS: Imagination, emotion, hope, potential, delusion, mystery, wishes, escape, entertainment, sustenance, water, longing, thirst

CHARACTERISTICS: Ethereal, spiritual, religious, otherworldly, emotional, moody

ROLES: Dancer, swimmer, photographer, celebrity, fashion designer, actor, artist

a fish. Similar to the Hans Christian Andersen fairy tale about the little mermaid, the family lived in a golden palace at the bottom of the sea. Poseidon had many love affairs and his children included the Cyclops, Pegasus, Theseus and Orion.

Poseidon often changed into other creatures, such as horses, and helped others to transform their shape as well. He was a moody deity, and could be very helpful at one time and angry the next. He used earthquakes, floods and shipwrecks to bring misfortune on others.

One story for which Poseidon is known is that of King Minos of Crete, who called on him to bring forth a bull from the sea for a sacrifice, to prove his divine right to be king. Poseidon provided the bull, but Minos became too fond of the beast to sacrifice it. Poseidon then played a cruel trick on Minos and asked Aphrodite to make the king's wife fall in love with the bull. From their union the ferocious Minotaur was created.

THE MEANING

Neptune represents the collective waters which contain all of the hopes, dreams, emotions, ideas and potential of humanity. Through Neptune we get beyond our current predicament and dare to dream of a better future.

Around the time of Neptune's discovery in 1846, the Industrial Revolution was still in full swing, and major developments in technology, such as the steam railway, were further transforming society and the landscape. Photography had just been invented, and early hoaxers were producing photographs of ghostly forms using double-exposure and claiming they were spectral beings. Hypnotism and the foundations of psychological theory were being developed. Socialism was on the rise in Europe, and the *Communist Manifesto* by Marx and Engels was published. Slavery was becoming an increasingly contentious issue around the world, leading to the American Civil War and abolition of slavery in the US by 1861.

Like Uranus, Neptune idealizes, but in Neptune's case the ideals tend to be based on a fantasy of someone or something who can save us from the pain of separation. At its heart there is a longing to escape the cold harsh reality of the world and return to the womb that sustained us before we were born.

This can be demonstrated when we return home after a long, hard day, close the doors and shut out the world, and immerse ourselves in a good book, film or other activity that takes us away from the daily grind and lets us escape for a while. Doing something that helps take our minds off our worries usually has a restorative effect, recharging our batteries.

But Neptune can get lost in this relaxing realm, and is not always good at stepping back into the real world, or knowing when to stop. When this happens, we may end up drinking more wine than intended, or staying up too late and sleeping through our alarm in the morning! Neptune is often associated with escapist and addictive tendencies.

People with a strong Neptune can be extremely religious, and have a natural affinity with spiritual practices and mystical experiences. They usually gain a lot of satisfaction from this, but may have a tendency to use spirituality as a crutch or as a means of escape from the everyday world and their responsibilities in it.

The planet also represents the yearning for a benevolent parent to save us from suffering and make everything better. This can take the form of a religious saviour – an all-powerful, all-loving God can be the ideal figure on which to place our yearning for a parent who will love us unconditionally, and who will provide solace from the pain of separation from our mother.

This yearning to be looked after can be reversed with a strong Neptune, and there is a tendency to sacrifice our own needs and look after others selflessly, becoming martyrs to ensure that others are indebted to us forever!

Fantasies of a perfect romance also fall under the realm of Neptune, and we can long for the perfect love relationship that will satisfy every need and make us feel happy and complete at last! The fantasy is again about returning to the womb and being looked after so that we never have to grow up and separate from our parental attachments, become independent adults or learn to face our responsibilities alone.

Acting, fame and glamour, along with the cult of celebrity, also belong to this realm, as do the modern media of photography, film and television. We idealize our favourite actors and celebrities and imagine they have perfect looks, relationships and lifestyles. Many of us dream of being famous, so that our lives could be perfect too. Yet the films these people star in are computer-animated, their images are airbrushed, and their perfection is only an illusion.

The realization that ideals can't be achieved can also lead to enormous disappointment and disillusionment with the world, and Neptune is associated with mood swings and destructive behaviour when reality doesn't match up to our expectations.

Unlike Saturn, Neptune is boundary-less and free to go with the flow, wherever it may lead. It is the classic embodiment of the artistic temperament, needing space and freedom to be playful and creative. Neptune blurs the lines between truth and fantasy and tries to bend the rules of reality. In this way our imagination is free to explore new ways of seeing and new ideas and creations can come out of it.

Neptune is associated with the mysterious realms of life, and questions that do not have a scientific explanation – such as where consciousness comes from – belong to its realm. The planet represents the unseen laws of correspondence that connect us all, and the inexplicable coincidences that occur in our lives. Conspiracy theories emerge out of Neptune's fuzzy realm, where nothing is quite as it seems, and there are many layers of possibility.

THE SYMBOL

Neptune's astronomical sign Ψ is an image of Poseidon's trident, a weapon which he famously carried. The planet is thought to be the co-ruler of the mutable water sign of Pisces, along with the sign's traditional ruler, Jupiter, and is at home in the adaptable and watery realm of this sign.

THE CYCLE OF NEPTUNE

Neptune takes around 165 years to orbit the Sun, and spends around 14 years in each sign (this varies, as Neptune's orbit is elliptical which means it will spend longer in some signs than others). While it won't make a revolution in a single lifetime, the cycle of Neptune means that it will make a square to its original position at around the age of 42, corresponding with the timing of the Uranus opposition and the Saturn square. The significance of the Neptune square at this age indicates that our sense of boundaries are dissolving, and we become more aware of life's more mysterious realm. It is a time when we are confused about who we are and where our lives are headed, which can lead to immense creativity and new possibilities that we did not imagine could be possible before.

In which sign was Neptune when you were born? How does the sign it was placed in correspond with your generation group, and how has it impacted upon your personal beliefs and yearnings?

Pluto the Sorcerer

THE SCIENCE

Pluto resides in a region of the solar system called the Kuiper belt, along with numerous other planetary bodies, asteroids and comets, many of which are still being discovered. The Kuiper belt extends from Neptune's orbit toward the outer regions of the solar system, beyond which is the Oort cloud.

Pluto is about five-and-a-half times smaller than the Earth, and less than half the size of Mercury. Like Mercury, Pluto has only a trace atmosphere. It appears brown in colour, and has three known satellite moons – Charon, Nix and Hydra.

Being the furthest from the Sun, it is the coldest body, the temperature of its surface atmosphere being around -223°C (-369°F). Like Uranus, it rotates on its side, where most other planets have their equator. Pluto's eccentric orbit means that it is sometimes closer to the Sun than Neptune, although the two are not in danger of colliding.

In 2006, the International Astronomical Union rede-fined what constitutes a 'planet' and it was decided that Pluto did not fall within this definition. It is now classed as a 'dwarf planet', along with Eris and Ceres.

THE MYTH

Pluto, known as Hades in Greek mythology, was the Lord of the Underworld. The word Hades was also used as the name for the underworld itself, and was also a reference to the realm of the dead. The underworld was a place where very few could enter unless they were deceased, and very few were allowed to leave once they were there. Even Hades spent most of his time there. But Hades did not represent death itself – this was thought to be the responsibility of the daemon Thanatos.

CYCLE: Pluto makes one rotation around the Sun approximately every 248 years

SIGNS: Pluto rules Scorpio (24 October– 22 November) (with Mars)

COLOURS: Black, white, red, maroon, purple

STONES & MINERALS: Hematite, obsidian

METALS: Plutonium

PLANTS: Cypress, rhododendron, aubergine, beetroot, pomegranate, narcissus, cacti

PARTS OF THE BODY: Sexual and reproductive organs, bowel

KEYWORDS: Unconscious, the unknown, fate, depth, detection, protection, secrets, truth, wisdom, life and death, birth, survival, waste, roots, annihilation

CHARACTERISTICS: Deep, intense, sexual, sensitive, probing, definite, wise, transformative, powerful

ROLES: Magician, midwife, detective, researcher, psychologist, spy, miner, treasure hunter

Hades ruled precious metals and anything that came out of the ground. He was known for his chariot drawn by four black horses, his possession of a helmet which made the wearer invisible, and his three-headed dog named Cerberus.

Hades' parents were Cronus (Saturn) and Rhea. He was the oldest of his brothers and sisters to be swallowed at birth by their father. His brother Zeus (Jupiter) was hidden by his mother at birth, and returned when he was old enough to castrate Cronus and free his siblings from his belly. Zeus then became king of the gods himself, and drew lots with his brothers to divide up the world between them. Zeus picked the sky while Poseidon (Neptune) picked the sea and Hades the underworld.

One day Cupid and Aphrodite were playing games when one of Cupid's arrows was accidentally released from his bow and hit Hades in the heart. This meant that he would fall in love with the next person he came across. His eyes fell upon a young girl, Persephone, who was out picking flowers. A great chasm opened up in the ground and Hades rode out on a chariot and abducted the girl, taking her into the underworld to be with him.

When Persephone didn't come home, her mother, Demeter, goddess of the seasons and the harvest (also one of Hades' sisters), began to worry and searched everywhere for her daughter. She couldn't find Persephone anywhere, so she destroyed all the crops and turned the Earth to barren winter in her anguish.

Zeus could not allow the situation to continue, and sent Hermes (Mercury) to the underworld to return Persephone to her mother. After much persuasion, Hades finally allowed it, but only on the agreement that Persephone would return to him. Persephone was obliged to return to Hades anyway, as she had eaten some pomegranate seeds during her time there, and this meant that she could not fully return to her childhood innocence and life with her mother again.

As a compromise, Persephone was allowed to stay with her mother for two thirds of the year, and Demeter restored the weather and allowed the crops to thrive again for this period. But when her daughter returned to Hades for one third of the year, Demeter turned the season to winter again, and this story describes why part of the year is winter.

THE MEANING

Pluto is associated with the realm of the underworld, our unconscious and the parts of our nature which we keep hidden and private. It represents the intimacy we have with loved ones whom we trust.

THE SYMBOL

Pluto was discovered in 1930 by a young astronomer, Clive Tombaugh, under the direction of Percy Lowell in his observatory in Flagstaff, Arizona, USA. Its symbol ♇ was partially chosen to represent the initials of Percy Lowell, and partly to indicate the first two letters of the planet's name.

This period was known as the 'Great Depression' in the Western world, when an economic crash led to widespread poverty and joblessness. It was also an age of extreme political views, and dictatorships at both ends of the political spectrum were thriving in Europe and Asia. In Germany, this climate laid the ground for the rise of the Nazi Party, which led to the Second World War in 1939. There were major developments in the weaponry used in warfare during this period and Hollywood and the film industry began to thrive. The Disney character Pluto was created in the same year and named in honour of the newly discovered planet. The radioactive element Plutonium was also discovered and named after the planet.

Although Pluto is now officially designated a 'dwarf planet' by astronomers, astrologers continue to class Pluto as one of the planetary pantheon which make up the astrological horoscope, and have not demoted its significance in any way.

In astrology, the planet has a reputation for being secretive and protective of its own personal security, and controls the information that it passes on, like a spy in wartime! It brings insight and understanding to the areas of life that lie beneath the surface, and can be excellent at tuning into the unseen world, cracking codes and getting to the heart of matters.

Pluto represents the ability to probe deeply into any matter and can bring a great depth of insight. People with a strong Pluto in their birth chart can make excellent psychologists, researchers and detectives, or anything which requires a good nose for finding things out and an unrelenting attitude which leaves no stone unturned!

Although it can hold back information and guard secrets when necessary, Pluto demands honesty from us at all times, and is fearless in the face of any truth, however hard to bear. In this way, Pluto can go to the places where angels fear to tread, and where other planets can't follow. For this reason it deals with the extremes of life, and is the planet of choice in times of crisis.

Pluto rules the survival instinct and has a strong will. It mainly works on an unconscious level and brings about what we need, often without us being aware that we need it. As a result, along the lines of the famous song by the Rolling Stones, we might not always get what we want with Pluto, but we tend to get what we need.

Transiting Pluto on personal planets in the chart can bring about unwanted or unimagined changes, which often involve the need to confront loss, as Demeter did in the myth. This may be a painful process, and we can go through a great deal of turmoil during the long periods Pluto spends at a particular point in the birth chart.

However, like the phoenix, we rise out of Pluto's ashes stronger and are transformed. We can then often look back and realize that the changes were necessary to our personal development, or to the wider society, and we may even feel grateful for the regeneration that was forced to happen, because we have gained something more valuable in the process.

However, Pluto can also refer to the most terrible and devastating experiences, such as murder, genocide and mass deaths due to war, accidents or natural disasters, which are so devastating and so brutal that there is no meaning to be found in them. Pluto is about the survivors and their experiences of fear, fury and the grieving process.

Pluto has a strong sense of justice and can unleash its wrath if crossed with any ill intent. The sign is also an expert at reading between the lines, and naturally picks up on anything we are feeling on an unconscious level. Sometimes Pluto can misinterpret the signs and become paranoid for no good reason! But it is a very sensitive planet and with wisdom and experience it can become a finely tuned instrument for detection of anything from people's underlying motives to underground treasure!

People with a prominent Pluto in their charts can have a lot of power and tenacity, and often get what they want. Because of its associations with controlling the will, and its vast reserves of wisdom and power, Pluto is associated with magic. Sometimes it can attract a lot of wealth, and the planet can signify money, riches and hidden treasures and indicate unexpected luck, inheritance and reward.

Pluto is the co-ruler of the sign of Scorpio, along with the sign's traditional ruler, Mars. Pluto takes approximately 248 years to make one complete revolution around the Sun. Because of its eccentric orbit, it can spend between twelve and thirty-two years in each sign.

Where is Pluto in your birth chart? This is where you can find great depth of understanding, wisdom and insight. It can also make you aware of the darker aspects of that sign in our lives and the society which we live in. It is our job to work creatively with Pluto's immense power, and use it to develop wisdom and compassion towards others and oneself.

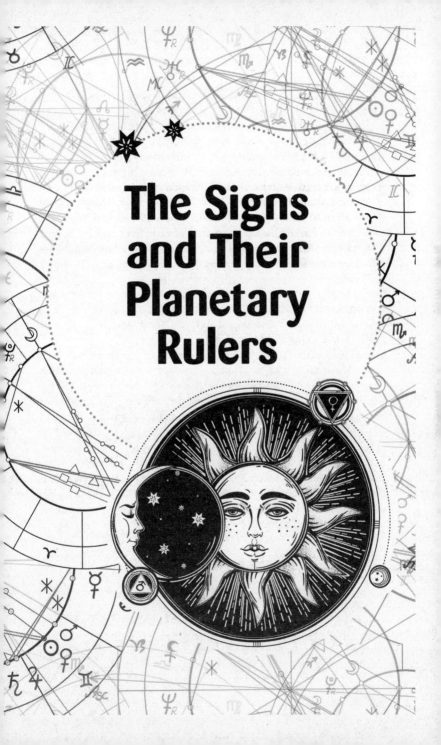

The Signs
and Their
Planetary
Rulers

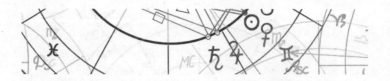

I n which sign of the zodiac are the Sun, Moon, Ascendant and planets placed in your birth chart? Look up the characteristics of the signs in this section and apply these to the various planetary principles to find out how they work in your life.

Remember that we normally display the qualities of our Sun, Moon and Ascendant signs most prominently.

If you have any planets placed in the signs they rule (such as the Sun in Leo, or Venus in Taurus or Libra), the qualities of those planets and signs will be particularly significant for you.

A NOTE ON COMPATIBLE SIGNS

Compatible signs are listed in the preliminary sections for each sign – these are the signs of the zodiac that tend to have common characteristics and similar approaches to life (for example, if my Sun is in Virgo and yours is in Capricorn, we may get along well and have a similar outlook). These compatible signs are intended to be used as a general guide only. It is important to remember that other sign combinations that are not listed can also work brilliantly, and relationships depend on the complete charts of the two people involved, rather than individual planetary signs. Also, some of us are looking for connections with others that are a little bit different, exciting and creative, so we might try some of the less conventional combinations, and these can work equally well.

ARIES
Positive – Fire – Cardinal
Planetary Ruler: Mars
Compatible Signs: Gemini, Leo, Libra, Scorpio, Sagittarius, Aquarius.
Parts of the Body: Head, jaw, brain and nerve centres.

Famous Individuals with Sun in Aries: Marlon Brando, Maria Callas, Charlie Chaplin, Russell Crowe, Bette Davis, Richard Dawkins, Rene Descartes, Celine Dion, Aretha Franklyn, Alec Guinness, Billie Holiday, Eric Idle, Henry James, Elton John, Heath Ledger, Elle MacPherson, Ewan McGregor, Spike Milligan, Sarah Jessica Parker, Emma Watson.

Positive Characteristics: Strong, fiery, energetic, active, dynamic, enthusiastic, optimistic, confident, assertive, courageous, heroic, inspiring, exciting, adventurous, decisive, warrior-like, fun-loving, pioneering, ground-breaking.

Negative Characteristics: Impatient, arrogant, headstrong, daring, self-serving, thoughtless, tactless, careless, insensitive, quick-tempered, aggressive, argumentative, loud, brash, unsubtle, self-absorbed.

Professions: Soldier, police officer, prison warden, security guard, fire fighter, lifeguard, paramedic, surgeon, midwife, company director, prime minister, athlete, boxer, football player, rugby player, racing car driver, lorry driver, drummer, manual labourer, blacksmith, ironmonger.

GLYPH ♈

The glyph for Aries represents the head and horns of a ram; it is also likened to a young shoot which has sprung out of the ground.

Ruled by the planet Mars, the warrior, Aries is an energetic go-getter! Those with the Sun, Moon, Ascendant, Mars or some of the other personal planets in Aries tend to be assertive and confident. Even when Arians are feeling timid on the inside, they come across as strong and authoritative on the outside. Full of ambition, Aries aims high and usually reaches its target out of sheer audacity and gall!

Arians often have the facial structure of a ram, particularly in the forehead and eyebrow area, which is represented by its glyph. This part of the body tends to be pronounced and the face is elongated. Arians also tend to have muscular bodies and broad shoulders.

Being the first sign of the zodiac, Aries is the pioneering spirit who charges forth into new frontiers to boldly go where no one has gone before! The sign symbolizes the moment of birth, when we push out of the womb and take our first breath. It is the impetus that drives us out of our comfort zones and into new areas of discovery.

Aries is the brand new soul stepping out into the world, and there is a fresh and uncomplicated quality about the sign. Life can seem very simple and straightforward to an Arian, but what they lack in experience, they more than make up for in enthusiasm. Aries wants to grab and try everything at least once, and often behaves like a kid in a candy store – there is so much to see and do, and no time to lose!

As babies we are born curious and surrounded by new toys with which to play and explore. Similarly, Arians can have a childlike curiosity about the world, and they sometimes display childish reactions, especially if something is denied to them! Tantrums are not uncommon for Arians of any age. But their anger can vanish as quickly as it came, and no sooner has the Arian's attention been diverted to something new than the matter is forgotten.

Aries children are often very daring and like to test their boundaries, which can be very alarming for parents and onlookers! Arians of all ages tend to be quite boisterous and often get into scrapes, but they learn how to take a tumble very quickly. They pick themselves up, dust themselves off and carry on, and the whole thing is forgotten in moments.

Arians also tend to bump into things and sustain cuts and bruises, often without noticing until you point it out, and then they usually can't remember how they came to be there! Aries rules the head, and Arians tend to bump their heads, or get headaches. They can literally behave like bears with sore heads and get into terrible moods, taking it out on all around them.

Arians like to take charge, and notoriously have difficulty with authority figures. Even as children, Arians may try to pit their wits against the authority figures around them. However, if handled with care and with the Arian's best interests at heart, Arian children will develop a respect for authority and find a way to earn it for themselves.

Arians have a strong sense of personal honour, and can be very gallant and chivalrous. The sign is the quintessential knight in shining armour, bravely prepared for battle and sent on a hero's quest. Aries finds the challenge irresistible and thrilling, the more impossible their task may seem at the onset, the better!

Aries is future-oriented and is not one to dwell on the past or bear a grudge. It is always thinking about where it is going next, not where it has been. Aries uses its primal passions and instincts to lead it along its path through life, chasing the incentives that are everywhere ahead of it! In fact, if you want to steer an Aries in a particular direction, 'dangling a carrot' may be a good way to guarantee success!

Like Leo and Sagittarius, Aries is a bright and optimistic fire sign, and, like the other fire signs, it tends to act spontaneously. Aries is excellent at initiating new projects and getting them off the ground where other signs might take too long to think and procrastinate, but they are not known for forward planning. They can quickly get bored with what they started and move on, leaving a trail of unfinished activities behind them. Other signs tend to run around, picking up after them, which can be infuriating!

Aries is headstrong and usually knows what it wants. Arians like to be in control of their own actions as well as everyone else's, and can often be found telling others what to do. They can develop a reputation for being bossy! Aries is not known for its cooperative or diplomatic skills, refusing to say or do anything it doesn't want to. They tend to lead rather than follow when in a group.

The sign hates to be dependent on others, and will only listen to the advice of those whom it admires and wants to emulate. Arians will often have long lists of heroes and role-models, which will include celebrities and athletes as well as people closer to them who take charge and show special abilities that the Arian would like to develop for themselves.

Aries is widely known as a selfish sign, tending to grab whatever it wants to satisfy its own needs. This quality is often looked down upon by the rest of the zodiac, but the fact that it is geared toward taking care of itself, and its own self interest, should be seen as a positive thing. Arians can teach us important lessons on the subject of survival and self-preservation. Many other signs could learn a lot from them in order to function better.

Aries has the confidence to behave however it wants, and does not apologize for it, or worry about what others might think. It is unencumbered by the crippling doubts and guilt that tend to hold others back. Of course, Arians have doubts and insecurities from time to time (because we are never purely one sign), but these thoughts are short-lived and don't tend to restrict them. This can't be a bad thing, and in this, the Arian sets an example for us all!

Indeed, we can all learn from Aries' free expression of Mars' fiery energy. The qualities associated with the planet and its ruling sign – assertiveness, self-interest, anger, strength and dominance – do not tend to sit well in our society, and so many of us choose to repress them, but at a cost to our confidence and sense of personal effectiveness and potency.

Aries does not pander well to people in need of constant reassurance or support, this can seem like an embarrassing display of weakness. Arians don't suffer whingers – the way they see it, if you want something, you should go and grab it, or you will only have yourself to blame! Aries has no tolerance for those who won't, or think they can't, achieve their dreams. There is no time to hang around complaining. Our lives are in our own hands, we make of them what we please, and it is up to us to go out and seize the day!

TAURUS
Negative – Earth – Fixed
Planetary Ruler: Venus
Compatible signs: Cancer, Virgo, Libra, Scorpio, Capricorn, Pisces.
Parts of the Body: Neck, throat, thyroid.

Famous Individuals with Sun in Taurus: Cate Blanchett, Bono, Charlotte Bronte, Cher, George Clooney, Penelope Cruz, Salvador Dali, Leonardo Da Vinci, Linda Evangelista, Sigmund Freud, Audrey Hepburn, Katherine Hepburn, Emmanuel Kant, George Lucas, Karl Marx, Michael Palin, Vladimir Putin, Queen Elizabeth II, Barbra Streisand, Uma Thurman, Rudolph Valentino, Orson Welles, Stevie Wonder, Renee Zellweger.

Positive Characteristics: Warm, loving, appreciative, sensible, practical, relaxed, placid, reliable, stable, steadfast, grounded, earthy, constant, secure, determined, comfort-loving, sensual, passionate, fertile, pleasure-seeking, tasteful.

Negative Characteristics: Stubborn, slow, lazy, predictable, inflexible, greedy, self-indulgent, jealous, possessive, resentful, touchy, unimaginative, sceptical.

Professions: Cook, baker, singer, musician, decorator, interior designer, furniture maker, landscape designer, gardener, farmer, builder, plasterer, sculptor, potter, beautician, masseur, financial advisor, accountant.

GLYPH ♉

The glyph for Taurus depicts the head and horns of a bull. Like the bull that represents the sign, Taurus is known for its patience and resilience. It is relaxed and placid, but when pushed or riled, it can 'see red' and charge with enormous force. You wouldn't want to stand in its way! Taureans are determined and target-oriented, and tend to have one goal which they will aim for to the exclusion of everything else.

Taureans tend to have strong and stocky physiques with well-built muscles in their neck and shoulders. They are known for their attractive and well-proportioned facial features and widely-spaced eyes, which exude warmth and have a look of determination about them. Taurus rules the throat area, and Taureans often have a beautiful voice and can make talented singers.

The sign tends to have great physical as well as emotional stability and core strength. Taureans have extremely steady hands and the ability to stand as firm and as stable as a pillar. They have a strong connection with the ground beneath them and are practical and secure individuals, bringing everyone down to earth and keeping things real.

Like Virgo and Capricorn, the other earth signs, Taurus takes its responsibilities seriously, and is extremely reliable and dependable. Some of the other signs even call them predictable! They have enormous stamina and staying power, and will see things through to the very end. Taurus likes routine and doesn't welcome sudden change, preferring events and ideas to slowly evolve, so that it has enough time to gradually adjust and get used to them.

Taureans don't take kindly to flightiness or unreliability in others. They have a calming influence on everyone around them, and are surrounded by an aura of safety and security, which can be extremely comforting, particularly to the less grounded signs.

Taurus is concerned with the here and now, and what is being experienced in the present. Taureans do not worry about what has passed or what might happen in the future.

Being realistic and practical, Taurus can be the doubting Thomas of the zodiac, having to see, touch, taste and smell something before it believes in its existence! This can be tricky when it comes to abstract concepts and Taurus tends not to have much time or patience with the 'unseen' realm. They are visibly irritated by anything abstract or irrational, and sceptical about things that can't be seen or experienced first hand.

Taureans are not often interested in religion and believe that everything must have a perfectly rational explanation. However, if they have a religious experience or witness something 'irrational' for themselves, then they can become fervent believers!

Taureans are connoisseurs of life: they have a fine appreciation of, and expertise in, anything from varieties of wine to furniture-making – anything that enhances the quality and pleasure one takes in life – and Taurus enjoys surrounding itself with sumptuous materials, fine dining and home comforts.

Ruled by Venus, Taurus is a loving and romantic sign, and Taureans are full of passion. They have a primal sensuality which can be very magnetic and erotic. They like to surround themselves with the seductive and can be easily seduced – this can include seduction by a comfortable chair or a sumptuous fabric as well as an attractive lover!

Taureans are deeply devoted and loyal to their loved ones and will support them through thick and thin. Taurus expects the same treatment in return, and is dismayed when others are not as constant as it expects them to be. It can take disloyalty very badly and can be ruthless in cutting others out of its life if they have crossed the line.

Jealousy can be a problem for Taurus, and it can be driven wild by any act of infidelity on the part of another. Even if the sign appears cool on the outside, its passions are raging underneath, and it can explode in a jealous rage if just cause is given.

Taurus has strongly-held opinions which it will stubbornly hold on to, and will not compromise on. While the sign is capable of strong and loyal bonds, it will sacrifice relationships if they do not fall in line with its demands.

Unlike the other earth signs, Taurus is not a worrier. Being typically slow and deliberate in its movements, the sign achieves what it sets out to do slowly but surely, and sees no urgency in anything. This can be infuriating for other signs that like to rush around and fit in as many activities and chores as possible.

Taurus may be slow, but it is not usually late, and if it arranges an appointment, it will allow a realistic amount of time to get there, and if Taurus says it will meet you at a particular place and time, then chances are it will, because Taurus is one of the most reliable and dependable signs of the zodiac.

Like a bull in a china shop, Taureans are not known for their subtlety, and can charge around 'bulldozing' anything that gets in their way, all very innocently and without meaning to! For this reason they are best kept away from delicate items, and need sturdy surroundings which can withstand their well-meaning clumsiness. Sometimes this translates into delicate social situations as well. Taureans tend to avoid social situations in which they have to use diplomacy and tact, as they are prone to making social faux pas.

Taureans are best left in environments to which they are accustomed, and the creature comforts which they like to surround themselves with, and like nothing more than to dress and behave casually in their own homes.

Having an affinity with materials and deriving great pleasure from physical experience, Taureans have an amazing talent with their hands, and can channel their passions through them to create objects, foods and images which delight, relax, tantalize and seduce all around them! Taureans have the gift of touch, and their talents can range from the kitchen to the bedroom – and their stamina comes in handy here too!

Another talent that arises from their incredible affinity with touch is massage, and there are many Taureans in the beauty and well-being industries, where they are particularly well placed to bring pleasure and relaxation to others.

GEMINI
Positive – Air – Mutable
Planetary Ruler: Mercury
Compatible signs: Aries, Leo, Virgo, Libra, Sagittarius, Aquarius.
Parts of the Body: Nerves, arms, shoulders, collar bones, lungs.

Famous Individuals with Sun in Gemini: Naomi Campbell, Joan Collins, Johnny Depp, Arthur Conan Doyle, Bob Dylan, Clint Eastwood, Ian Fleming, Judy Garland, Paul Gaugin, Allen Ginsburg, Thomas Hardy, Angelina Jolie, John F. Kennedy, Nicole Kidman, Paul McCartney, Kylie Minogue, Marilyn Monroe, Queen Victoria, Joan Rivers, Salman Rushdie, Brooke Shields, Donald Trump, Walt Whitman.

Positive Characteristics: Intelligent, bright, quick-witted, multi-tasking, imaginative, talkative, charming, congenial, sociable, curious, quick, lively, energetic, enthusiastic, stimulating, entertaining, playful, fun-loving, adaptable, versatile, youthful, risk-taking.

Negative Characteristics: Mischievous, changeable, unreliable, inconsistent, untrustworthy, dishonest, unfocused, non-committal, fickle, superficial, immature, nervous, uptight, easily bored.

Professions: Writer, correspondent, journalist, reporter, columnist, social commentator, presenter, teacher, researcher, storyteller, matchmaker, human resources manager, events organizer, wedding planner, comedian, entertainer, jester, magician, counsellor, psychotherapist.

GLYPH ♊

The glyph is thought to indicate the number two and represent duality, as well as the twin stars Castor and Pollux, which are in the constellation of Gemini.

The sign of Gemini, represented by the twins, can be like two different personalities in one, and sometimes Geminis have two (or more) very different lifestyles and identities which are kept separate from each other. The dual nature of the sign also indicates the need for relationships and the importance of connecting and exchanging ideas with others.

Variety is very much the spice of life for this sign. Geminis like to try everything at least once, and usually a number of times, just to be sure! They like to adapt to the moods of others and their environments and usually find it easy to relate to people from all walks of life.

Geminis are gregarious and extroverted, and make an effort to talk to almost everyone they meet. With a genuine interest in all types of people, Gemini isn't discriminatory when it comes to friends and acquaintances. As long as they have plenty of social invitations and opportunities to expand their network, Geminis are happy!

Planets in Gemini can be fast and expressive, curious and experimental. Like their ruling planet, Mercury, Geminis are quick in thought, speech and action. They have strong wits and can make enjoyable and stimulating company, keeping us entertained with their stories and in stitches at their jokes. They need lots of stimulation and can have very short attention spans, leaving the slower signs spinning in an effort to keep up.

Gemini is extremely flexible and happy to change its plans at the drop of a hat, allowing life to take the lead and always hoping for an unexpected adventure. They behave with spontaneity and are full of optimism about what the future holds.

There is something eternally youthful about Geminis, and they tend to have Peter Pan syndrome – forever young and looking for adventure, refusing to grow up and become a responsible adult. However, since this sort of behaviour has become fairly commonplace in Western society, these eternal youths no longer look out of place.

Gemini doesn't like to put all its eggs in one basket, preferring to spread them out and cover all its bases, just in case! In friendships, this translates as having as many acquaintances as possible, and Gemini have contacts everywhere, which can make them very influential and useful people to know.

Geminis like to help people out by putting them in contact with one another, and often know who to connect with whom for the best results. This is a remarkable skill which can be extremely beneficial and can help others find the right information, job, marriage partner or path in life. For this reason, Geminis can make skilled networkers, and excellent matchmakers.

It is hard for Geminis to stay constant, and committing to someone or something can be problematic. They can go through periods of frequently switching lifestyles and jobs and giving their lives a complete overhaul. Geminis tend to travel light and accumulate few possessions so that they can move on whenever they need to.

Wherever they go, Geminis like to stay close to the exit points in case they need to slip out or make a quick getaway! One moment you can be talking to a Gemini, the next they have disappeared. This sign doesn't like to stay in one place for too long, or it can start to feel stifled. It doesn't mean Geminis don't care about you and can't wait to get away, and you can tell if they like you as they will keep returning, like a boomerang or a bad penny! But they do need the freedom to stretch their wings and fly off when the fancy takes them.

The sign has a reputation for being two-faced and fickle in romance, and Geminis may express their undying love for us one minute and then we can catch them asking someone else to the dance the next! Geminis love to play with words and ideas and create an imaginary reality that sometimes takes a departure from the 'real world' as others understand it. It can be difficult to get an honest or straight answer from them.

However, once Geminis have made a genuine commitment, they can stay perfectly loyal in relationships, although they will still need variety and spontaneity in their lives, and should have plenty of freedom to pursue their other friendships and interests.

Those with Gemini prominent in their charts can't always keep on the straight and narrow – they like to play pranks on others and get up to a little mischief every now and again. However, Geminis need to be careful not to take things too far. They can be so wrapped up in the world of clever ideas that they lose sight of reality and the consequences of their actions, and can end up hurting others as well as themselves without meaning to.

Geminis love all the types of communication that are available to us today, from meeting face-to-face, to chatting on social networking sites. Geminis also love being in demand, and thrive on receiving texts, emails and phonecalls.

Gemini likes to know what is happening with everyone, and has a genuine interest in every detail of their lives. It wants to know what they have been doing, to share information and swap contacts. But although curious about everything under the Sun, Gemini tends not to be very comfortable around difficult or painful emotions – either their own or those of others.

Like Libra and Aquarius, the other air signs, Gemini does a lot of thinking and debating with others, but is not as comfortable with emotional intimacy. It is often inclined to think about and analyse rather than feel its own emotions.

Being naturally optimistic and upbeat, Geminis can attempt to brush off the more difficult emotions whenever they arise in order to try to cheer themselves, and others, up. Geminis are great at solving other people's problems, but not so good at giving expression to their own feelings. Geminis do have a way with words, however, and can say just the right thing to help a person gain some perspective on a problem and turn it around. They are also good at shining a light on a situation and helping us see it in a new way. For this reason, they can make excellent magicians, as well as counsellors and psychotherapists.

CANCER

Negative – Water – Cardinal
Planetary Ruler: The Moon
Compatible signs: Taurus, Leo, Virgo, Scorpio, Capricorn, Pisces.
Parts of the Body: Stomach, mammary glands.

Famous Individuals with Sun in Cancer: Pamela Anderson, Ingmar Bergman, Richard Branson, George W. Bush, Barbara Cartland, Tom Cruise, Princess Diana, Harrison Ford, Henry VIII, Ernest Hemingway, Lindsay Lohan, Franz Kafka, Helen Keller, The Dalai Lama, Courtney Love, Nelson Mandela, George Michael, Camilla Parker-Bowles, Nancy Reagan, Sylvester Stallone, Ringo Star, Donald Sutherland, Prince William, W.B. Yeats.

Positive Characteristics: Caring, gentle, loving, nurturing, home-loving, selfless, sensitive, emotional, nostalgic, patriotic.

Negative Characteristics: Overprotective, smothering, insecure, overly sensitive, paranoid.

Professions: Midwife, nanny, nurse, carer, homemaker, landlord/ landlady, cook, baker, cake decorator, librarian, historian, museum curator.

GLYPH ♋

The glyph for Cancer is thought to represent a woman's breasts, or a mother and child in an intimate embrace. It may also represent the two pincers of a crab.

Cancer, like its symbol of the crab, is known for having a hard shell which protects its soft interior from harm. The sign is ruled by the Moon, which is the traditional symbol of the mother and femininity (next to the Sun, which represents the masculine principle, or the father). Like their ruler, Cancer's moods can be changeable and in constant flux. They are in touch with their emotions and tend to be soft-hearted and easily upset.

Cancerians are the caring and nurturing mothers of the zodiac, and the qualities associated with the sign apply to both men and women who have Cancer prominent in their birth chart. Whether male or female, these individuals tend to make loyal friends and confidantes and excellent hosts, wanting to take care of others at every opportunity.

The parts of the body associated with Cancer and the Moon include the soft tissue of the breast area as well as the stomach, which we fill with food that nurtures and sustains us and helps us to grow. Typical Cancerian features include large round eyes and a round face with clear and delicate skin. Female Cancerians may also have an ample bosom! Both males and females have gentle and delicate facial expressions that provide a giveaway as to the nature of the sign.

Cancer is a sensitive and watery realm, and the sign symbolizes the primordial waters from whence we all came. It is therefore linked with mother and mothering, and our home, family and personal background. It also describes our nation and our heritage, and the history of our families and relatives before we were born. It is important for Cancerians to learn about their own family trees and histories so that they can connect with their own roots and feel part of something larger. This will help to build up their all-important sense of identity.

Cancerians are interested in the past – particularly their own past – and they have excellent memories. This sign can be very nostalgic and Cancerians like to reminisce about old times with good friends. Looking at old diaries and photo albums is a favourite pastime. Cancerians tend to hoard a lot and hold on to things, so that they stay connected with the past. They often like to live in the family home in which they grew up, and they resist redecorating, so that any memories are kept intact.

Although Cancer is a cardinal sign, its strong connection with the past can cause a resistance to change (normally associated with the fixed signs). Cancerians need to feel safe and secure in order to allow change into their lives, and this process of adjustment cannot be rushed.

Cancer needs a lot of love and appreciation from those around it and depends on the close bonds it has with its nearest and dearest to sustain it. Cancerians do not like to feel abandoned, and will take desperate measures to avoid being left alone – from becoming indispensible by taking care of loved-ones, to using guilt and emotional blackmail if necessary.

Cancerians are suspicious of people they don't know very well, and aren't very good at having acquaintances, preferring a few close confidantes whom they can trust. They tend to be particularly close to family and friends whom they have known since childhood.

Cancer is extremely sensitive, and can take things personally. Consequently Cancerians are easily hurt by other people's words and actions, even if they were not intended to cause harm. They tend to blow things out of proportion, and things can seem much worse to them than they might actually be. It is important for Cancerians to bear this in mind, in order to avoid becoming paranoid about what others might be saying or thinking about them.

Cancer has a strong shell with which to defend itself against harm – it has to or its delicate insides will get squashed very easily. The shell can easily turn into excessive defensiveness, however, and Cancer needs to take care that it does not shut people out or treat any kind of change as a threat.

It is important for Cancerians to have more positive expectations from other people and the world outside, so that they do not always fear the worst, as this can become a self-fulfilling prophecy. It can be very difficult for them to allow themselves to be vulnerable in this way, but it is important to keep their defences down unless absolutely necessary, so that they can keep themselves open to new possibilities.

Cancerians make loyal and loving friends and partners. They are at their best when they have built up their self-confidence and sense of security, so that they don't need to rely on other people's assurances to believe in themselves and realize how wonderful they are! Cancerians should also do their best to allow their loved ones the freedom they need to grow and explore their own paths. Like a parent allowing her children to grow up and leave home, it can be very hard to let go, but it is essential for their development, and they always return!

Like a crab, Cancerians move in a sideways direction, and they tend to approach and navigate obstacles in indirect ways. This can be useful in certain situations, and Cancerians can be good at lateral thinking and problem-solving, and tend to bring a lot of insight and empathy to a situation. However, they are not always good at being straight with people or direct in their behaviour when it is called for. Rather than being open about what they think, Cancerians may drop hints and hope that people pick up on what they are trying to say. They like to avoid direct confrontations where possible and prefer someone else to be their mouthpiece when such action is needed.

Cancerians tend to be quiet and shy individuals, preferring to keep a low profile and blend in wherever they go. They are known for their kindness, however and can't bear to watch anyone suffer. They would immediately jump to anyone's defence if needed, and can be quite ferocious if the situation requires it!

LEO

Positive – Fire – Fixed
Planetary Ruler: The Sun
Compatible signs: Aries, Gemini, Cancer, Libra, Sagittarius, Aquarius.
Parts of the Body: Heart, spine and back.

Famous Individuals with Sun in Leo: Neil Armstrong, Lucille Ball, Emily Bronte, Sandra Bullock, Fidel Castro, Kim Cattrall, Coco Chanel, Bill Clinton, Robert De Niro, Alfred Hitchcock, Whitney Houston, Aldous Huxley, Mick Jagger, Carl Gustav Jung, Philip Larkin, Jennifer Lopez, Madonna, Helen Mirren, Barack Obama, Robert Redford, J.K. Rowling, George Bernard Shaw, Arnold Schwarzenegger, Percy Bysshe Shelley, Alfred Lord Tennyson, Andy Warhol, Mae West.

Positive Characteristics: Creative, lively, fun-loving, playful, passionate, generous, magnanimous, open, sociable, gregarious, glamorous, graceful, faithful, loyal, noble, honourable, dignified.

Negative Characteristics: Arrogant, egotistical, self-centred, attention-seeking, insensitive, risk-taking, lazy, loud, controlling, demanding, bossy, stubborn, dogmatic, intolerant, snobbish, patronising, judgemental.

Professions: Actor, presenter, MC, host, model, artist, clothes designer, company director, PR manager, advertising executive, event planner, firefighter, lifeguard, dignitary, nobleperson, monarch.

GLYPH ♌

The glyph represents a lion's mane, and is roughly in the shape of the constellation of Leo.

Ruled by the blazing Sun at the centre of the solar system, Leo is the divine child of the zodiac and likes to be noticed. This sign will soak up all the love and attention it can get, and Leos tend to be sunny, joyful and enormous fun to be around. With a reputation for being extroverts, a typical Leo is generous, gregarious and larger than life.

Leo is represented by the symbol of a Lion, the king of the beasts, and Leo likes to strut around regally. Those with the sign prominent in their charts often have a thick and curly mane of hair, with the graceful movements of the lion, and a lion's bite when their passionate rage is aroused! Also like a lion, they tend to have powerful and muscular physiques, with broad shoulders and narrow hips.

Leo rules the heart, back and spine areas, and tends to hold up its torso with a look of courage and pride. Being big-hearted, Leos will give generously to others in any way they can, often volunteering their time to do charity work or to support voluntary organizations. They have a strong sense of purpose and need a focus or a mission to sink their teeth into.

Leos tend to be confident and extroverted, although some Leos can be quite shy and don't really enjoy being in the public eye at all. However, even the more private Leos will tend to have an inner sense that they are meant for great things, and they possess a quiet confidence that shines through. People with Leo prominent in their birth chart tend to be youthful and playful at any age, and have a well developed sense of fun, wanting nothing more than to enjoy life to the full. They have enormous stores of energy and exuberance, which they use to fuel their active lives and busy social calendars.

Like the other fire signs, (Aries and Sagittarius), Leos are highly creative and original. Being natural performers, they tend to make excellent actors and presenters, and have a strong presence on stage and screen, and will enjoy the glamour of working in the media, advertising or in public relations.

While many Leos dream of fame – particularly these days while the cult of celebrity is riding high – they don't have to become involved in show business to achieve the appreciation they long for. Whatever work they do, it is particularly important for Leos to be recognized for their achievements, and develop their own unique gifts and talents, with a sense that they are forging their own path in life and achieving their potential.

One of Leo's talents is the gift of the gab, and this sign can charm the birds from the trees! With their self-confidence and charisma, Leos tend to be successful in all that they do. They need to be careful and keep a sense of proportion, however, and remember that everyone is unique and special, while taking care that success doesn't go to their heads!

Leos love space and operate on a large scale – big houses, expensive cars, designer clothes and, of course, plenty of jewellery – usually gold and precious stones, of course! Leos love to be able to show off, and the sign makes a gracious host, of the sort that makes sure everyone's plate is full and glasses are overflowing. They tend to throw lavish parties, whether they can afford to or not, because one of the main priorities for Leo is to live life to the full. Those born under the sign tend to attract a large income, or have wealthy partners, to help them maintain their fairytale lifestyles. But however much they earn, Leos often live beyond their means, because of an unerring belief that life is too short not to enjoy everything in abundance!

Leos tend to be direct and decisive and are born leaders. They will often have a strong will and a commanding voice, which others tend to obey. They should be very careful what they ask for, because chances are they will get it! Sometimes this sign can get a little too big for its boots, and earns a reputation for being bossy, a quality it needs to keep in check.

Leos have a tendency to talk down to those who are not part of their own social circles, who are more timid or don't have the same levels of energy as they do! They also tend to have the loudest voice in the room, and this can dominate the more gentle, quieter signs.

Leos are not known for their cooperative qualities. They often 'play up' in an argument and insist on getting their own way. The sign can be obstinate, prone to extremism, and intolerant of other people's viewpoints. This can make it difficult to resolve any problems that arise.

Dignity is important to Leos, and they follow a noble code of conduct which seems very old-fashioned by today's standards. Faithful and loyal, brave and quick to come to the aid of their loved ones, Leos expect the same treatment in return, and do not take kindly to betrayal or to being let down by those they love and trust.

Like its ruling planet, the Sun, Leo is the hero of the zodiac. Like the Batman or Wonder Woman of this world, Leos have special qualities and can achieve the impossible. They treat life like it is a challenge or an opportunity to show what they are made of and test their mettle. Through these challenges Leos grow and discover who they are. They teach us that such goals are within everyone's reach.

VIRGO
Negative – Earth – Mutable
Planetary Rulers: Mercury
Compatible signs: Taurus, Gemini, Cancer, Scorpio, Capricorn, Pisces.
Parts of the Body: Intestines, nervous system.

Famous Individuals with Sun in Virgo: Lauren Bacall, Ingrid Bergman, Tim Burton, Agatha Christie, Leonard Cohen, Sean Connery, Roald Dahl, Cameron Diaz, Queen Elizabeth I, Colin Firth, Stephen Fry, Greta Garbo, Richard Gere, Hugh Grant, Prince Harry, Jeremy Irons, Michael Jackson, Stephen King, Beyoncé Knowles, Sophia Loren, Keanu Reeves, Claudia Schiffer, Mary Shelley, Peter Sellers, Mother Theresa, H.G. Wells.

Positive Characteristics: Intelligent, thoughtful, witty, humble, quiet, shy, subtle, sensible, hardworking, helpful, useful, reliable, conscientious, focused, careful, discerning, critical, communicative, organized, tidy, clean, hygienic, pure.

Negative Characteristics: Over-critical, fussy, pernickety, judgemental, perfectionist, habitual, nervous, tense, uptight, hypochondriac, obsessive, antisocial, self-deprecating, embarrassed, proud.

Professions: Teacher, writer, editor, publisher, translator, linguist, critic, librarian, judge, advocate, quality controller, consultant, administrator, events organizer, columnist, craftsperson, tailor, tradesperson, cleaner, nutritionist, nurse, doctor, vet, homeopath.

GLYPH ♍

The glyph is thought to represent the intestines, which Virgo rules. The glyphs for Virgo and Scorpio are similar, except for the right side of the sign – in Virgo's case the end is enclosed, suggesting the feminine principle.

Virgo is represented by the image of a maiden holding a sheaf of wheat, apparently based on the Greek and Roman goddesses Demeter and Ceres. The maiden is a symbol of fertility and nourishment, and guarantees the crops will grow and the cycle of life is maintained.

The virgin maiden is a symbol of self-containment and purity, and Virgo is an independent sign. Virgos have a strong sense of self-assurance, which ensures that their sense of worth is ultimately not based on other people's opinions.

The Sun is in Virgo from late August to late September, during the time of the harvest in the northern hemisphere. Virgos are known for their powers of discrimination, and are very good at working out what is useful from what is not, separating the wheat from the chaff. They tend to be able to assess situations in their own context, and make excellent judges and advocates.

Virgos tend to be discerning about everything they do, especially the way they treat their bodies and their general appearance. For this reason, they are usually extremely well turned out and groomed to within an inch of their lives.

Very critical of others as well as themselves, and with sometimes impossibly high expectations, Virgos are often disappointed. They hate to let others down, and work incredibly hard to avoid doing so. None of us is perfect, although Virgos like to try! They must avoid comparing themselves to others, and recognize that everyone has their good, and not so good, qualities.

Virgos love efficiency and hate waste, wanting to make the best use of everything. One of the things they most want to avoid wasting is time, they like to keep interactions real and to the point. They also hate wasting food, energy, money and any other resources. This can show itself in any form, from re-using teabags to avoiding people who talk too much. Virgo has plans for every tool at its disposal, and is always plotting the best way to use the resources at its fingertips.

Virgo is a shy and modest sign, while at the same time being quietly capable, hardworking and industrious. This makes Virgos excellent and dependable employees. They also make good team players, but they can be overly considerate of others in the workplace. Sometimes the more ambitious and assertive signs will see them as easy pushovers and take Virgo for granted, giving them all the difficult tasks and paying them less. For these and other reasons, Virgos sometimes prefer to work alone.

Virgos have their own way of doing things, and they usually do them well. They tend to find fault in the methods of other people. In fact, they prefer not to allow anyone else to do anything for them at all, as Virgo is so dissatisfied with most other people's workmanship that their motto is 'if you want a job done properly, do it yourself!' A lot of people call this perfectionism or control freakery, but this is a reflection of Virgo's high standards, which they apply to their own output as well as that of others. They can't help it if they tend to do things better than other people.

Virgo is about mastery through practice and careful attention to detail. This can be mastery of materials – Virgos make excellent craftspeople, and are often involved in traditional crafts and other highly skilled trades. Creating something useful and doing it well gives Virgo a lot of pleasure, and Virgos have patience and tenacity in getting to know their materials.

Virgos are also good at mastering language and ideas. The sign is known for its witty sense of humour, and has a way with words, delivering lines at exactly the right time for the greatest comic effect! Virgos have a strong command of language, and make particularly good writers and editors. They are also talented at debating, and have clear and logical minds that can get to the heart of a matter, and make it look easy.

Organization is another area in which Virgo excels. But Virgo doesn't work all the time, it will schedule in time for rest and play as well! Although shy and introverted, Virgos can shine in social situations, where their wit and cleverness can be most enjoyed and appreciated by others.

Virgos make loving and attentive partners, and enjoy one-to-one relationships in which they can get to know another person really well, and be known in turn. In this way Virgos will gradually open up, like a lily, to the person they learn to love and trust, and allow themselves to be truly understood and appreciated for who they are.

They should take care not to go down the route of constant criticism or nagging. Instead they need to open their hearts and learn to accept their partners for who they are, foibles and all.

Like the other earth signs (Taurus and Capricorn), Virgos tend to be honest and down to earth. While usually calm and even-tempered on the outside and clear-headed on the inside, Virgos are not very comfortable in the emotional realm, and tend to set their emotions to one side for processing later, when there is time in their busy schedules.

Because of this, Virgos may sometimes feel like their emotions have a life of their own, and the build up of emotional stress often leads to physical pains and ailments for Virgo – usually in the form of headaches, stomach problems and indigestion. It is very important, therefore, for Virgo to look at the emotional source of their ailments and find some kind of outlet for their stress, in order to help relieve their physical symptoms.

Being an earth sign and concerned with the body, Virgos take nutrition seriously, and want to ensure that their bodies are running as efficiently as the rest of their lives. Virgos are drawn to healthy foods such as wholegrains, fruit and vegetables. They are often vegetarians or have special diets of one sort or another.

Virgos also take ethical considerations into account when it comes to food, and often cut out large food groups or enrol themselves in a gruelling regime which is difficult or antisocial to follow. With a little organization, Virgos manage their alternative diets alongside their busy schedules, carrying special foods and vitamins around with them wherever necessary!

General health also holds enduring interest for Virgos, and they are often walking medicine cabinets, knowing the best treatment for each common ailment, as well as some that are less common.

Virgos are also notoriously concerned with hygiene, and are known as the handwashers of the zodiac! This, combined with their concern with getting things right and doing them well, leads Virgos to develop routines and repeat certain behaviours and rituals which can astonish, amuse and sometimes cause concern to any other sign observing them!

In esoteric philosophy, our everyday habits are thought to lead to our destinies, and Virgos use repetition as a way of achieving their aims and maintaining balance in their lives. However, daily routines can also become stale with time, and Virgos can get stuck in ruts.

Change is generally welcomed by Virgo, which is a mutable sign, and it is adept at revisiting habits and making changes wherever necessary to improve output! When change is imposed by external factors, however, Virgo has a considerable knack for being resourceful and will manage change as it does everything else – with aplomb!

LIBRA

Positive – Air – Cardinal
Planetary Rulers: Venus
Compatible signs: Aries, Taurus, Gemini, Leo, Sagittarius, Aquarius.
Parts of the Body: Kidneys.

Famous Individuals with Sun in Libra: Brigitte Bardot, Silvio Berlusconi, David Cameron, Simon Cowell, Michael Douglas, Eminem, Brian Ferry, Mohandas K. Gandhi, Bob Geldof, Charlton Heston, Catherine Zeta Jones, John Lennon, Arthur Miller, Danii Minogue, Friedrich Nietzsche, Gwyneth Paltrow, Christopher Reeve, Cliff Richard, Anita Roddick, Will Smith, Margaret Thatcher, Archbishop Desmond Tutu, Oscar Wilde, Kate Winslet.

Positive Characteristics: Charming, sociable, communicative, loving, romantic, diplomatic, tactful, beautiful, graceful, balanced, harmonious, moderate, peaceful, optimistic, idealistic, objective, clear, logical, just, fair, agreeable, pleasant, friendly, cooperative.

Negative Characteristics: Vain, lazy, indecisive, disillusioned, disappointed, dependent, easily-led, contrary, argumentative.

Professions: Architect, town planner, engineer, mathematician, accountant, salesperson, designer, photographer, make-up artist, ballet dancer, model, beautician, hairdresser, florist, relationship counsellor, mediator, judge, advocate, ambassador, diplomat.

GLYPH ♎

The glyph for Libra represents the scales of justice.

Like the scales that represent the sign, Libra is associated with justice and fairness, and Librans are always concerned with seeing two sides to everything, weighing them both up and finding the middle ground. Natives of this sign make efforts to keep things in balance in their lives, and amble along peacefully, enjoying everything in moderation.

Ruled by Venus, Librans love beautiful things, whether in appearance, behaviour or ideas. In turn, a person with a prominent Venus or strong placements in Libra can have strikingly beautiful features, a well-proportioned figure and a great sense of style, knowing how to enhance their looks with the right clothing, make-up, hairstyle and so on. Librans often have dimples in their cheeks or chins, which add to their delightful charm!

The first six signs are concerned with the personal realm of self, home and family life, while the last six signs are focused on the 'other', the external world and the vast 'collective' to which we all belong. Libra is the first of these external signs, and is concerned with our relationships with significant 'others'; our partners in love and business.

Librans are concerned with relating, and thrive on being loved and appreciated by others. They are shy but sociable creatures and enjoy parties, good conversation and the company of others. They can suffer terrible loneliness if they are alone for too long.

As an air sign (along with Gemini and Aquarius), Libra is concerned with the realm of ideas and ideals, one of their highest ideals being love – and Libra is well-known for being in love with the idea of love. Always focused on relationships, Librans look for a companion who can perfectly complement them.

Romantic relationships are of primary importance to Libra. However, their relationships do not always match up to the ideals they hope for and dream about, and Librans can have a problem with fully committing to their partners, believing that the ideal is out there somewhere.

However Librans may prefer to stay with a partner even when things aren't working out, just so they can avoid being alone. If they do eventually decide to leave, they may try to make sure they have someone else lined up, so they can hop straight into another relationship.

In relationships there is often a fine line separating love and hate, and along with those we love, Libra is also thought to represent our enemies and nemeses in life!

Libra is the seasoned diplomat of the zodiac. With one of the sign's primary aims being to foster harmonious relations between opposites, Librans make excellent mediators between two disagreeing parties. They use their charm to build connections between people, and so can be excellent mediators in peace talks.

Being an air sign, Libra is also concerned with logic and communication. Librans can help people to talk through their concerns, listen to their viewpoints, look at their situations in a wider context, and take a more philosophical approach, which can be enormously helpful in turning a negative situation around.

Those who have Venus and Libra featuring strongly in their charts tend to be gentle folk, and the sign is naturally easy-going, kind and cooperative. Libra can also be quite a lazy sign and – like one of its natives, John Lennon – would support staying in bed for peace!

However, while peace-loving in principle, Librans are no strangers to argument, and tend to pose the opposite viewpoint to every opinion they hear expressed. This can make them seem argumentative, but if we take a closer look we can usually find that Libra is only arguing the opposite point of view to show us that there is another perspective to which we are not giving due consideration.

They hold a mirror up to every point of view, so that we can understand ourselves and our positions more clearly. Although this can be very helpful, Librans are often criticized for being inconsistent and seemingly not having opinions of their own.

When pressed for a decision, Librans will often take the lead from others rather than make their own choices. This can be great if they are with someone who is happy to take the lead, but if the Libran is with another appeasing sign such as Cancer or Pisces, or with another Libran, they might have a very long wait! This difficulty in general decision-making can lead to problems in everything from choosing an item from the menu in a restaurant, to deciding on a career path.

Librans can have excellent judgement, however, and usually just need to take more time to make a decision so that they can be sure it's the right one.

Librans make charming hosts and have many friends. They are pleasant company and are easy to be around. However, always being so kind and reasonable can lead to a lot of pent-up anger, which can explode in private, or cause stress. Rather than trying to please others all the time (which is not possible), Librans should remember to stay in touch with their own feelings and opinions and find a way to express them honestly to others.

SCORPIO

Negative – Water – Fixed
Planetary Rulers: Mars (Traditional) and Pluto (New)
Compatible signs: Aries, Taurus, Cancer, Virgo, Capricorn, Pisces.
Parts of the Body: Sexual and reproductive organs.

Famous Individuals with Sun in Scorpio: Bjork, Richard Burton, Albert Camus, Prince Charles, John Cleese, Hilary Clinton, Peter Cook, Marie Curie, Leonardo DiCaprio, Art Garfunkel, Bill Gates, Goldie Hawn, Scarlett Johansson, John Keats, Grace Kelly, Calvin Klein, Vivien Leigh, Claude Monet, Demi Moore, Pablo Picasso, Sylvia Plath, Tim Rice, Julia Roberts, Winona Ryder, Martin Scorcese, Paul Simon, Dylan Thomas, Voltaire, Bill Wyman.

Positive Characteristics: Charismatic, passionate, sexy, powerful, insightful, shy, quiet, mysterious, sensitive, receptive, deep, intense, focused, concentrated, still, wise, compassionate, emotional, strong, determined, authoritative, controlled, loyal, devoted, honest, brave, fearless, investigative.

Negative Characteristics: Dark, negative, depressive, brooding, demanding, controlling, unrelenting, unsociable, secretive, deceitful, vengeful, cunning, jealous, possessive, obsessive, cruel, hard, destructive, extreme, stubborn, impossible.

Professions: Accountant, tax collector, oil tycoon, deep sea diver, archaeologist, miner, tunnel maker, underground train driver, metal detector, refuse collector, jeweller, goldsmith, surgeon, radiologist, midwife, researcher, psychotherapist, magician, occultist, detective, private investigator, investigative reporter, spy, code-cracker, politician, campaign manager, spin doctor.

GLYPH ♏

Scorpio's symbol, like Virgo's, represents the intestines. It is thought to be the masculine version of the glyph, with a Scorpion's sting in its tail.

Scorpio is symbolized by the scorpion, a creature with strong survival instincts, which can withstand extreme temperatures and terrains. With Mars and Pluto as its rulers, Scorpio is associated with the extremes of life – birth, death and sex.

Scorpio is a passionate and complex sign, and from the beginning it is clear that the lives of Scorpios are never going to be boring! They are known for their smouldering sexiness, enigmatic charm and lashings of charisma, and we are drawn to them like flies to honey!

Those with a strong Pluto or an emphasis in Scorpio often have a dark and brooding appearance and a powerful and piercing stare. Scorpios are careful and controlled in their movements and often have a rare and graceful poise.

Scorpios are usually shy and quiet, and like to be alone or in a one-to-one situation with another person. They spend a lot of time trying to understand their own thoughts and feelings, and those of others. Although they may have lots of friends and acquaintances, Scorpios like to have one close confidant.

Romantic relationships tend to be close, intimate and serious with Scorpios. They yearn for a partner who understands them and whom they can rely on to stay faithful. They become jealous very easily and need to be careful to keep this in check, otherwise they risk driving partners away.

Natives of the sign usually don't like being among groups of people, and are able to move around so quietly and carefully in public spaces that they can go unnoticed if they want to! To get noticed, however, Scorpios need only to turn on their charisma, and they will stand out from the crowd again in a second.

Everything we say and do provides a Scorpio with food for thought. They don't tend to talk a lot, and are good listeners. This is because they like to concentrate on one thing at a time. When we talk to a Scorpio, they are usually all ears and give us their full attention. We really feel like we are being heard when we talk to a Scorpio, especially when we find out that they still remember what we said fifteen years later. This sign is sometimes described as obsessive!

Scorpios, like elephants, never forget the words or actions of others – or at least the gist of them – especially those that cause hurt or harm, which they will take very badly. Those with an emphasis on Scorpio in the birth chart are deeply affected by injustice. Unlike Aries – which shares the rulership of Mars – Scorpios don't tend to react immediately when hurt, but will retreat for a while to play out scenarios in their minds until they have worked out the best course of action to take.

Taking some sort of action is essential for a Scorpio, who takes being mistreated very badly, and needs to know that justice will be done. If such matters are ignored or brushed aside, the anger eats away at the Scorpio and can turn into depression.

Like a still pool of water, Scorpio's feelings are not visible on the surface, but underneath are raging waters that run deep. Although Scorpios may not give this away, it can be seen when we really look into their eyes, for a Scorpio's gaze carries all the passion, complexity and determination that is raging inside them.

Scorpio is concerned with the unseen elements in life – all that is secret, underground and hidden from others. We sweep our secrets under the carpet and try to hide them from view, only for Scorpio to stumble upon them! The sign has finely tuned receptors which can sense the subtext in our behaviour, and knows what is going on behind the scenes. For this reason, Scorpios tend to just know things.

A fixed water sign, Scorpio has a strong and focused will. Scorpios go about getting what they want in a professional manner, and will use every trick in the book to achieve their desired outcome. They instinctively know what to say and when to say it to manipulate a situation in their favour. Because of these cunning methods, Scorpios can be accused of being deceitful and Machiavellian.

Scorpio's skills can be extremely useful to certain professions such as research, detective work, the secret services, politics and in any organization where it is necessary to work the system in order to succeed. Scorpios tend to attract a lot of money and wealth through their talents.

There is something about a Scorpio which draws others to spill their deepest secrets to them. We have a sense that Scorpios can handle the truth like no one else can, and we instinctively know that they have the insight which can shed some light on the situation and give us the advice we are searching for.

With all the advance planning that they do, Scorpios tend to be brilliant in times of crisis, and usually know the best way to handle emergency situations. They are tremendously brave and can go where angels fear to tread.

Scorpios have the choice of using their abilities for good or ill in the world, and part of being a Scorpio entails developing the wisdom and compassion that accompanies their power, to help soothe the wounds in others as well as themselves.

Scorpio is concerned with delving deep into the psyche and shedding light on the parts of our internal lives that other signs can't reach. For this reason, people with planets in Scorpio tend to be very good at psychotherapy. They can also be adept at working with very dark and painful experiences, and assisting with the client's healing and transformation.

Scorpios are drawn to astrology, the tarot and similar mantic systems. Studying these subjects can help a Scorpio to develop their wisdom and insight.

SAGITTARIUS

Positive – Fire – Mutable
Planetary Ruler: Jupiter
Compatible signs: Aries, Gemini, Leo, Libra, Aquarius, Pisces.
Parts of the Body: Thighs, hips, liver.
Famous Individuals with Sun in Sagittarius: Christina Aguilera, Woody Allen, Jane Austen, William Blake, Noam Chomsky, Winston Churchill, Arthur C. Clarke, Walt Disney, Kirk Douglas, Jimi Hendrix, Boris Karloff, Bruce Lee, C.S. Lewis, John Milton, Jim Morrison, Nostradamus, Brad Pitt, Keith Richards, Christina Rossetti, Charles M. Schultz, Frank Sinatra, Britney Spears, Steven Spielberg, Ben Stiller, Tina Turner, Mark Twain, Ludwig van Beethoven, Tom Waits, Jay-Z, Frank Zappa.

Positive Characteristics: Frank, open, honest, optimistic, lucky, jolly, fun-loving, enthusiastic, energetic, inspiring, faithful, religious, philosophical, objective, broad-minded, curious, intrepid, audacious, adventurous, progressive, visionary, expansive.

Negative Characteristics: Insensitive, tactless, blunt, careless, indiscrete, unemotional, disinterested, restless, impatient, bored, non-committal, irresponsible, fickle, fanatical.

Professions: Student, researcher, teacher, professor, philosopher, commentator, explorer, innovator, astronaut, travel agent, travel writer, travelling salesperson, casino worker, bookie, gambler, stuntman, racing driver, jockey, athlete, archer, overseas correspondent, pilgrim, guru, monk, nun, priest.

GLYPH ✒

The glyph for Sagittarius represents the archer's arrow, and is based on the shape of the constellation.

Represented by the figure of a centaur archer, Sagittarius has the upper body of a human and the bottom half of a beast. The human top half is aiming an arrow upwards toward the sky and getting ready to fire. Sagittarians are always aiming for the distance and love nothing more than to explore new terrain and expand their minds, whether through travel or education. The part of the sign that is beast reminds us that Sagittarius has an instinctive, spontaneous and unpredictable side which needs the space to run wild, and can't be pinned down.

The typical Sagittarian is slender, athletic and muscular in build, with short limbs and faun-like features. Although it's true that they have strong constitutions, Sagittarians sometimes behave as though they are invincible. They don't always take care of their bodies or what they put into them. Natives of the sign should take care that they maintain their physical resilience by keeping unhealthy habits in check.

Sagittarians are progressive thinkers and innovators, who dislike narrow-mindedness, or anything that restricts their behaviour or thinking. They need the freedom to take on new challenges, often for little reason other than because such challenges exist. They value the journey and the knowledge that they pick up along the way as much as arriving at their destination. They thrive on adventure and making new discoveries.

Sagittarians want to learn and understand as much as possible about the world, and treat everything as though it is a phenomenon they are observing from a great distance. In this way they learn a lot about the world which isn't apparent from a closer perspective. Natives of the sign need to be careful that they are not missing out on the benefits of being an 'insider', and part of the community that they have come from.

Many Sagittarians do settle down and build roots, but even then they are drawn to travel and exploration through their minds, and satisfy their curiosity instead by reading, scouring the Internet, taking courses and meeting people from other countries and all walks of life. This helps them maintain the broad perspective that they thrive on.

Sagittarians have an incessant inquisitiveness. As children they ask penetrating questions like 'why is the sky blue?' and point out all the things around us that we take for granted. In some ways, Sagittarians are like aliens on this planet, and require an explanation for everything.

Like Aries and Leo, Sagittarius is a bright and optimistic fire sign. Sagittarians are future-oriented, and tend not to worry about the past, or even remember much of it! Natives of the sign tend to be too busy thinking about the endless possibilities of the future, where they will go next and what they will do there.

One of Sagittarius' main concerns is the search for meaning. Sagittarians are fascinated with the religious urge in humans, and will explore all the religions of the world, as well as secular philosophies, to find out about how humans have explained the phenomenon of life and found purpose in it.

Sagittarians retain their childlike qualities and put off growing older and the onset of maturity for as long as possible! The sign has an excellent sense of humour and is naturally very jovial. Sagittarians like to play pranks and get up to one kind of mischief or another as they get older, just to maintain their playfulness and keep life from becoming too serious.

Intimacy can be an unchartered realm for Sagittarians, and they can find romantic relationships a minefield, largely because they feel trapped and tied down by them, preferring to avoid anything serious for a very long time.

Like the other fire signs, Sagittarians are competitive, and like to win. Preferring to be the ones doing all the chasing in relationships, they try their luck and punch above their weight. When they succeed, this partly serves to boost their confidence, and partly is intended to ensure that their partner does not become too attached, and won't be requiring a long-term commitment.

Sagittarians will often prefer to be alone, so they don't have to make any allowances or compromises for anyone else. This tends to change as they get older, however, and provided they find an unconventional and freedom-loving partner like themselves, they can form satisfying and long-lasting connections.

Like their ruling planet, Jupiter, Sagittarians represent exuberance, a positive approach and a 'can do' attitude! They like to bound around, seeking adventure. This makes them lots of fun to be around, although the other signs will become worn out long before Sagittarius relents.

Sagittarians like to dress very casually, and are often outdoors. Walking shoes and boots are a necessary item in their wardrobes, as are waterproofs and a hat. Sagittarians like to get out and do plenty of exercise, and will often cycle or walk long distances rather than use mechanized forms of transport.

Natives of this sign are open and honest to a fault! They tend to answer questions very earnestly with the first thing that comes to mind, even if this is the most inappropriate thing to say. They are not inclined to sugar-coat or protect other people's feelings, and are known for being utterly tactless at times. However, they have no malice, and are easily forgiven!

Sagittarians do not take hints very easily, and need things to be spelt out and explained directly to them. Unlike Scorpio (and most of the other signs), Sagittarians have no inbuilt radar that allows them to pick up signals and undercurrents. They usually believe warnings of danger to be exaggerated, and are prone to mock others' fears. This attitude can, and usually does, work in their favour – problems seem to disappear before a Sagittarian feels their effects, and they have an uncanny knack of escaping any dangerous situation unharmed, or, at least, unharmed by anyone else's standards.

Sagittarians make excellent teachers, and can be an inspiration to all who know them. They bring out our curiosity and teach us how to think and act for ourselves.

CAPRICORN

Negative – Earth – Cardinal
Planetary Ruler: Saturn
Compatible signs: Taurus, Cancer, Virgo, Scorpio, Aquarius, Pisces.
Parts of the Body: Bones, knees, teeth, hair, nails and skin.
Famous Individuals with Sun in Capricorn: Muhammad Ali, Shirley Bassey, Orlando Bloom,

Humphrey Bogart, David Bowie, Gérard Depardieu, Mel Gibson, Cary Grant, Stephen Hawking, Janis Joplin, Martin Luther King Jr., Annie Lennox, Kate Moss, Elvis Presley, Jude Law, Marilyn Manson, Henri Matisse, Paul Merton, Dolly Parton, Edgar Allan Poe, J.R.R. Tolkien, Denzel Washington, Tiger Woods.

Positive Characteristics: Practical, capable, successful, mature, sensible, smart, formal, professional, gregarious, ambitious, career-focused, high-powered, achieving, hard-working, dedicated, responsible, stable, steady, reliable, conscientious, disciplined, determined, prudent, careful, realistic, reserved, traditional, official, appropriate, dignified, cautious, contained, conservative, controlled, authoritative, punctual.

Negative Characteristics: Pessimistic, critical, miserly, hard, callous, inflexible, demanding, regimented, controlling, authoritarian, pressurized, outdated, restrained, repressed.

Professions: Banker, accountant, politician, governor, judge, lawyer, police officer, army general, sports coach, head teacher, examiner, civil servant, bureaucrat, manager, director, chiropractor, osteopath, doctor, dentist, priest, bishop.

GLYPH ♑

The glyph for Capricorn is thought to represent the head and body of a goat and the tail of the fish.

Capricorn is represented by the symbol of the goat, or the mythical sea-goat, with the upper body of the animal and the tail of a fish. The goat is a hardy and sure-footed animal and can climb the steepest and craggiest terrains, aptly describing the capable and ambitious characteristics of the sign. The association with the mythological sea-goat may have come from the fact that the Sun travels trough Capricorn during the rainy season. This symbol represents the more sensitive and emotional side of Capricorn, a side that is not always apparent when we first meet them.

Capricorns tend to be healthy and lean in appearance, and are typically tall, with a strong and pronounced bone structure, as well as healthy hair, skin and nails. They can be prone to stiff joints, particularly in their knees, and should take care to relax and find ways to release the stresses and strains of everyday life.

Ruled by Saturn, Capricorn is highly disciplined and takes its responsibilities very seriously. The sign is concerned with personal achievement, and is extremely hard-working, stopping at nothing to achieve its goals. When Capricorns experience setbacks, they will pick themselves up and find a way to get back up the ladder.

Giving up is never an option for this sign! Capricorns may occasionally have to adjust their plans, but they are realistic enough to ensure that, with hard work and application, their goals are achievable from the start. Making allowances and moving goalposts further down the line makes Capricorns feel like they have let themselves down, so they don't like to do it too often.

Like the other earth signs, Taurus and Virgo, Capricorn is a practical sign, and often (though not always) tends to measure its achievements by the amount of money it earns. Capricorns enjoy the trappings of success – a nice house in a good area, an expensive car, private schooling for their children, and so on. This helps them to feel secure in the knowledge that their life is on track.

If they fall upon hard times, Capricorns are more than capable of turning things around in time, and achieving success through persistence and dedication, if they really want it. The trick is to work out what they want most of all, and then aim for it!

Capricorns are consummate professionals, maintaining appropriate boundaries and not allowing their personal life to get in the way of duties at work. They will want to fulfil their public duties to the letter of the contract, for their own peace of mind and they don't like to cut corners.

Fulfilling social expectations is also highly important to Capricorns, and they respect the social mores and institutions that make our society. The sign likes to follow rules and uphold the traditions of the past, and values tried and tested systems. If it works, Capricorns do not believe in fixing it, and will resist changing time-worn practices unless they find a very good reason to do so.

With their strong work ethic, Capricorns do not often take holidays, and time off may feel like a guilty pleasure. However, Capricorns know how to play hard when they do let their hair down and allow themselves to kick back and relax.

Capricorns like to be sociable when time permits, and usually have a wide circle of friends. Dating and relationships tend to be approached cautiously, with many practical considerations to be taken into account, such as their partner's social standing and earning potential, and they will err on the side of finding a partner who will improve their own position in some way. Once they have found a suitable partner, they tend to be committed for the long term, and take marriage vows very seriously.

Capricorns like to dress well, and they look smart and professional at all times, wearing formal clothes at social functions, even when the dress code is casual. They can find it difficult to dress down in their leisure time, and will often plan outfits in advance so that they are impeccably turned out, even when taking the dog to the park. Designer clothes hold a lot of appeal for Capricorns, who enjoy their quality and tailoring, as well as the prestige of wearing expensive labels.

Capricorn's ruling planet is Saturn, the lord of time, and time is of the essence for Capricorns. They are good at timekeeping and use the clock to structure their lives and keep their plans on course. Saturn is also associated with the aging process, and Capricorns tend to be mature and sensible from an early age. They have a strong affinity with their grandparents and the elderly during their childhood. They tend to come into their own as they get older, particularly after their first Saturn return (around the age of 29/30).

We learn self-discipline through our authority figures, and Capricorn teaches us that we won't get far in life without guidance. It is the parent who forces us to go to school when we feel like having a day in bed, or the teacher who sets a test every morning to make sure we have done our reading the night before.

Capricorns seem to intrinsically understand that where there is 'no pain' there is 'no gain', and that there is a deeper purpose to all our hard work – which is self-development and growth. They know that we must work hard chipping away at the rough stone in order to reach the diamond at our core. The path of those born under this sign may seem like a difficult one, but the rewards are great, and they have peace of mind and integrity that comes with knowing that they have earned their achievements.

Capricorns make loyal and dependable friends, colleagues and companions. Although they can be surprised to discover that not everyone lives by the same priorities and high standards as they do, it is helpful if they try to understand other people's points of view and remember not to judge others – or themselves – too harshly.

AQUARIUS

Positive – Fixed – Mutable
Planetary Rulers: Saturn (Traditional) and Uranus (New)
Compatible signs: Aries, Gemini, Leo, Libra, Sagittarius, Capricorn.
Parts of the Body: Shins, ankles, circulation.
Famous Individuals with Sun in Aquarius: Jennifer Aniston, Robert Burns, Lord Byron, Lewis Carroll, James Dean, Charles Dickens, Farrah Fawcett, Clark Gable, Germaine Greer, Paris Hilton, Alicia Keys, Abraham Lincoln, David Lynch, Bob Marley, Wolfgang Amadeus Mozart, Ronald Reagan, Franklin D. Roosevelt, Nicolas Sarkozy, Justin Timberlake, John Travolta, Oprah Winfrey, Virginia Woolf.

Positive Characteristics: Independent, lively, communicative, friendly, congenial, helpful, humane, humanitarian, principled, socially conscious, rebellious, idealistic, revolutionary, activist, earnest, honest, unusual, different, surprising, eccentric, scientific, inventive, innovative, original, fair-minded, tolerant, even-tempered, cool, clear, detached, intelligent, cutting edge, visionary.

Negative Characteristics: Cold, idiosyncratic, contrary, obstinate, demanding, intolerant, extreme, fanatical, marginalized, shocking, unrealistic.

Professions: Scientist, academic, mathematician, physicist, astronomer, meteorologist, astronaut, pilot, air steward, inventor, politician, MP, activist, reporter, community worker, charity worker, volunteer, electrician, engineer.

GLYPH ♒

The glyph for Aquarius represents radio or air waves.

The well-known image of the water-bearer associated with this sign represents the waters of rejuvenation that Aquarius pours out of its vessel and onto the earth. Aquarius is an air sign, and rejuvenation is achieved through the ideas and innovations that it brings to the world. It is thought that the association with water may have come about because the Sun travelled through Aquarius during the rainy season in ancient Mesopotamia.

Aquarian natives have a striking appearance, with crystal clear eyes and sharp features. The face usually has an expression of curiosity. Aquarius rules the ankle and shin area, as well as the circulation. Aquarians sometimes feel the cold terribly.

Aquarians are not afraid to be different from the norm. In fact, they can't help but follow their own path in life. They are well known for marching to the beat of their own drums.

Aquarius is an idealistic and humanitarian sign, and people with personal planets placed there, particularly the Sun and Moon – as well as the Ascendant – are often involved in some form of activism or another. They can be found protesting against unethical behaviour and outdated institutions, or volunteering their time to support the causes that they believe in.

Aquarius is inventive and likes to remain on the cutting edge of society. Its rulers, Saturn and Uranus, are concerned with social issues, how best to govern and how to reinvent the old ways so they keep up with the new. While Aquarius respects the old traditions, it is concerned with updating them and bringing change where it is needed.

Aquarians are socially and environmentally conscious, and will go to great lengths to ensure that their actions are as ethical as possible. They were the first to start recycling schemes and will walk to work to reduce their carbon footprint. They often have unusual diets, dress sense, habits and living arrangements, usually on principle, to make a political point.

Aquarians tend to have an independent and logical mind. They value facts and 'truth', and you can depend on an Aquarian to give their honest opinion on anything. They often follow politics and current affairs, and will spend a lot of their time arguing and debating the latest burning issues with anyone who is willing to pull up a chair and participate!

Aquarians are open-minded about people, and have a wide range of friends across the full spectrum of social demographics. They don't pay much attention to age, cultural background, social status, etc., and seem to look at the human being behind the outward appearance. Very little seems to surprise an Aquarian. Sometimes it feels as if we could gallop around them dressed in a pantomime horse costume and they wouldn't pay much attention!

The opinions of Aquarians can become dogmatic, however, and while they support tolerance in principle, in practice they can become intolerant of others' viewpoints, making them difficult to negotiate with. For this reason many Aquarians either have extremely understanding partners, or find that it is easier to live on their own.

Freedom and liberty are precious to Aquarians, especially their own, and they tend to be extremely independent. However, they need a lot of contact with other humans and animals, and can get very lonely without it.

Aquarians can feel like outsiders and 'different' to the rest of society, often having a sense of rejection from their peers and feeling marginalized from an early age. This can be difficult for them, and sometimes Aquarians avoid groups altogether as they can feel uncomfortable. However, when they find a community of people who support the same ideas as they do, they can experience a great sense of brotherhood, and feel like they have finally arrived home. Aquarians tend to treat everyone equally – whether family, friend, animal or alien from another planet! This is sometimes hardest on partners and children, who like to feel that they have a special place in their Aquarian loved one's heart. They do, of course, although it doesn't always show.

Often Aquarians will be happy to consider playing the part of step-parent or adopting children, as they do not need to be blood relatives to feel like they are kin with others. With Saturn and Uranus as its rulers, Aquarius believes in self-control and prefers to use logic to solve problems, rather than feel overwhelmed by the emotions that accompany them. This results in Aquarians typically being quite cut off from experiencing their own feelings, and they are often caught unawares by them.

Aquarians make excellent friends, and like to be helpful, but their difficulties with intimacy mean they don't always know how to relate to other people or connect with them on an emotional level. Aquarians are uncomfortable with emotional displays, and feel like they are being unfairly manipulated by others. They seem to treat other people's emotions as an unwelcome distraction or as a major infringement of their rights!

Aquarians are often academically gifted and are drawn to all branches of science and research, where their logical thinking, inventiveness and desire to progress humanity can be channelled in the right direction. Sudden flashes of inspiration can be commonplace for Aquarians, and they can make incredible discoveries.

However, Aquarians can sometimes devote their lives to work, and their personal lives and relationships, as well as their general health and well-being, can suffer as a result.

Like Gemini and Libra, the other air signs, Aquarius is idealistic, and Aquarians are forever aiming for the ideal, a trait which guides them in everything they do. As is the case with ideals, however, they don't seem to match up to reality very often, and they end up disappointed, disillusioned and discouraged at times.

It can be useful for Aquarius to remember that, as the saying goes, we should change the things we can, accept the things we can't, and develop the wisdom to know the difference.

PISCES

Negative – Water – Mutable
Planetary Rulers: Jupiter (Traditional) and Neptune (New)
Compatible signs: Taurus, Cancer, Virgo, Scorpio, Sagittarius, Capricorn.

Parts of the Body: Feet.

Famous Individuals with Sun in Pisces: Douglas Adams, W.H. Auden, Drew Barrymore, Juliette Binoche, Jon Bon Jovi, Michael Caine, Karen Carpenter, Johnny Cash, Frederic Francois Chopin, Kurt Cobain, Cindy Crawford, Albert Einstein, Mikhail Gorbachev, George Harrison, Eva Herzigova, Jack Kerouac, Eva Longoria, Michelangelo, Liza Minnelli, Patrick Moore, Lou Reed, Dr Seuss, John Steinbeck, Elizabeth Taylor, Bruce Willis.

Positive Characteristics: Gentle, emotional, loving, compassionate, kind, helpful, caring, sensitive, passive, permissive, sacrificing, creative, artistic, imaginative, dreamy, surreal, impressionable, spiritual, religious, visionary.

Negative Characteristics: Sensitive, vulnerable, vague, unclear, impractical, unreliable, unrealistic, impossible, manipulative, easily-led, escapist, melodramatic, overwhelmed, addictive.

Professions: Nurse, carer, anaesthetist, hypnotist, mental health worker, social worker, regression therapist, actor, mimic, poet, artist, painter, photographer, sailor, lifeboat rescuer, swimming instructor, musician, clairvoyant, medium, priest, monk, nun, mystic.

GLYPH ♓

The glyph for Pisces is thought to represent two fishes.

Pisces is represented by the symbol of two fish swimming in opposite directions, and the stars in the constellation of Pisces are blurry and widespread, without a clear boundary.

Pisces is a universal and all-encompassing sign, like the sea waters around the Earth, and it holds within it all the potentials, dreams, hopes and yearnings of collective humanity.

Pisceans have compassionate and watery eyes, that are often pale or deep blue in colour.

They tend to have soft and sensitive skin which can burn easily and is prone to allergic reactions. Pisces rules the feet, and the foot area is often sensitive. Sometimes Pisceans can have unsteady footing, and need to be mindful when they walk.

Pisces is a mutable water sign, and the last sign of the zodiac. What started out fresh and new in Aries has now come to the end of its cycle. If Aries was the moment when we burst forth into the world, then Pisces is the end point, the sign through which we return to the eternal waters from whence we came. Thus, Pisces has a world-weary quality about it, and people with an emphasis on the sign in their birth chart can seem like old souls who have seen everything under the Sun.

Pisceans may appear quite passive and lacking in aims and ambitions. This is not necessarily the case, because while they have many hopes and dreams for the future, they are adept at accepting what life offers, rather than trying to impose their will on it. Pisceans tend to 'let go and let God'. They should be careful, however, not to give up too easily or avoid trying in the first place, and remember that

God helps those who help themselves!

As a water sign, Pisces is attuned to the emotions and operates somewhere between the conscious and unconscious realms, where the veil between the worlds is thin and mysteries are revealed. Pisces is a very sensitive sign, and can pick up on unspoken messages and underlying feelings between people.

Pisceans are instinctive but not very observant of their environment. They tend to sense their way around, and may not always know where they are going, or remember the journey. But they do manage to end up in the right place – eventually!

Pisceans' eyes tend not to be focused on anything in particular, but seem to be taking in everything at once. Often they will daydream and zone out, sometimes following things in the room which aren't apparent to others, in the way that cats do!

They often wander around in a bubble, unaware of what is happening in their vicinity. This bubble partly serves as a form of protection from the outside world, or a way to escape or hide away from it. Whatever the case, it is an involuntary reaction, and however much a Piscean may want to keep a grip on reality and stay in touch with their surroundings, they find themselves floating off into the world of their imagination.

The sign's rulers, Jupiter and Neptune, are concerned with finding meaning in the world, and exploring the big questions of who we are and where we came from. Pisceans can hold strong religious beliefs and often cultivate an interest in spirituality and mysticism. They tend to enjoy visiting religious sites and going on pilgrimages or retreats, whether or not they are religious! Pisces is a highly compassionate and caring sign, and many Pisceans can be found in the caring professions. Those born under this sign have a natural tendency to take care of others, often at the expense of their own needs. However, as with oxygen masks on an aeroplane, Pisceans are advised to put their own mask on first, and make sure they are able to breathe before seeing to the welfare of others.

Pisceans also need to remember not to wear themselves out, and should not work for free or without receiving worthwhile reward for themselves, as this sort of giving will start to take its toll on their health and well-being, particularly as they get older. They may be forced to give up such work due to ill health, and illness is the only way a Piscean's body can communicate with their mind sometimes. Pisceans would do well to listen to their bodies when this is the case.

Pisceans are often physically sensitive, developing bodily reactions such as allergies in response to emotional problems and disturbances to the natural environment. Many Pisceans develop illnesses related to machinery, mobile phones and other modern day technologies and pollutants. Mysterious ailments which are undiagnosable and unexplainable by modern day medicine belong to the realm of Pisces and its ruler Neptune, and may be better explored through complementary therapies if conventional routes have not been helpful.

Pisceans have great difficulty coping with the harsh realities of life. They will seek to escape the pain of awareness through addictions, and can get trapped in a cycle of self destructive behaviour. Pisceans need to realize that they must save themselves from this cycle, and look to the healing waters inside them to push them up to the surface and out of harm's way.

They should also be careful to avoid using such self-destructive behaviour to manipulate others into letting them have their own way, as there are much more effective and mutually beneficial ways to do this.

Pisces is a wonderfully creative and receptive sign, and is the natural home of the talented artist as well as the mystic. Pisceans can be extremely imaginative and have a natural talent for music and the creative arts.

Pisces is also thought to be a psychic sign, dealing as it does with the blurry space between worlds. They tend to see ghosts and sense psychic disturbances.

Pisceans prefer everything that is old and second-hand, and will tend to live in old houses and wear second-hand clothes. This is partly because they like to be surrounded by the spirits and echoes of the past, and partly because they don't like the responsibility of looking after new things, as they know the items will inevitably get worn out or destroyed in their possession.

Although not known for its powers of logic or linear thought, Pisces gains knowledge and understanding through using its sensitive receptors. In this way, Pisceans can access information that other more logical and realistic signs can't. Pisces can often tell if someone is lying or cheating, for example, just by noticing subtle signs that others wouldn't.

Pisces is adaptable and will fit in with everyone else. When Pisceans are with other people they tend to completely focus on them and lose touch with their own opinions and needs. Because of this, Pisceans can find the company of other people quite draining, and gain relief by being alone.

However, like the other water signs, Pisces has a deep yearning for emotional connection, and gains a lot of comfort from the company of others, tending to feel abandoned if left alone too long.

Pisces is about the magic and mystery of life, and Pisceans understand these realms better than any other sign. They are often criticized for being notoriously chaotic, messy and confused, often doing inexplicable things like finding themselves lost on their own street, or using sugar instead of salt to season their food. However, without these kooky qualities Pisceans would not have the incredible gifts and talents which the other signs only dream about. As with those of every other sign, these talents deserve to be celebrated and nurtured.

Day-by-Day Oracle

Aries
21 March–20 April

21 MARCH

This is the first day of the astrological year, and so 21 March natives tend to be pioneering individuals. If this is your birth date you are brave, independent and outspoken, although you would prefer to be alone than in the company of people with whom you have nothing in common. Others tend to see you as passive because you don't feel the need to justify your views or your actions to them. This is a mistake on their part because, like a wolf in sheep's clothing, people can underestimate you at their cost. Release your pent-up energy with vigorous walks in the country.

AFFIRMATION: Mercury lights the path ahead, and Mars makes me brave enough to take it.

PLANETS: Mercury and Mars

KEYWORDS: Dynamic, determined, independent

22 MARCH

Those born on 22 March are quietly self-assured and once they are set on a particular path, are not easily sidetracked. Consequently they can be highly successful in the business arena. Security is paramount to anyone born on this day. Fiercely protective of the things and people they hold dear, they quickly become prickly if these are compromised in any way. If this is your birthday, you should be mindful of committing to projects before thinking them through thoroughly because once you begin, you'll feel deeply uncomfortable if you have to divert, or abandon your course later on.

AFFIRMATION: The Moon gives me insight while Mars drives me onwards.

PLANETS: Moon and Mars

KEYWORDS: Emotional, dedicated, protective

23 MARCH

If you were born on this day, you are a natural leader with a big personality and exude a self-confidence that others find attractive. Your creativity and infectious curiosity inspire the people around you. You're happy to take the odd risk if you think it will lead to victory, and this sometimes leads you down a dangerous path. Your lust for success means you can be a workaholic. You find it hard to assign tasks to others because, deep down, you feel you would do a better job yourself. Try to be a little more humble in your dealings with others, especially colleagues. Learn to appreciate and use their talents and you will reap the rewards.

AFFIRMATION: The Sun sends his warmth to draw people to me, and the spirit of Mars helps me to help them.

PLANETS: Sun and Mars

KEYWORDS: Uplifting, passionate, unwavering

24 MARCH

Spontaneous, productive and busy, 24 March people are highly active with bags of energy and a naturally childlike air that others find endearing. They are modest and quiet, and it's easy to mistake these qualities for passivity. If this is your birth date, you don't enjoy speech for its own sake, so when you do say something it's always worth listening to. Sometimes your positivity and openness can be interpreted as naivety. For success in business, team up with people who can balance this side of your nature with a healthy dose of cynicism; they won't be able to resist your childlike creativity and you will benefit from their practical know-how.

AFFIRMATION: Mercury is the child full of infectious energy; Mars harnesses that energy and builds upon it.

PLANETS: Mercury and Mars

KEYWORDS: Straightforward, cheerful, hardworking

25 MARCH

If this is your birth date you can be accurately called 'unstoppable', as you have one of the most active and energetic birthdays in the zodiac. The hero in your own life story, some see you as self-centred and you are definitely something of a lone wolf, but look beneath the surface and one will find a kind-hearted soul whose childlike demeanour others find irresistible. You may be tempted to remain alone, but romantic relationships are very important to you, and if you can settle with one partner you will be fulfilled on every level. Look for a partner who shares your lust for life – beginning at the gym.

AFFIRMATION: Mars lends me limitless energy, while Venus drives me to find a soulmate.

PLANETS: Venus and Mars

KEYWORDS: Vigorous, tenacious, loveable

26 MARCH

Those born on this day are naturally tuned in to the way things, and people, work, and are often willing to share their insights with others. They have the ability to stand back and look at things without prejudice, preferring to see the simple reality of a situation. They are usually self-sufficient and work at their own pace regardless of what is going on around them. Occasionally, 26 March people are seen as impervious to the stress of others. They don't always perceive urgency. If this is your birth date you are a good person to have around in a crisis because your sense of humour remains intact when that of others fails.

AFFIRMATION: Pluto sets me apart from others, while Mars helps me to soldier on unwavering.

PLANETS: Pluto and Mars

KEYWORDS: Insightful, magnetic, enterprising

27 MARCH

If you were born on 27 March you are self-reliant and see yourself primarily as an individual rather than belonging to any particular group or tribe. You are agile-minded and adapt what you've learned to suit your own ideas instead of conforming to dogma. Jupiter's influence means that, if this is your birth date, you have a strong adventurous streak which, combined with your natural self-reliance, could see you travelling all over the world. Your excellent instincts and realistic outlook will help you to safely navigate whatever difficult situations you may find yourself in. If this is your birth date, remember that your family will offer you support when you need it most, so be careful not to lose touch.

AFFIRMATION: Jupiter leads me on an adventure, while Mars gives me the tools I need to stay safe.

PLANETS: Jupiter and Mars

KEYWORDS: Intuitive, intrepid, independent

28 MARCH

Those born on this day are so focused it is difficult to distract them from the task at hand, even when absolutely necessary. They can be insensitive to the feelings of others but people tend to respect their honesty, so they don't usually find themselves ostracized. Saturn is linked with authority and rules, and its influence on 28 March natives can mean they are a bit uptight. If this is your birth date, learn to relax from time to time. Take a walk in the open air – you'll feel better for it and this will be reflected in your relationships. Remember to take lunch breaks during your working week. They help you to recharge.

AFFIRMATION: Saturn helps me set firm goals; Mars gives me the energy I need to achieve them.

PLANETS: Saturn and Mars

KEYWORDS: Diligent, truthful, entrepreneurial

29 MARCH

People born on 29 March like to hold up their end of the bargain, and can be relied upon in any situation. If you were born on this day, other people admire your unwavering loyalty and your commitment to the causes you believe in. You are a charming idealist but can be extraordinarily stubborn, and as far as you are concerned the world is black and white. You believe totally in your own moral rectitude and this can lead others to perceive you as small-minded. Try to rise above the temptation to judge others. Remember nobody is perfect, not even you.

AFFIRMATION: Uranus challenges me to question my beliefs; Mars gives me the strength to rise above my shortcomings.

PLANETS: Uranus and Mars

KEYWORDS: Definite, unquestioning, visionary

30 MARCH

Those born on this date are driven to succeed, and won't let anything get in their way. Undaunted by the prospect of failure, they will try over and over again until, eventually, they get what they want. When the future looks unpromising, it is the 30 March native who picks everyone up, dusts them off and gives them the energy to get on with the task in hand. If this is your birth date, use your incredible positivity for worthwhile causes, and you will do a lot of good in the world while inspiring others to do likewise. Volunteering for a charity in your spare time suits you down to the ground.

AFFIRMATION: Mercury gives me a message to carry; Mars makes sure it reaches its destination.

PLANETS: Mercury and Mars

KEYWORDS: Adaptable, supportive, enthusiastic

31 MARCH

Like their neighbours from the previous day, 31 March people are tenacious in the extreme, and will stop at nothing to achieve their goals. Do not attempt to dethrone someone born on this day; it will be nigh on impossible to do so. If this is your birth date, you are most comfortable being the boss, and don't like to play second fiddle to anyone, but your actual talent often lies in a supporting role, rather than a leading one. Remember it can be lonely being the one at the top; sometimes the people lower down the pecking order have more fun. Let loose and have fun with friends and loved ones; they will enjoy it and so will you.

AFFIRMATION: The Moon enables me to support others, while Mars pushes me forward from the rear.

PLANETS: Moon and Mars

KEYWORDS: Determined, loyal, pragmatic

1 APRIL

Those born on this day have true star quality, but being in the limelight is not important to them. However, they do enjoy being in the midst of the action. Their pioneering spirit wins through again and again, taking

them to places most of us would never dare to go. People born on
1 April are unique in the zodiac because, astrologically speaking, their
birth date lies at number one in the first sign. Hence, they are often seen
as heroes in the eyes of the people around them. This can lead them
to expect too much of themselves. If this is your birth date, be wary of
biting off more than you can chew.

AFFIRMATION: Mars redoubled propels me to new heights.

PLANETS: Mars and Mars

KEYWORDS: Bold, adventurous, curious

2 APRIL

People born on 2 April are engaging and self-assured, and it is these
qualities that others find sexy. They are idealists, and are capable of
doing great things, but they occasionally need to stop discussing things
and get on with putting their plans in motion. They are keen to talk
about their utopian vision for the universe at every opportunity, which
some people can find tiresome. If you are a 2 April native, try not to
'hold court' with friends and family; instead learn to listen attentively
and let them take the floor from time to time. They may have a thing or
two to teach you.

AFFIRMATION: Venus attracts people into my life and Mars enables me
to hold them there.

PLANETS: Venus and Mars

KEYWORDS: Confident, alluring, sincere

3 APRIL

If you want to find a 3 April person, look for the centre of the action.
There they will be, doing everything they can to appear indispensible.
They hate to be ignored. If this is your birth date you are essentially good-
natured and full of *joie de vivre*, but others tend to see you as naïve. Don't
let other people's bad attitudes get you down, simply rise above it. Your
positive 'can do' approach to life sometimes inspires jealousy in those
who feel they have less to be happy about. Organizing a soirée sees you
putting all that cheeriness to good use and spreading a little joy.

AFFIRMATION: Mercury has given me a message of joy; Mars drives me
to share it with others.

PLANETS: Mercury and Mars

KEYWORDS: Persuasive, fun-loving, unassuming

4 APRIL

The lives of 4 April natives are often full of challenges, but these people have the ambition, charisma and initiative needed to overcome whatever life throws at them. If you were born on this day you are a natural leader of people, and others often look to you for the positive energy you share with whoever is in your company. You're a tough cookie, but the Moon's influence means that you also have a well-developed sensitive side. You need to surround yourself with genuine friends, not flatterers and 'yes' people, if you want to be happy and truly fulfilled.

AFFIRMATION: The Moon gives me the tools to mother myself, so I can overcome life's challenges.

PLANETS: Moon and Mars

KEYWORDS: Lively, ambitious, charismatic

5 APRIL

Just as the Sun is consistent in rising and setting each day, so are 5 April natives in the way they approach life. If you were born on 5 April, you possess star quality in abundance, and this comes across, not as arrogance, but as self-confidence. You have the tenacity to keep going until you've finished what you started, even if no one else sees the point in your endeavours. When others fail to see the relevance of all this hard work, simply ignore them. It may not pay off today, nor even tomorrow, but eventually you'll be feeling the benefits and they'll be ready to eat their words.

AFFIRMATION: The Sun is warm and consistently giving; Mars is tenacious and confident.

PLANETS: Sun and Mars

KEYWORDS: Dependable, determined, self-assured

6 APRIL

If this is your birthday, your talents lie in organization and precision, but you can also be highly original – even visionary – in your approach to creative tasks. You tend to scrutinize everything, and everyone, that you come into contact with. This critical streak is what keeps you safe when others stray into turbulent waters. You are highly protective of anything you've worked hard for, and can't stand the thought of losing it as the result of an impulsive error of judgement. It is healthy to have high standards for yourself and others, but learn to silence that inner critic and overlook occasional flaws and you'll find you feel more settled.

AFFIRMATION: Mercury tells me to go easy on myself in order to achieve my mission.

PLANETS: Mercury and Mars

KEYWORDS: Modest, orderly, magnetic

7 APRIL

Natives of 7 April display enthusiasm in everything they do. They have a passion for life that attracts other people to them, and in turn, they respond well to positivity in others. Venus's influence means they value partnership, and thrive in a relationship, but they can also be jealous. If you were born on this day, learn to tackle these possessive instincts and you will find contentment. Don't use anger to fuel the fire in your love life, as it will leave you, and your lover, feeling exhausted. A replenishing activity, like feeding birds in the park, sees you rediscovering your nurturing side.

AFFIRMATION: Venus brings love into my heart; Mars gives me the passion to keep it alive.

PLANETS: Venus and Mars

KEYWORDS: Hopeful, passionate, fiery

8 APRIL

If this is your birthday you have a very caring nature, which you express in all manner of ways. But, although you are able to touch others' lives with your generosity, Pluto's influence means that it is sometimes hard for them to touch you. This can make it difficult for you to build intimate relationships, and it is something you may want to work on if you are to find true happiness. Set aside some time you can dedicate to building bridges between you and the people you love. A well-written and heartfelt letter, or a good long chat, will help to heal old wounds.

AFFIRMATION: Pluto draws others to me, while Mars breaks down barriers so I can let them in.

PLANETS: Pluto and Mars

KEYWORDS: Giving, captivating, resolute

9 APRIL

If this is your birthday you have a voracious appetite for life, and whatever you do, you do with 100 per cent of your energy and enthusiasm. Spontaneous and fun-loving, you are the sort of person who books a holiday at a moment's notice. Calm in any crisis, you will not get stressed if you arrive at the airport and realize you've forgotten to do some important task. Adventure is your middle name and when things, occasionally, don't go to plan, you are resilient enough not to let it shake your resolve. Celebrate your wild, impulsive side and never let anyone call you reckless.

AFFIRMATION: Jupiter brings me good fortune; Mars overcomes obstacles.

PLANETS: Jupiter and Mars

KEYWORDS: Progressive, strong-minded, adaptable

10 APRIL

Life with a 10 April native is never dull. They are born with the courage to be themselves no matter what, and this rare quality will stay with them throughout their lives. They are exciting and spontaneous individuals who think nothing of gambling with things that others regard as far too important to risk. If you were born on this day, you must search for your true calling. You aren't really as foolhardy or as reckless as other people think, so you can trust your own judgement. Don't let others divert you from whatever path you feel is the one for you.

AFFIRMATION: Saturn fuels my ambition. Mars gives me the strength I need to realize it.

PLANETS: Saturn and Mars

KEYWORDS: Adventurous, daring, determined

11 APRIL

Those born on this date are useful to have around in a crisis, because they can be relied upon to salvage whatever seems unsalvageable. They are diplomatic and caring individuals who tend to take responsibility for other people's development. They are perfectly suited to a management role in a large organization because they are great at taking others under their wing. If this is your birth date, you may find you are the type of person who picks up waifs and strays: make sure you set firm boundaries in your personal life so you don't feel invaded.

AFFIRMATION: Uranus allows me to change what others cannot.

PLANETS: Uranus and Mars

KEYWORDS: Direct, useful, compassionate

12 APRIL

Those born on this day tend to be integral to society and are finely attuned to the public mood. They are great diplomats with a natural talent for debate, and they often find themselves speaking up for, or on behalf of, colleagues and family members. They make great union representatives, because they are prepared to fight for the plight of the common man. If you are a 12 April native, make sure you know where you end and the world begins. Don't lose yourself in the crowd. It is important that you get to know yourself at a deeper level before trying to speak for others.

AFFIRMATION: Neptune gives me insight that I use to help others.

PLANETS: Neptune and Mars

KEYWORDS: Honest, insightful, ingenious

13 APRIL

Like their neighbours from 12 April, natives of 13 April tend to act as spokespeople for others and feel at their most happy and successful when busy trailblazing. They are perfectly suited to pioneering social reform and working with people who are less fortunate than themselves. The Moon's influence means they are tuned in to the feelings of others, and this makes them brilliant politicians. If this is your birthday, you are capable of going the distance, and when you finally reach your destination, you'll make sure all your doubters know about it.

AFFIRMATION: The Moon gives me the power to nurture and protect.

PLANETS: Moon and Mars

KEYWORDS: Empathetic, instigating, defiant

14 APRIL

If you were born on this day you have a keen sense of the past, and hold traditional values dear, especially when it comes to the family and your place in society. You inherently believe that everyone has their own special place in the grand scheme of things. You like to know where your niche is, and fit it well, but take the time to expand your horizons every once in a while and you may surprise yourself. Do something that seems out of character – try cooking a brand new recipe, or enrol in a creative evening class – the novelty will give you the boost you seek.

AFFIRMATION: The Sun gives me authority and a sense of history, but Mars goes forward with a pioneering spirit.

PLANETS: Sun and Mars

KEYWORDS: Traditional, orderly, honourable

15 APRIL

If this is your birth date you are a realist to the last; in fact, you could probably do with letting a little fantasy into your life. You are organized and tend to your tasks like a nurse tends to her patients – conscientiously and methodically. Others feel secure in your company, and look to you for guidance, protection and healing. Constantly looking after others can be extremely draining and leaves you little time to look after yourself. It is very important that you take time out to replenish some of that energy. Relaxing in a luxurious bubble bath with a good book will rejuvenate you.

AFFIRMATION: Mercury helps me adapt to meet others' needs.

PLANETS: Mercury and Mars

KEYWORDS: Controlled, efficient, nurturing

16 APRIL

Those born on this day wear their hearts on their sleeves and have a keen sense of humour. They can find the funny side of any situation and this makes them popular and likeable. They can always be relied upon to ease tensions by making people laugh, and this can prove to be a valuable asset in the workplace as well as among friends and loved ones. People born on 16 April are generous to a fault, but can be so accommodating that they let people walk all over them. If this is your birth date, don't let others take advantage of you. Left unchecked, your permissive nature will encourage their bad behaviour and make matters worse.

AFFIRMATION: Venus shines her light on me, so I can laugh when others frown.

PLANETS: Venus and Mars

KEYWORDS: Accommodating, loving, self-deprecating

17 APRIL

An iron will and an innate sense of importance are qualities shared by those born on 17 April. If this is your birth date you hate to be ignored, but you rarely are, because you carry yourself in a way that inspires respect. Your influence is far-reaching and others look to you for moral, spiritual and ethical guidance. You would make an excellent teacher or religious leader, because you are great at getting your voice heard. You hate bullies and will rush to the defence of anyone you perceive as being victimized. You never forget where you came from, and cherish your family and your roots for what they are, without nostalgia.

AFFIRMATION: Pluto and Mars give me the power to break down barriers.

PLANETS: Pluto and Mars

KEYWORDS: Principled, powerful, protective

18 APRIL

Like knights in shining armour, those born on this day offer protection to those around them, and can often be relied on to save the day. If this is your birth date, you are a progressive thinker and will fight for what you believe is right, but you can be argumentative. You are generous and have a well-developed sense of fun – you like to be at the centre of the party. Direct and uncomplicated, others know where they stand with you and that makes you feel comfortable. Learn to steer clear of disagreements that are unimportant or petty: concentrate on the causes that mean something.

AFFIRMATION: Jupiter invites understanding and good fortune.

PLANETS: Jupiter and Mars

KEYWORDS: Dependable, optimistic, bubbly

19 APRIL

Earthy, grounded and in control are all phrases that describe people born on this day. This may sound a little dull, but these people also have a fun side, and like to party with the best of them. The 19 April native has staying power, is good with their hands and respects earthiness in others. They don't have much time for the intangible, preferring things they can actually grab hold of. If this is your birth date, resist the temptation to try and mould everyone you meet into exactly who you want them to be. The world will be much more enjoyable when you learn to appreciate others for who they are.

AFFIRMATION: Saturn loves structure and solidity, but Mars gives me the courage to look beyond the obvious.

PLANETS: Saturn and Mars

KEYWORDS: Fun-loving, humble, stable

20 APRIL

Natives of 20 April are natural leaders. They are dynamic people with a lust for power that drives them on an upward trajectory through life. If this is your birth date, you have a strong imagination and this lends you an air of magic that people find attractive. You'll usually find an ingenious solution to whatever obstacle you encounter. The challenges thrown at you do nothing to dampen your spirits – in fact they usually spur you on. Your day is not complete without a bit of problem-solving, so do some DIY, or spend some time completing a difficult crossword, to blow the cobwebs away.

AFFIRMATION: Venus is magnetic; Mars is dynamic.

PLANETS: Venus and Mars

KEYWORDS: Creative, exciting, inspiring

Taurus
21 April–21 May

21 APRIL

Those born on this day have a way with words. This, together with their air of dignity and professional commitment, makes them able salespeople, whether or not they actually choose to go into sales as a career. If this is your birth date, you are renowned for your good taste – you have your finger on the pulse and people tend to come to you for style advice. Venus in your chart reinforces this love of physical beauty, and you appreciate it in people as well as things. Try to look beyond the material once in a while. Remember that true beauty comes from inside as well as out.

AFFIRMATION: Venus brings beauty into my life while Mercury helps me communicate it to others.

PLANETS: Mercury and Venus

KEYWORDS: Chic, persuasive, caring

22 APRIL

If this is your birth date, you may not be the life and soul of the party, but you certainly know how to organize one, and this is often your function, either professionally, or within a family or social group. You don't seek to steal the limelight, and may even be seen as a bit of a loner, but you gain fulfilment from bringing enjoyment to others, and

this makes you an excellent host and friend. Don't be hurt if people undervalue your efforts to please them: some people won't understand what motivates you, so move on and find others who do. With your supportive, caring nature, you will never be short of friends.

AFFIRMATION: The Moon shuns the spotlight, but Venus draws people in.

PLANETS: Moon and Venus

KEYWORDS: Strong, organized, dependable

23 APRIL

Natives of 23 April natives have the strong influence of the Sun in their chart and so radiate warmth and security. If this is your birth date, you have a well-established sense of tradition, and thrive when held in the bosom of a large and respected organization. Your career is likely to be something of a slow burner, with gradually building recognition rather than instant fame and fortune. The message here is to 'play the long game'. Ignore any outlandish impulses and instead keep plugging away and eventually success will be yours. Be persistent, but not complacent.

AFFIRMATION: Venus draws people out of the cold to bask in the warmth of the Sun.

PLANETS: Sun and Venus

KEYWORDS: Warm-hearted, secure, attractive

24 APRIL

People born on 24 April like others to know what they are thinking, and tend to communicate their ideas and emotions by making beautiful things. They have an excellent eye for detail, and enjoy working with their hands, so make great craftspeople. They often exhibit caring qualities and are natural parents, but this urge to nurture often extends to friends, colleagues and even strangers. If this is your birth date, you may need to learn when to take a step back. You cannot ultimately be held responsible if others choose not to take your advice and, if you think about it carefully, did they ask for it in the first place?

AFFIRMATION: Venus brings love into my life; Mercury helps me to share it with others.

PLANETS: Mercury and Venus

KEYWORDS: Thoughtful, expressive, caring

25 APRIL

When a 25 April person enters the room, everyone knows about it. They have a physical presence that remains with them throughout life and touches every part of their existence, from their careers, to their friendships and romantic relationships. People born on 25 April are doers. They may not be great at smalltalk, but they always deliver on their promises and are brilliant people to have around in a stressful situation because they know how to bolster flagging confidence. If this is your birth date, have patience with those who appear weaker than you; their strengths simply lie elsewhere.

AFFIRMATION: Venus gives me strength where others fail.

PLANETS: Venus and Venus

KEYWORDS: Dominant, dynamic, reassuring

26 APRIL

People born on 26 April are the caretakers of the zodiac. Their greatest skill is in maintaining and preserving things. This may sound pretty mundane, but the reality is far from it – without its cleaning ladies and conservationists, the world would begin to fall apart! If this is your birth date, you can be stubborn, sometimes preferring to plug away at a pointless task rather than be seen to change direction. Try to remain open to new ideas: sometimes it is better to admit defeat and walk away than waste your life on a fruitless endeavour. Allow your inspirational side to shine through by passing on your knowledge and skills.

AFFIRMATION: Pluto allows me to be reborn.

PLANETS: Pluto and Venus

KEYWORDS: Independent, passionate, determined

27 APRIL

One of life's natural adventurers, those born on this day never lose their passion for life and will always walk on the wild side – within reason. They never sit still for long and continue learning into old age. If they didn't go to college, they will revisit their education later in life, by attending evening classes, becoming mature students or simply learning a new skill. If this is your birth date, you are independent and a bit of a wanderer; you take comfort in your own company. You may not need other people, but Venus's influence in your chart means that others gravitate to you anyway.

AFFIRMATION: Jupiter the gypsy brings good fortune.

PLANETS: Jupiter and Venus

KEYWORDS: Self-sufficient, unpredictable, bold

28 APRIL

Those born on this day are among the zodiac's most determined individuals. Once they have embarked on a task, they will not abandon it for love nor money. This can make them great people to work alongside on a project, as long as you agree with their preferred course of action. If you oppose them you will end up frustrated, and probably defeated. If this is your birth date, you are decisive and driven, but would it really hurt to defer to another's judgement every now and again? You may find people are more receptive to your ideas when you listen to theirs.

AFFIRMATION: Saturn gives me ambition and drive; Venus can balance this with love and humility.

PLANETS: Saturn and Venus

KEYWORDS: Steadfast, single-minded, patient

29 APRIL

People born on 29 April know how to present themselves and are highly aware of their public profile, so they are naturally adept at any kind of social networking. People see them as confident and in control and this can have many benefits in a professional arena. They are dominant personalities who often take the leading role, but all this can start to feel restricting. If this is your birth date, release some of that pressure by dancing around the house or playing party games – the sillier the better. You may feel stupid to begin with, but it will help you to lighten up a bit.

AFFIRMATION: Uranus and Venus combined, balance independence with bonding energy.

PLANETS: Uranus and Venus

KEYWORDS: Reliable, sensible, self-assured

30 APRIL

Like their neighbours from 29 April, those born on this day have dominating personalities, but they are also charming and witty. They like to be in charge and enjoy working for a living, but can sometimes be tempted to follow the rules at the expense of common sense, or people's feelings. If this is your birth date, you don't like uncertainty and only really feel secure when you are around the friends and family you hold most dear. Your sense of duty is so strong that you will follow them to the ends of the earth. A long dinner with loved ones sees you cracking jokes and thoroughly enjoying yourself.

AFFIRMATION: Venus brings me charm and good fortune; Mercury shows me the bigger picture.

PLANETS: Mercury and Venus

KEYWORDS: Playful, loyal, humorous

1 MAY

If this is your birth date you enjoy nothing more than people-watching, and you tend to notice things like body language and other so-called 'secret' behaviour, that others do not. You are not overly talkative (chatting distracts you from your favourite pastime), but you usually make what you say count. Your natural wit has a way of disarming arrogant people: you know just how to bring someone down a peg or two, and others admire this in you. Your love of observing others can mean that you forget to participate yourself. Getting involved in a group activity of some kind may help you to interact a little better.

AFFIRMATION: Mars stands alone but Venus gets involved.

PLANETS: Mars and Venus

KEYWORDS: Calm, perceptive, subtle

2 MAY

If this is your birth date, you love beautiful things and enjoy indulging yourself. A tactile and sensual person, you naturally gravitate to luxurious textures and can often be found trawling boutiques for glamorous garments, or at the perfume counter, sampling a new scent. Many 2 May people find themselves working in the fashion industry, where their perfectionism is a valued trait, and they can be as forthright and outspoken as they like. Try to relax from time to time; your sense of beauty will shine out in whatever you do, and sometimes the more effortless it appears, the better.

AFFIRMATION: Venus takes life in her stride.

PLANETS: Venus and Venus

KEYWORDS: Direct, tasteful, idealistic

3 MAY

Do you often find yourself at the centre of an argument trying to broker peace between two opposing sides? Do people tend to look to you to break the bad news? Do you keep your feet on the ground rather than embarking on flights of fancy? If you answered 'yes' to all three, then you may be a 3 May native: diplomatic, charming and peace-loving. You know how to look on the bright side, and invest a lot of energy in your relationships, but you worry too much about stepping on other people's toes. It doesn't hurt to say what you really think from time to time.

AFFIRMATION: Mercury gives me the ability to communicate and Venus, the capacity to love.

PLANETS: Mercury and Venus

KEYWORDS: Tactful, clever, fair

4 MAY

Natives of 4 May are natural teachers or trainers and often inhabit positions of responsibility. However, their calm and collected exterior often hides a well-developed wild side. They can be risk takers, or dig their heels in rather than comply with the wishes of others, so they are not to be trifled with. If this is your birth date, concentrate on developing the nurturing side of your personality, rather than your inner wild-child, but don't ignore him completely. Find an outlet for the adrenalin junky in you: visit an indoor climbing wall or try go-karting to let off steam.

AFFIRMATION: The Moon gives me the insight I need to nurture others.

PLANETS: Moon and Venus

KEYWORDS: Nurturing, determined, adventurous

5 MAY

Those born on this day can usually offer a piece of advice in any situation, but however good that advice is – and usually it is very good – some people won't want to take it. People born on 5 May are practical and insightful thinkers with the best intentions at heart. They have a lot to offer, both professionally and in social circles, but people sometimes mistake their interest for meddling. If this is your birth date, learn to take a step back and leave people alone for a while. They will soon see the error of their ways and welcome your input with open arms.

Physical activity is rewarding for you and gives you a chance to focus on yourself.

AFFIRMATION: The Sun gives me strength to overcome obstacles.

KEYWORDS: Persuasive, insightful, helpful

PLANETS: Sun and Venus

6 MAY

People born on 6 May appreciate the simple things in life, and often experience the urge to go 'back to nature'. They like to be direct and hate being bogged down in red tape, paperwork or petty politics. They are sensitive and imaginative people, whose creative minds are best put to good use rather than left to wander aimlessly. If this is your birth date, you are an insightful individual with a sixth sense that others find fascinating. Try a camping weekend if urban life becomes tiresome: the fresh air, peace and quiet will do you good.

AFFIRMATION: Venus encourages harmony; Mercury proliferates it.

PLANETS: Mercury and Venus

KEYWORDS: Responsive, intuitive, earthy

7 MAY

When 7 May people commit to something, they commit for life. If you are attracted to a 7 May native, don't look to them for a harmless fling, because you are likely to end up with more than you bargained for. Their devotion inspires people, as does their love of music and beauty in all things. They are lucky individuals who seem to attract gifts and windfalls, so if they put a bet on a horse or a sporting event, it might be a good idea to follow their tip. If this is your birth date, your deeply ingrained sense of loyalty can render you blind to the facts of a situation, so remember to keep your eyes open at all times.

AFFIRMATION: Venus brings me good fortune and a love of beauty in all things.

PLANETS: Venus and Venus

KEYWORDS: Devoted, fortunate, self-possessed

8 MAY

The 8 May native is not afraid to take direct action, or to speak up when others stay silent. They tend to defend the wishes or aspirations of a group of people, and are fearless in their pursuit of fairness. They rarely back down from a fight – in fact they relish the challenge. They make faithful partners and harbour a love of material beauty, so their homes are usually harmonious and enjoyable places to be. If this is your birth date, learn to take yourself a little less seriously and show the odd chink in your armour. People will relate to you better when they realize you are as imperfect and as vulnerable as they are.

AFFIRMATION: Pluto gives me renewed energy.

PLANETS: Pluto and Venus

KEYWORDS: Outspoken, courageous, tasteful

9 MAY

Natives of 9 May are especially endowed with typical Taurean traits, including a love of material beauty and nature, but don't be fooled into thinking they are among the zodiac's softies. They are also formidable opponents, and not the kind of people you'd want to get on the wrong side of – in fact their tempers can be fearsome. If this is your birth date you hate bullying or exploitation of any kind, and will stand up for anyone who is being treated unfairly. You make good politicians, lawyers and policemen, but it is essential that you get on top of your anger management issues, if only for the safety of those in the immediate vicinity when you erupt.

AFFIRMATION: Wherever Jupiter takes me, Venus's love will follow.

PLANETS: Jupiter and Venus

KEYWORDS: Fair, adventurous, influential

10 MAY

Those born on this day tend to be lone wolves, and this can attract criticism, not to mention jealousy, from others as they progress through life. They lead by example, but travelling in their wake is often difficult. It is best not to take on a 10 May person unless you are absolutely confident of victory, because once they've defeated you they'll make sure you never forget it. However, they can also be graceful, charming and capable of seducing almost anyone, even their enemies. If this is your birth date, learn to trust your instincts – they are often correct.

AFFIRMATION: Saturn gives me the will to succeed; Venus gives me the allure I need.

PLANETS: Saturn and Venus

KEYWORDS: Passionate, intuitive, alluring

11 MAY

Do you find your appearance, words and actions attract attention even when you wish they wouldn't? Do people sometimes describe you as eccentric, or even odd? Then you could be an 11 May native. People born on this day tend to stand out. Some learn to like it and positively court controversy, whereas for others it is the bane of their existence. If this is your birth date, just smile and accept that you are different from others. There is nothing you can do about it so you may as well learn to enjoy it. Besides, would you really have it any other way? Isn't it better to be unique than the same as everyone else? Concentrate on finding a soulmate who embraces your unique outlook.

AFFIRMATION: The power of Uranus and Venus combined allows me to be myself.

PLANETS: Uranus and Venus

KEYWORDS: Unconventional, fun-loving, liberal

12 MAY

It's that twinkle in your eye that gives it away – you are a 12 May person. Your love of mischief tends to land you in trouble with friends, family members and colleagues, but your devilish sense of humour and air of self-assurance hold a certain allure. Like an errant TV detective, you are often described as a bit of a maverick, but you get results, so people ultimately respect and, secretly, admire you. People may love your innate talent and your naughtiness, but try to follow the rules on occasion and never break them just for the sake of it. They are usually there for a reason. Team sports help to keep you in line and do you a world of good.

AFFIRMATION: Neptune allows me to break with convention; Venus ensures that I do so with love in my heart.

PLANETS: Neptune and Venus

KEYWORDS: Ingenious, playful, attractive

13 MAY

If you are a 13 May native, you have a natural and fun-loving manner that people find attractive. Like a swan gliding serenely across the water, you seem to do everything with ease, even if you are paddling away like anything underneath. Most of the time, though, you are a leisurely and lyrical sort of person whom others love to be around, especially at parties and social gatherings, where your mischievous side really comes out to play. You are easily led astray and need to set yourself firm boundaries, and surround yourself with good influences. Remember that ultimately you are in control of your own behaviour – the decisions you make are your own.

AFFIRMATION: Venus attracts people into my life, the Moon allows me to see whether or not they should stay there.

PLANETS: Moon and Venus

KEYWORDS: Bubbly, popular, easy-going

14 MAY

Those born on this day are very tuned in to where they stand in time. They always seem to have one eye on the past and another on the future, but they live and work squarely in the present. They have a childlike curiosity about the world, are quick to adopt trends and like to follow events in the news. They think nothing of breaking with tradition and seem to be always on the go. If this is your birth date, try to find a calm space to relax in once in a while. A week, or even a day, away from all kinds of media, especially the Internet, will help you to regroup.

AFFIRMATION: Venus invites calm; the Sun gives me the will to seek it out.

PLANETS: Sun and Venus

KEYWORDS: Youthful, active, caring

15 MAY

Like their neighbours from 13 and 14 May, those born on this day have a natural and easy manner that attracts people into their lives. But those from 15 May are particularly magnetic and people are drawn to them, sometimes without even knowing why. If you were born on this day, others tend to see you as down-to-earth, and even a bit ordinary, but they know little about the powerful astrological forces at work in your horoscope. You are naturally creative and able to use everyday objects to create extraordinary things. A woodworking class would suit your earthy personality down to the ground.

AFFIRMATION: Mercury and Venus create harmony and share it with the world.

PLANETS: Mercury and Venus

KEYWORDS: Imaginative, attractive, practical

16 MAY

The 16 May native is naturally flamboyant and outrageous, and, even if their upbringing discourages it, their true self will eventually shine out for all to see, and continue to become more obvious as time goes by. If this is your birth date, and an idea or project appeals to you, then go with it and don't pay any attention to what anyone else thinks. Your critics are probably just jealous of your innate star quality. You have a volcanic temper, and when you lose it, it's not a pretty sight. Find a way to let go of all that tension; with your well-developed flair for self-expression, a night on the dancefloor might help.

AFFIRMATION: The strength of Venus means I can be whoever I want to be.

PLANETS: Venus and Venus

KEYWORDS: Extrovert, outlandish, passionate

17 MAY

People born on 17 May like to get to the heart of the matter, and have a natural intensity that will either repel or attract others. Whichever way it goes, there is no denying the power they project out into the world. They are direct, thorough and intelligent thinkers who can make profound and simple statements of truth that may take others aback. On the other hand, their tactlessness can be grating to those people who would prefer not to hear the truth. If this is your birth date, you tend to see things as black and white, but sometimes life just isn't like that. Try to appreciate the various shades of grey too – your life will be all the richer for it.

AFFIRMATION: Pluto breaks down barriers and allows me to see the truth of the matter.

PLANETS: Pluto and Venus

KEYWORDS: Strong, elegant, powerful

18 MAY

Jupiter's influence means that 18 May people need to explore new horizons in every area of life. They are natural revolutionaries – great to have around when you need to shake things up, but not when it's time to hunker down and get on with completing a task. They get carried away easily, preferring to fight the system than accept authority, and when confronted with this fact they find it difficult to accept and nigh on impossible to change. It can be exhausting fulfilling this role. If this is your birth date, make sure you take time to recharge those batteries. The fight can wait for another day.

AFFIRMATION: Jupiter gives me the energy I need to fight for change.

PLANETS: Jupiter and Venus

KEYWORDS: Passionate, unconventional, motivating

19 MAY

Are you the sort of person who is constantly active, always running this way and that, like the white rabbit in Alice's wonderland? Do you sometimes feel as if you're losing your grip because you are just too busy to get everything done? Then you could be a 19 May native. You might think that all this energetic output looks a bit like mania in others' eyes, but it doesn't. People see you as controlled and authoritative – so that's one less thing for you to worry about. You have great leadership potential and, if you can harness it, you could go very far indeed. Perhaps a life-coaching course might help you meet your goals more efficiently.

AFFIRMATION: Saturn gives me the power to succeed in my goals.

PLANETS: Saturn and Venus

KEYWORDS: Vital, influential, dynamic

20 MAY

Those born on this day enjoy the finer things in life, and love nothing better than an excellent meal in a good restaurant, chased down with a bottle of vintage wine. They are naturally stylish and revel in luxurious surroundings but are at once kind and approachable – a rare quality in the sort of environment they are usually at home in. They can be easily bored, and need to learn to finish things, as well as find physical exercise they enjoy, if only to work off those rich meals. If this is your birth date, you would do well to abide by the rule 'everything in moderation'. Try escaping to a health resort once in a while to combine luxury with a more frugal regime.

AFFIRMATION: Venus loves life and all it has to offer.

PLANETS: Venus and Venus

KEYWORDS: Friendly, indulgent, tasteful

21 MAY

People with a birth date of 21 May combine an imaginative and childlike nature with the will to get things done, and their tenacity makes them unusual, not to mention valuable. In the tradition of all earth signs, they have a strong need to make their ideas tangible and they often find themselves literally sculpting something out of nothing. Natives of 21 May make great craftspeople. If this is your birth date, you have a tendency to worry about other people and neglect yourself and your own needs in the process. A little meditation will help you to focus on problems you can actually solve, instead of the ones you can't do anything about.

AFFIRMATION: Mercury and Venus mean I can make my ideas a reality and spread my vision.

PLANETS: Mercury and Venus

KEYWORDS: Visionary, engaging, youthful

Gemini

22 May–21 June

22 MAY

Do you ever feel as if you've bitten off more than you can chew? Do your loved ones ever accuse you of obsessive-compulsive behaviour? Do you find you tend to repeat the same mistakes in life over and over again? Those born on this day are typically drawn towards epic tasks and find it impossible to delegate, preferring to take on all the responsibility themselves. If this is your birthday, you are great with kids and thrive when part of a big extended family, but can be moody, especially when all that responsibility starts weighing on your shoulders. Concentrate on doing what you do best, and leave the rest to someone else.

AFFIRMATION: The Moon belongs to the Earth, and is held in its embrace for all time.

PLANETS: Moon and Mercury

KEYWORDS: Friendly, loving, generous

23 MAY

Those born on 23 May have boundless energy and this impacts upon every area of their lives. They give 100 per cent in everything they do, and make brilliant parents because they are naturally playful and can keep up with their children even after a long day at work. Those born on this day emit a rare kind of warmth that surrounds them with light and attracts people in; others enjoy spending time with them and their sex appeal is undeniable. If you were born on this day, your need for attention and flattery can get out of control. Remember that the only opinions that really matter are your own, and those of the people you love.

AFFIRMATION: The Sun's rays are warm and far-reaching; he always gives without receiving.

PLANETS: Sun and Mercury

KEYWORDS: Enthusiastic, agile, warm

24 MAY

Opinionated, witty and outspoken, 24 May people can't help but say what they think, and so tend to end up in the limelight. They may at first come across as outgoing and sociable, but often this is not the case. They like privacy and any communication must be on their terms, not yours. If this is your birth date, you are good to have around in tense situations because you clear the air by voicing what most other people keep to themselves, but be careful not to land yourself in trouble – you could end up being used as a scapegoat if others won't back you up. Be prepared to stick to your guns when this happens. Your peers will respect you for it.

AFFIRMATION: Mercury redoubled allows me to speak when others stay silent.

PLANETS: Mercury and Mercury

KEYWORDS: Humorous, honest, reflective

25 MAY

The phrase 'freedom fighter' perfectly sums up the 25 May native. They are naturally fervent, ethical individuals who believe that everyone deserves equal treatment and are drawn to activism in support of their beliefs. They won't compromise their principles and will leap over any obstacle to prove their point, even if it makes them unpopular. If this is your birth date, you're not as brave as you seem on the surface; you hate rejection, even by people you don't like very much. Try to be more forgiving of others – the phrase 'judge not lest ye be judged', is a good one to live by.

AFFIRMATION: Venus and Mercury bring a message of love and tolerance.

PLANETS: Venus and Mercury

KEYWORDS: Bold, principled, dignified

26 MAY

People born on 26 May are sometimes misunderstood. At their core they are warm-hearted people but they are also complex, treading a fine line between their traditional values and their attraction to a more outrageous, unconventional way of life. They have difficulty expressing how they feel and can appear serious to those around them, but they are also graceful and magnetic. Friendship and loyalty are two of the most important factors in the lives of 26 May people. If you were born on this day, you may need to be easier on yourself as well as others – it will make your life run much more smoothly.

AFFIRMATION: Pluto breaks down barriers and lets people in.

PLANETS: Pluto and Mercury

KEYWORDS: Generous, complex, attractive

27 MAY

If you were born on this day, chances are you have made, or will have to make, a choice between a cause, organization, or social group and your own personal development. Whichever your choice, you are unlikely to abandon it later on, as you like to stick with your decisions until they pay off. You have an unconventional view of the world, which is primarily expressed in your sense of humour. Most people appreciate your peculiar way of looking at things, but don't get so wrapped up in talking that you forget to listen. It drives people mad and, in the long run, alienates them from you.

AFFIRMATION: Mercury listens as well as speaks.

PLANETS: Jupiter and Mercury

KEYWORDS: Humorous, zany, tenacious

28 MAY

Those born on 28 May are self-starters. They are happiest at the beginning of a new project but they also have the ability to hang in there and finish what they start, and this is what sets them apart from other innovators. Those born on this day usually achieve success in business through their excellent manners and their innate aptitude for logical thinking. If this is your birth date, you really should take advantage of your natural skills. Don't underestimate how far a little elbow grease and a good head for figures can get you. Work off excess energy with a little strenuous sport: squash or climbing will suit your agile mind and stretch you physically.

AFFIRMATION: Saturn sets challenges for me to overcome.

PLANETS: Saturn and Mercury

KEYWORDS: Creative, diligent, intelligent

29 MAY

Have you ever been accused of being a drama queen? People born on 29 May tend to be drawn towards any crisis, and could be described as confrontational in their dealings with others. However, they're always ready to stand up for the underdog, and that can be very valuable in a tense situation. If you were born on this day, Mercury's influence means that you value charm, wit and humour, all of which you have in spades – but you do need to express your physical self too. Racket sports, such as tennis, badminton or squash, mirror the banter you enjoy so much.

AFFIRMATION: Mercury makes me a strong communicator; Uranus encourages me to speak for change.

PLANETS: Uranus and Mercury

KEYWORDS: Revolutionary, outspoken, funny

30 MAY

Mercury is the planet of communication and, for those people born on this day, its influence is strong. They love to keep in touch with others and are perfectly suited to modern life, as it's now so easy to communicate with the world all day and all night long. People born on 30 May are information-hungry and easily bored. They like new things, and quickly lose interest in anything they consider 'old hat'. If this is your birth date, try to find some stillness in your life. Gardening combines your love of constant change with peaceful surroundings, allowing you to regroup and create something beautiful.

AFFIRMATION: Mercury can create as well as comment.

PLANETS: Mercury and Mercury

KEYWORDS: Social, adaptable, energetic

31 MAY

People born on this day often portray a hard exterior, but underneath that façade is a soft-hearted, often sentimental individual. The 31 May native makes a perfect spokesperson, as they can express easily what other people find difficult to put into words. Activity and energy pervade everything they do and they certainly stand out from a crowd

with their charm and good looks. Those with families will experience great joy through their children's achievements, and the nurturing influence of the Moon means they are caring, thoughtful parents. If this is your birth date, try not to take what people say too seriously – smile and do a little yoga to help you relax.

AFFIRMATION: The Moon helps to keep your emotions under control.

PLANETS: Moon and Mercury

KEYWORDS: Compassionate, rational, communicative

1 JUNE

The 1 June native appears bubbly and outgoing, but what you see is not always what you get. Underneath it all, 1 June people tend to be private individuals who crave attention and company but have trouble letting others get close to them. Their fingers are well and truly on the pulse, and they have an instinctive sense for what the public wants, so they are well-suited to working in public relations or sales, but they could do with working on their patience and learning to enjoy their own company. If this is your birth date, keeping a diary will help you touch base. Spend a little time each day getting to know yourself.

AFFIRMATION: Mars gives me the courage to let others in.

PLANETS: Mars and Mercury

KEYWORDS: Trendy, reserved, shrewd

2 JUNE

Geminis tend to have an element of duality about their personalities, and 2 June people are no different. They can be at once materialistic and spiritual, and are comfortable in the heart of a city or in remote countryside, as long as they aren't alone. Like their neighbours from 1 June, 2 June natives thrive as long as there are others about, but dislike their own company. This needs to be addressed if they are to really enjoy life. If this is your birth date, begin to test yourself: try going on an outing, all on your own. It may feel awkward at first, but it will help you to see that 'alone time' can be rewarding.

AFFIRMATION: Venus likes company, but is strong enough to survive without it.

PLANETS: Venus and Mercury

KEYWORDS: Adaptable, busy, complex

3 JUNE

People born on 3 June are natural communicators, and are never short of the right word or phrase to use. They don't hesitate to get into a debate, and once drawn into an argument, they will not back down. When excited or riled they can be extremely blunt, and this can ruffle a few feathers, but they are also charming and seductive. If you were born on this day, the opposite sex love you, as you love them, but don't expect to be able to talk your way out of any difficult situation. You can't take back harsh words said in anger, you can only regret them at leisure. Try to think carefully before saying something you might regret.

AFFIRMATION: Mercury uses reason, not rage.

PLANETS: Mercury and Mercury

KEYWORDS: Persuasive, articulate, seductive

4 JUNE

Never happier than when they are learning, 4 June people are natural students and will go on improving themselves throughout life. They are quietly ambitious and will often gravitate to the upper levels of a career path. However, given the choice between becoming the boss, or remaining in the position of empowered underling, they tend to go with the latter, because they feel more secure in this role. If this is your birth date, try to use your natural communicative skills for good causes. If you're going to speak directly and risk making enemies in the process, it may as well be for a good reason.

AFFIRMATION: The Moon gives me insight and the will to speak for the greater good.

PLANETS: Moon and Mercury

KEYWORDS: Flexible, intelligent, direct

5 JUNE

Those born on this day are playful, lively and imaginative. They like a good yarn and tend to prefer fiction to fact. Their stories enthral and delight everyone who hears them, but they aren't necessarily heavy on the truth. However, those born on 5 June do have a keen sense of integrity – their stories are for entertainment only, and everyone around them knows it. If this is your birth date, have patience with people who seem not to understand you; they just need a little more time to get to know your playful ways. Why don't you jot down some of those tall tales in a diary, so that future generations can enjoy them too?

AFFIRMATION: The Sun's strength lies in tolerance.

PLANETS: Sun and Mercury

KEYWORDS: Creative, communicative, dignified

6 JUNE

Those born on this day are driven by a personal vision so central to their lives that it is almost all-encompassing. Their relationships, career, even their families go on the back burner when something they think is more important comes along. Natives of 6 June natives can try to balance their obsession and moderate their behaviour, but it is integral to who they are. They will always go to the ends of the earth in pursuit of their desires. If you were born on this day, you may need to take a step back and rebalance. Performing a kind gesture for a loved one takes you out of yourself, if only for a short time.

AFFIRMATION: Mercury is interested in exchange, not isolation.

PLANETS: Mercury and Mercury

KEYWORDS: Driven, visionary, vital

7 JUNE

Those born on this day have a well-developed imagination and are happy to while away whole hours daydreaming. They are not the most practical people in the zodiac – they're always locking themselves out, or turning up late for appointments, but what they lack in organizational skills they more than make up for with oodles of charm. So they are usually forgiven. Like a lot of Geminis, 7 June natives have their fingers on the pulse, so people often look to them for style advice. If you were born on this day, invest in a system that will help you organize yourself a bit better and you'll be able to raise your game significantly.

AFFIRMATION: Venus is my good luck charm.

PLANETS: Venus and Mercury

KEYWORDS: Endearing, trendy, creative

8 JUNE

Natives of 8 June are usually at the top of the class at school and often go on to achieve highly in the world of work. Their balanced approach to crisis makes them great leaders, especially in a domestic setting. When a family meal is turning into a disaster, you can rely on an 8 June person to cool everyone down and look at things rationally. Those born on this day need periods of quiet to recharge their batteries. If this is you, make yourself a space at home where you can do this; put a 'do not disturb' sign on the door and read a newspaper, or brainstorm ideas. A few minutes to yourself will do you a lot of good.

AFFIRMATION: Pluto chooses solitude, but Mercury needs love and friendship.

PLANETS: Pluto and Mercury

KEYWORDS: Resilient, strong, clever

9 JUNE

People born on this day tend to be forthright and robust in one area of their lives, and strangely passive in another. They may be the boss at work, but a big softie at home, or vice versa, so you never quite know where you stand with them. For this reason they can be unpredictable, and even frustrating. On the other hand, 9 June people have agile minds and are very capable and logical. They balance this with a childlike attitude to relationships, which can be perceived as playful or irritating, depending on the partner. If this is your birth date, you may need to spend a little more time thinking things over rather than jumping in with both feet. A quiet walk alone will help you gain perspective.

AFFIRMATION: With Jupiter comes optimism, so use this to your advantage.

PLANETS: Jupiter and Mercury

KEYWORDS: Impulsive, endearing, adaptable

10 JUNE

Life is a roller coaster for 10 June people, and they may occasionally feel exhausted by its twists and turns. But it is at those times – when the constant ups and downs are driving them mad – that they come into their own, because 10 June people have it within them to be immensely brave and resilient. Some of those born on this day have a very deep understanding of the forces at work in the universe and this gives them an air of mystery and magic that others respond to. If this is you, don't allow yourself to become embroiled in other people's dramas – you have quite enough on your plate, with your own.

AFFIRMATION: Saturn is strong and can overcome anything.

PLANETS: Saturn and Mercury

KEYWORDS: Courageous, complex, alluring

11 JUNE

Like their 10 June neighbours, 11 June people are courageous. They are the kinds of people who will give 100 per cent to whatever they do, plus a little bit more given the chance. They are great problem solvers, and are excellent people to have on a committee or an events team, because they have a knack for logistics. If this is your birth date, you don't share the same contradictory nature of many other Geminis and this definitely stands in your favour. You are able to focus, so make the most of it and devote yourself to an area of study or a profession that really inspires you.

AFFIRMATION: Uranus, the planet of invention and innovation, gives me the focus I need.

PLANETS: Uranus and Mercury

KEYWORDS: Brave, tenacious, organized

12 JUNE

People born on 12 June are natural optimists, preferring to see the good in people and situations wherever possible. However, this positive outlook takes a lot of energy and, underneath, there's a melancholy side that must be acknowledged. Those born on this day are sensitive to the emotions of others, sometimes too sensitive. They can become brooding and sad if they don't set firm boundaries between them and the people they care about. If this is your birth date, your rich imagination and creative talent should be developed. Buy yourself a sketchbook and get drawing, as participating in the visual arts can release those inner demons and leave you feeling refreshed.

AFFIRMATION: Neptune is insightful and sensitive, Mercury helps me express my feelings.

PLANETS: Neptune and Mercury

KEYWORDS: Creative, caring, emotional

13 JUNE

Has your social schedule ever distracted you from what really matters? Do you have a powerful imagination but often wonder why reality doesn't quite match up to the fantasy? Have you ever told your family and friends that you are simply too busy to find someone special and settle down? Then you may well be a 13 June person; constantly seeking the next big thing without ever looking at the bigger picture. If this is your birth date, take some time to reflect. If you want something, go out there and don't stop until you get it – that includes the love of your life. You need someone to act as a sounding board and help you gain perspective; choose someone you trust and ask them to listen while you figure things out aloud.

AFFIRMATION: Mercury, the planet of reason, gives me the gift of clarity.

PLANETS: Moon and Mercury

KEYWORDS: Active, ambitious, insightful

14 JUNE

People born on 14 June are tough cookies and formidable opponents. It's wise not to rile them unless you are geared up for a fight, but make friends with them, and they'll be fighting your corner forever. Intensely loyal, determined and direct, those born on this day make great employees, as long as you don't mind the odd bit of egotistical behaviour. They are well suited to any profession where the ability to argue is a prerequisite. They keep a cool head in the most stressful of circumstances, which can make them even more frustrating to argue with. If this is your birth date, physical exercise will help you to manage that aggression.

AFFIRMATION: The Sun can be fearsome but loving at the same time.

PLANETS: Sun and Mercury

KEYWORDS: Resilient, calm, rational

15 JUNE

Those born on this day have clever and active minds. They are natural students and will go on learning in one form or another throughout their lives, but this serious side is balanced out by a highly developed sense of humour and fun. When it comes to romance, 15 June people like the thrill of the chase, and their form of seduction is overt rather than subtle. Their charm is the most effective weapon in their arsenal, because they need the company and appreciation of others in order to feel content. Natives of 15 June often rank money high on their list of priorities. If this is your birth date, you know that money is nice, but try to remember that it's not everything.

AFFIRMATION: The strength of Mercury means I communicate well in all situations.

PLANETS: Mercury and Mercury

KEYWORDS: Intelligent, amusing, likeable

16 JUNE

It has been said that those born on this day are 'true capitalists', since they are often able to turn misfortune to their advantage. They get the most out of all situations, and that is a rare and valuable trait. If a 16 June person invests his, or her, money in a particular bank, you may be wise to follow suit, but their uncanny abilities extend beyond finance to all areas of life, including friendships, social life, relationships and jobs. They are natural gardeners, as they instinctively know how to make things grow and prosper. If you were born on this day, you feel most alive when taking calculated risks, but have you thought about ways in which you might use your skills for the benefit of others?

AFFIRMATION: Venus, the planet of love and luck, brings positive energy into my life.

PLANETS: Venus and Mercury

KEYWORDS: Clever, nurturing, generous

17 JUNE

People born on this day are naturally skilled strategists, with good heads for business. They are very competitive and tend to thrive in relationships based on mutual respect and admiration. Their partners must be equal to, or better than them, at most things, as they find verbal sparring sexy and will not be attracted to weak or flimsy personalities. Natives of 17 June are inspiring individuals, who take themselves seriously – perhaps too seriously. If this is your birth date, you could do with lightening up a bit. A evening out at a comedy club may encourage you to relax and have a giggle. Who knows, you may even learn to laugh at yourself too.

AFFIRMATION: The regenerative power of Pluto allows me to change and grow.

PLANETS: Pluto and Mercury

KEYWORDS: Bright, sporty, witty

18 JUNE

Those born on this day have powerful personalities, and can often enforce their will on the world without actually doing very much at all, such is their psychic strength. They tend to shun the limelight, preferring to work in the shadows, pulling strings from the sidelines to get what they want. This might sound sinister, and it is true that 18 June natives can be given to manipulative tendencies, but on the whole, they work for the common good. If this is your birthday, you are a natural optimist, with the ability to overcome even the biggest obstacle with sheer perseverance and good spirit. Hence, people find you endearing and likeable.

AFFIRMATION: Jupiter, the traveller, keeps me young in heart and soul so I can leap life's hurdles.

PLANETS: Jupiter and Mercury

KEYWORDS: Strong, reserved, psychic

19 JUNE

Natives of 19 June can make great personal trainers, because they act as catalysts in all sorts of situations. If a friend needs support after a nasty break-up, or a colleague needs motivating, call a 19 June person and they'll be raring to go within minutes. Because of this ability to provoke intense reactions in others, those born on this day are an acquired taste. In other words, people either like them or loathe them. If this is your birth date, you don't mind this reaction. You like to be direct and uncomplicated and you like your relationships to be that way too. Try to find people who live life as fully as you do, and you will avoid feeling frustrated.

AFFIRMATION: Saturn, the planet of ambition, drives me forward and Mercury helps me guide others.

PLANETS: Saturn and Mercury

KEYWORDS: Active, positive, definite

20 JUNE

Those born on this day tend to attract excitement and adventure and this makes them great people to socialize with; wherever they go, so does the party. People born on 20 June have a profound effect on those around them; they can inspire them to greatness or set them on completely the wrong track. They are the sorts of people your mother warned you about, but it isn't deliberate. Natives of 20 June are commonly unaware of the trail that is left in their wake. If this is your birth date, you need to be aware of the effect you can have on those around you and moderate your behaviour accordingly, but don't try to repress who you are, because it won't work.

AFFIRMATION: Venus brings people into my life; it is my job to nurture them.

PLANETS: Venus and Mercury

KEYWORDS: Energetic, pioneering, influential

21 JUNE

People born on 21 June always want more of whatever there is to go round, be that adventure, success, love, food or money. They can't get enough of life and make sure they live every minute to the full. They are jolly and amiable people, whose unquenchable curiosity can lead them straight to the top, or down a rocky or even dangerous road, depending on their ability to reason. Those born on this day are drawn to social causes, and it is a good idea for them to throw their passion and energy into this line of work. If this is your birth date, you may need to learn to back off every now and again. If you can work out how to tone down that intensity at will, you will be all the more successful.

AFFIRMATION: The Moon remains a certain distance from the Earth, and is all the more beautiful for it.

PLANETS: Moon and Mercury

KEYWORDS: Strong, passionate, enthusiastic

Cancer
22 June–22 July

22 JUNE

Those born on this day are naturally perceptive and can easily tune in to the feelings of others. They are born romantics who will chase that 'butterflies in the stomach' feeling for as long as they live. They need excitement, but also make excellent homemakers. Problems can arise when their domestic responsibilities drastically outweigh the amount of time they have to devote to adventure. When this happens, 22 June natives will isolate themselves in a fantasy world rather than deal with the mundane nature of real life. If you were born on this day, don't let that happen; put aside an hour or two a week to do something that replicates that excited feeling in a safe environment.

AFFIRMATION: The Moon's influence gives me insight and receptivity.

PLANETS: Moon and Moon

KEYWORDS: Emotional, insightful, intrepid

23 JUNE

Do you enjoy using social networking sites to chat with friends or dish the dirt? When you're in love, do you shout it from the rooftops? Then you could well be a 23 June person. Relationships are of the upmost importance to those born on this day – both their own and those of other people. They like nothing better than involving themselves in other people's lives and this can lead others to accuse them of being nosey, but that is not the case. People born on this day just love the idea of love and everything concerned with it, including art, music and literature. If you you are a 23 June native you are a great listener and therefore make a great friend – if you can resist the temptation to pass on things you have been told in confidence.

AFFIRMATION: The Sun rules the heart – he gives out warmth, never scorn.

PLANETS: Sun and Moon

KEYWORDS: Romantic, caring, fun-loving

24 JUNE

Home is extremely important to all Cancerians, and 24 June people are no different, although they are more likely than most to use their home as a place from which to engage in the thing they hold most dear, their vocation. If this is your birth date, you are 100 per cent committed to one thing, be it a job, a hobby, a cause or an art form, and this will always come first on your list of priorities. You are kind and loving towards your families and partners, but you can find their presence frustrating because you need peace and quiet in order to achieve what you feel you were put on the earth to do. Ethics are important to 24 June people, so managing a fair trade, eco-business would suit you perfectly.

AFFIRMATION: The Moon nurtures and cultivates.

PLANETS: Mercury and Moon

KEYWORDS: Motivated, diligent, caring

25 JUNE

If this is your birth date, you were born to nurture everything and everyone around you. You take real delight in the enjoyment of others and consequently make a great host. When you throw a party or event people will still be talking about it for weeks afterwards. People born on 25 June are the vessels of the zodiac; they draw influences from all around them and these can have a strong positive, or negative, effect on their personalities. If this is you, be wary of who you get close to, and if you feel someone is consistently draining your energy every time you meet, delicately sever ties with them.

AFFIRMATION: The Moon gives me the power of insight and, ultimately, good judgement.

PLANETS: Venus and Moon

KEYWORDS: Receptive, mothering, entertaining

26 JUNE

Natives of 26 June provide strong foundations on which to build
a family or friendship group. They can be physically, as well as
emotionally, stable and can withstand a great deal. Interestingly, they
are also sensitive souls, who see their homes as a sanctuary from
a harsh and brutal world. For this reason they sometimes develop
expensive tastes and fill their spaces full of objects they can't really
afford. They make great parents, but can be overprotective at times.
If you were born on this day, learn to have confidence in others. The
best tool a parent can give their children is the ability to take care of
themselves, so release some of that worry and let them get on with it.

AFFIRMATION: The Sun rules the heart; he gives out warmth, never
scorn.

PLANETS: Pluto and Moon

KEYWORDS: Resilient, emotional, caring

27 JUNE

People born on 27 June will check that every door and window in the
house is locked, and double locked, before they venture outside. This
is because their home is particularly important to them; they see it as
a safe base from which to explore the world, and without its security
they feel lost. Similarly, 27 June people value their moral convictions
and like to feel that everything they do is 100 per cent right. Their
principles underpin everything they do. If this is your birth date, try to
remember that not everyone shares your black-and-white view of right
and wrong, and open yourself up to others' points of view. Jupiter's
influence brings good fortune, but in order to benefit you have to
follow its lead every now and again.

AFFIRMATION: Jupiter encourages me to trust in the universe.

PLANETS: Jupiter and Moon

KEYWORDS: Protective, sensitive, virtuous

28 JUNE

Those born on this day tend to take a lead role in most situations. They
make natural leaders because they are solid and dependable characters

who, once set on a course of action, will soldier on no matter what. Like their neighbours from 27 June, they can be very good parents but they tend to be too authoritative at times. On the other hand, they also have a well-developed sensitive and romantic side. They need a partner who can stand up to, as well as stand beside, them. If this is your birth date, be mindful of the way you talk to others – make sure you give them the respect they deserve, just as they respect you.

AFFIRMATION: Saturn puts me in control, but the Moon allows me to show my vulnerable side.

PLANETS: Saturn and Moon

KEYWORDS: Strong, pioneering, determined

29 JUNE

People born on this day are often daydreamers, but this doesn't mean they never get anything done. In fact, those born on this day are very capable of finding practical ways to use this innate imaginative ability, and often come up with the money to fund their hare-brained schemes. They are shrewd businesspeople but will not exploit their co-workers or employees because they believe that everyone is created equal. Those born on 29 June make great bosses. If this is your birth date, you tend to be too over-protective, and can appear clingy. When this happens, take a step back and re-assess the situation. Go for a walk to clear your head.

AFFIRMATION: Intuitive Uranus brings success.

PLANETS: Uranus and Moon

KEYWORDS: Imaginative, resourceful, savvy

30 JUNE

People born on this day are technically skilled and highly motivated individuals who are prone to stubbornness and can be frustrating to live with. You will not make a 30 June native do anything he, or she, doesn't wish to. They make wonderful family members, parents and partners because they love to nurture. They care deeply about their homes and the area in which they were brought up, but can be too nostalgic and yearn for the past when they should be living in the present. If you were born on this day, learn to enjoy what you have, rather than what you could have had, and stop investing so much money and energy in technology; you don't really need it. Treat the people you love instead.

AFFIRMATION: Mercury, the planet of communication, encourages me to give.

PLANETS: Mercury and Moon

KEYWORDS: Loving, loyal, intelligent

1 JULY

People born on this day have a well-developed feminine side; even men born on 1 July have mothering instincts and sometimes take on traditionally female roles both at home and at work. They get a great sense of satisfaction from making life comfortable and enjoyable for others, even if their efforts go unnoticed. They are spontaneous and fun-loving, adaptable and open to new ideas, all of which makes them pleasurable to be around and valued by colleagues and loved-ones alike. If this is you, don't ignore your ability to see beyond the surface to the heart of the matter: being insightful is not the same as being melancholy.

AFFIRMATION: Passionate Mars and insightful Moon give me the power to see beyond the obvious.

PLANETS: Mars and Moon

KEYWORDS: Nurturing, impulsive, sensitive

2 JULY

People born on this day are naturally receptive to the feelings of others, and this can have both positive and negative effects on their lives. On the one hand, people are drawn to their open personalities; they make friends very easily and are usually seen as bright and breezy by their peers. On the other hand, 2 July people can be over-critical of themselves and have difficulty separating their own views from those of other people. If this is your birth date, remember that the universe has granted you power over your emotions. You have the ability to rise above these self-confidence issues and succeed in whatever you put your mind to. A short assertiveness course may help you to develop the skills you need.

AFFIRMATION: I invite Venus, the planet of love, to stop me making an enemy of myself.

PLANETS: Mercury and Moon

KEYWORDS: Insightful, open, empathetic

3 JULY

Typically a well-rounded individual, a 3 July person values balance and will strive to achieve it. They are very adaptable people and roll with life's punches with effortless finesse. Like all Cancerians, they are perceptive and sensitive types, but they are also able to survey situations from a distance. Consequently they often have an air of 'higher authority' about them. People tend to listen to whatever 3 July people have to say, and will act on their advice without fuss. If you were born on this day, try to embrace the lighter things in life a little more and don't be afraid to get 'stuck in', especially when there is fun to be had.

AFFIRMATION: Mercury encourages me to get out there and get involved.

PLANETS: Mercury and Moon

KEYWORDS: Authoritative, stable, direct

4 JULY

People born on 4 July are proud of their roots. They never forget (and neither will they let anyone else forget) how far they have come along life's path. This gives them a clear sense of perspective, but also makes it hard for them to see things from other people's point of view, so they can come across as a little narrow-minded. Natives of 4 July are at their most comfortable when representing a group of people with the same background as them; they are fiercely loyal and make great union representatives, councillors and keen sports fans, but need to steer clear of fanaticism in all its forms. If this is your birth date, remember that it is our differences that make us unique and beautiful, you included.

AFFIRMATION: The Moon sheds light on life's rich tapestry.

PLANETS: Moon and Moon

KEYWORDS: Patriotic, dignified, generous

5 JULY

Life with a 5 July person is anything but boring. Like a butterfly, they enjoy flitting from one project to another, and are always on the move. However, when in love, they are generous and devoted, as long as the object of their affections is willing to drop everything to come along for the ride. They don't enjoy being pinned down, or having responsibility heaped upon them – so don't ask them to water your plants while you are on holiday! If you are a 5 July native, you may need to develop your staying power: try setting yourself small and achievable goals. The satisfaction you get from reaching them will help to spur you on.

AFFIRMATION: The Sun rises and sets each day, but no one accuses him of being 'predictable'.

PLANETS: Sun and Moon

KEYWORDS: Spontaneous, interesting, loving

6 JULY

Do you sometimes feel as if an outside force is controlling your movements, so that events in your life seem beyond your control? Has anyone ever told you they are attracted to you without knowing why? Do you consider yourself particularly fortunate, or tuned in to patterns that others don't notice? If you answered yes to all of these questions, then you are a typical 6 July person, and your inner magnetism is already apparent to you. If not, then the chances are it has yet to reveal itself, but it is there. People born on 6 July have a lucky streak, and others sense this and want to be around you. On the other hand, you tend to attract waifs and strays, so you need to set strong boundaries.

AFFIRMATION: Mercury enables me to take control of my inner magnetism and turn it to my advantage.

PLANETS: Mercury and Moon

KEYWORDS: Strong, intense, attractive

7 JULY

The 7 July native likes to uncover the truth in things and cannot abide pretence in any form. Like a good detective, they can usually trust their hunches and so if a 7 July person tells you they don't trust someone, but can't put their finger on exactly why, it may be a good idea to follow their lead; the reason will show itself in good time. Those born on this day will devote their time to making sure the workings of their business or family life are as transparent as possible. It goes without saying that you should not try to keep secrets from them, because they will find you out, and when they do, they'll lose respect for you. If this is your birth date, try to be more sensitive to people's wishes. Some things are private and just don't need to be shared.

AFFIRMATION: Venus gives me compassion for others.

PLANETS: Venus and Moon

KEYWORDS: Inquisitive, intelligent, honest

8 JULY

Those born on this day have to see it in order to believe it. They don't have a lot of time for theories or ideas, preferring tangible products. So if you want them to invest in your business, show them the actual figures, not a pie-in-the-sky business plan. Natives of 8 July are powerful pragmatists and usually rise to the top of their chosen profession through sheer determination and hard work. Their partners and children may have to put up with not seeing them much during the working week, but when they are at home they give family life 100 per cent. If this is your birth date, try to let go a bit: play a silly game with your children or go out with friends.

AFFIRMATION: Pluto can help me reinvent myself with play.

PLANETS: Pluto and Moon

KEYWORDS: Practical, grounded, generous

9 JULY

People born today are natural engineers. They are fascinated by the unseen forces of nature and their lively, analytical brains are always asking questions of the universe. Their ability to look at life from a new perspective makes them great people to have around and, though their efforts to push back boundaries often go unnoticed or unappreciated, the people that matter will eventually recognize their talents. If you are a 9 July native try to make time to keep a diary. Write in it regularly and date your entries; future generations may well be interested to follow your lines of inquiry. However don't let these interests consume all your energy – save something for those who care about you.

AFFIRMATION: Jupiter, the gypsy, takes me on a journey into uncharted territory.

PLANETS: Jupiter and Moon

KEYWORDS: Intelligent, questioning, brilliant

10 JULY

Those people born on 10 July have a keen sense of duty. They are law-abiding, loyal and will always go out of their way to help a friend. Natives of 10 July are often quiet and modest individuals, who live most of their lives in a backstage role, but will suddenly emerge and do something reckless or passionate when they arrive at one of life's 'flashpoints' such as adolescence or middle age. They hate to cause a fuss or hurt others' feelings and will sometimes go too far to avoid doing so. This invariably leads to trouble. If this is your birth date, be aware of this and try to say what you think when necessary. An assertiveness course will help you to find the middle ground.

AFFIRMATION: Saturn will find the courage to overcome shyness.

PLANETS: Saturn and Moon

KEYWORDS: Faithful, dignified, sensitive

11 JULY

People born on 11 July are highly social beings, who know exactly how to get what they want from any situation. They are master manipulators: every piece of information they have at their disposal is imparted on a need-to-know basis. On the other hand, these people will have a close circle of friends with whom they usually communicate openly and honestly – up to a point. Natives of 11 July may not, on the surface, seem like team players, but they do best when acting as part of a group. If this is your birth date, try dropping the 'smoke and mirrors act' and just show people the real you – you will reap the rewards if you do.

AFFIRMATION: Uranus joins the personal to the collective consciousness.

PLANETS: Uranus and Moon

KEYWORDS: Intelligent, subtle, communicative

12 JULY

Those born on this day are creative and imaginative with sensitive souls, but they are also strong characters with a keen sense of logic and a shrewd business mind. Natives of 12 July don't like to answer to anyone, especially not those they distrust or dislike, and so they will often chose self-employment over working for a large organization. They are motivated chiefly by what they see as the 'common good', but what that constitutes is subjective. If this is your birth date, you are very influential and capable of making difficult decisions, but you can be a little over-bearing at times. Learning to step back occasionally will ultimately increase your influence, not lessen it.

AFFIRMATION: Neptune, the planet of psychic power, can help me exert my influence in a more subtle way.

PLANETS: Neptune and Moon

KEYWORDS: Independent, strong, dominant

13 JULY

Opportunities abound for 13 July people, and many know exactly how to make the most of them. They seem to have a natural sense of timing – they will move house at just the right time to make the most of the market, or change jobs just before a swathe of lay-offs. People regard them as lucky and will often follow their lead, but 13 July natives rely on a feeling of self-confidence to carry them forward. If they have a knockback, it can take them a while to get back into their stride. If this is your birth date, do whatever it takes to maintain that good mood. Affirmations and visualization are both great tools for success and, what's more, they're both free.

AFFIRMATION: The Moon's power gives me all the strength and insight I need to make good choices.

PLANETS: Moon and Moon

KEYWORDS: Fortunate, wise, self-assured

14 JULY

People born on this day have an air of credibility that stays with them throughout their lives, and the power this gives them cannot be underestimated. As the father figure in the zodiac, it is the Sun's influence that lends them authority, although they may not be aware of it, because these gifts are not used consciously. Those born on 14 July often find themselves in positions of command, but there is a downside to this special treatment. All this responsibility can weigh heavily on their shoulders, especially early in life, when they need to be allowed to make the same mistakes as everyone else. If this is your birth date, make sure you forgive yourself the odd slip-up – you are still human after all.

AFFIRMATION: The Sun is the master of the heavens, but he isn't responsible for anyone but himself.

PLANETS: Sun and Moon

KEYWORDS: Trustworthy, charming, welcoming

15 JULY

Like a sculptor with his clay, 15 July people have a strong link with the material world and possess the power to mould and manipulate it to suit them. They are often good with their hands and gravitate towards hobbies that enable them to use this innate talent, but their abilities go beyond mere things; they are also great at getting the best out of people too. Natives of 15 July work very well in managerial or training roles, as they'll happily muck in when a crisis arises and it's 'all hands on deck'. If this is your birthday, resist the impulse to hoard useless objects. Make sure you have a garage sale or take unwanted things to a charity shop when the clutter begins to get on top of you.

AFFIRMATION: The power of Mercury helps me to communicate my vision.

PLANETS: Mercury and Moon

KEYWORDS: Skilled, wise, generous

16 JULY

Those born on this day have the strong influence of Venus in their charts, and so are preoccupied with adventure and matters of the heart. They tend to fall in love often and with passion, but these obsessions can be short-lived. They are idealists, who prioritize drama and romance over everyday life, so they can quickly become frustrated when the reality doesn't live up to the fantasy. If this is your birth date, you must either stop making promises you can't keep, or find a partner who has enough staying power to make up for your lack of it. When you meet someone new ask yourself this question: am I actually in love with this person, or am I in love with the idea of them?

AFFIRMATION: Venus creates harmony, not crisis.

PLANETS: Venus and Moon

KEYWORDS: Fun-loving, venturesome, attractive

17 JULY

It is the influence of Pluto in their charts that makes 17 July people strangely compelling. They are private people who like their own space and will protect it fiercely. This is because they are extremely receptive to the feelings of others; negative energy rubs off on them easily and so they retreat to the sanctuary of their own homes, where they feel emotionally in control. Those born on this day may be private, but they aren't risk-averse or retiring types. They love adventure and can be outgoing, but it has to be on their terms. If this is your birth date, learn to use your magnetism to attract the right people to you. Meditation can help in this task.

AFFIRMATION: The regenerative power of Pluto encourages me to rise above my insecurities.

PLANETS: Venus and Moon

KEYWORDS: Intriguing, protective, sensitive

18 JULY

Those born on this day have two clear sides to their personalities. The side they present to the public is generous, carefree and outgoing, and others respond well to that – people may even have them down as one of life's jokers. Their private side, however, is more complicated. They can suffer acutely from insecurities and take rejection very hard indeed. Their self-confidence is supported by their work, and if they don't have a fulfilling vocation they can wilt and fail like plants without sufficient water. If this is your birth date, you need to find a job that can give you the satisfaction you seek. A session with a life coach may help to point you in the right direction.

AFFIRMATION: Jupiter can help me find balance and self-understanding.

PLANETS: Jupiter and Moon

KEYWORDS: Changeable, motivated, affectionate

19 JULY

If you were born on this day you value grace and form, and are highly physically aware. You are happiest when exercising and anything that involves sculpting the body, such as dance, yoga or pilates, is great for you. People born on 19 July cannot bear to be hurried, especially when it comes to romance, so your partners need to know when to back off and give you space. You may not always be ready on time to leave for a party or dinner, but when you are ready you'll give 100 per cent and do so while looking fabulous. Saturn's influence suggests that these people believe in Karma and like to live by its rules.

AFFIRMATION: Saturn understands that the laws of nature apply to every living being.

PLANETS: Saturn and Moon

KEYWORDS: Elegant, soulful, peaceful

20 JULY

Life with a 20 July native is always interesting but can get bit hectic, to say the least. They don't tend to inhabit the middle ground, swinging instead from one extreme to the other, depending on their ever-changing mood. This can be exhausting for people who aren't used to going from 'high as a kite' to 'down in the doldrums' in the space of a second or two. If this is your birth date, you love to surround yourself with beautiful things, and like nothing better than spending your free time shopping for life's little luxuries. Use shopping trips as a chance to get away from it all. Take your time: have a coffee, relax and chat. An afternoon out will help you to regain a sense of composure and balance your emotions.

AFFIRMATION: Venus craves beauty, but true beauty can only exist in harmonious surroundings.

PLANETS: Venus and Moon

KEYWORDS: Tasteful, adaptable, sensitive

21 JULY

If you were born on this day, people tend to come to you with their problems. You have a natural sense for the feelings of others and are able to empathize with them. This makes you an extremely valuable person to have as a friend; everyone loves to spend time with someone who genuinely wants to know about them, rather than listening for a gap in the conversation to fill with their own troubles. Fulfilling this role in people's lives can be exhausting though. When you feel irritable and stressed, write a letter addressed to Mercury, the planet of communication. Pour out your feelings and afterwards, burn it. Releasing that negative energy will help you to recover.

AFFIRMATION: Mercury can help me communicate more effectively.

PLANETS: Mercury and Moon

KEYWORDS: Understanding, flexible, kind

22 JULY

People born on 22 July are determined to succeed and can overcome any obstacle. They are brave, direct and competitive people who simply refuse to play second fiddle to anyone, especially people they can't respect. They are creatively talented because they have a well-developed sensitive side that, although it may not show itself in their professional lives, dominates the inner workings of their souls. The Moon's influence is responsible for this side of their character, but as their birth date falls on the cusp between Cancer and Leo, they may not like others to acknowledge this side of them publicly. If this is your birth date, don't be afraid to embrace the softer side of your nature.

AFFIRMATION: The Moon's power is strong and vulnerable at the same time.

PLANETS: Moon and Moon

KEYWORDS: Resilient, courageous, artistic

Leo
23 July–23 August

23 JULY

Leos are usually confident people, but 23 July natives tend to struggle with insecurities. Whether they choose to go on suffering, or rise above such problems, is up to the individual. If they are determined, they will get over their confidence issues and fulfil their potential, but if they allow their doubts to cast a shadow over their lives, they will never be able to claim their place in the limelight. Those born on this day are conservative at heart and have a keen interest in history, as well as highly developed investigative skills. If this is your birth date, researching your family tree will indulge these interests and may give you a confidence boost if an ancestor has achieved something great.

AFFIRMATION: The Sun radiates confidence, and so must I.

PLANETS: Sun and Sun

KEYWORDS: Intelligent, respectful, courageous

24 JULY

Those born on this day appear perfectly serene and confident, but underneath the surface is a bubbling cauldron of self-doubt and criticism. Others see them as articulate, dedicated and inspiring, but they are so busy over-analyzing and questioning every decision that sometimes they appear to change direction without warning, throwing everyone else off course. If this is your birth date you have a choice: either you can go on blaming these idiosyncrasies on your 'artistic temperament', or you can learn to shut out that destructive voice that tells you you've messed up, when actually you're doing just fine. The latter is the preferable option for you, and everyone who cares for you.

AFFIRMATION: Mercury tells me to expel those negative voices, and so release them to the universe.

PLANETS: Mercury and Sun

KEYWORDS: Creative, exciting, warm

25 JULY

Natives of 25 July are born triers, and although they may not always achieve success in their endeavours, they always continue to be idealistic. They never let what might generously be called a 'mixed result' put them off trying again. Romantic to a fault, 25 July people may not be the most practical, but they are great fun to be around and can lift anyone out of a bad mood. Unless, of course, that person is in a bad mood because the 25 July person's unfettered idealism has caused something to go wrong. If you were born on this day, you have immaculate taste and a vibrant outlook on life, but you might need to develop a more sensible side to balance things out a bit.

AFFIRMATION: Venus and the Sun combined, help to protect my idealism.

PLANETS: Venus and Sun

KEYWORDS: Positive, determined, loving

26 JULY

People born on 26 July are highly influential individuals who carry a lot of weight, either within a familial group or in a business situation. They are ambitious and competitive people, who will work extremely hard to rise to the top of their field, but in doing so they are sometimes accused of being ruthless and narrow in their outlook. In their personal lives, 26 July people are very loving. They fall in love easily and deeply, but rarely give themselves completely to a partner. This can lead to feelings of distrust and, ultimately, to separation. If this is your birth date, try to let your partner see your vulnerabilities a little more often.

AFFIRMATION: Pluto's influence means I can start again, and let people see the real me.

PLANETS: Pluto and Sun

KEYWORDS: Tenacious, strong, romantic

27 JULY

Those born on this day have a real wanderlust, and they are able to indulge it because their warm personalities and natural organizational skills mean they are welcomed wherever they go. People flock to 27 July natives because they radiate positivity and self-belief, and it is for this reason that they often find themselves responsible for making decisions on others' behalf. If this is your birth date, you should learn to hand this responsibility back where appropriate. It is not fair for others to expect you to make their choices for them, especially if they eventually blame you when things don't go to plan. Find a way to express this viewpoint, and you'll be free to live your own life unimpeded.

AFFIRMATION: Jupiter allows me to be free from the shackles of undue responsibility.

PLANETS: Jupiter and Sun

KEYWORDS: Adventurous, confident, authoritative

28 JULY

People born on 28 July respect traditional values and tend to feel nostalgic for the formality of the past. They feel most at home in highly structured environments, and so will often seek employment in an age-old institution like a long-running family law firm or publishing house. They like to get to know people well before they reveal their real selves, so will be in favour of long engagements before marriage. They may well live in the same road and stay in the same job for years, shying away from the transient existence so enjoyed by their neighbours from 27 July. If you were born on this day, you need to embrace new things as well as old, and do not neglect your computing skills in favour of dying technologies and methods.

AFFIRMATION: Saturn gives me the discipline and ambition I need to move on.

PLANETS: Saturn and Sun

KEYWORDS: Dignified, stable, kind

29 JULY

Do you often find your hunches about a person or a situation turn out to be correct? Do others look to you to tell them which side of the fence to jump? Have you ever been accused of prejudiced thinking? If you answered yes to these questions, then you sound like a typical 29 July person. Your loyalty knows no bounds, and no one would ever question your uncanny business instincts, but you do have blind spots when it comes to certain elements of society – particularly the group you, yourself, fall into. People don't always fit so squarely into the category you put them in; that's what makes humankind so interesting! Try having a conversation with someone who is as different to you as possible.

AFFIRMATION: Uranus, the planet of intuition, helps me to see clearly.

PLANETS: Uranus and Sun

KEYWORDS: Influential, patriotic, shrewd

30 JULY

Mercury's influence gives 30 July people the ability to speak from the heart, a skill that is often undervalued in this day and age, where soundbites often seem to count for more than honest communication. Natives of 30 July are solid and dependable people who don't have it in them to be anything other than what they are. Others respect them for this, even when they are being awkward and unyielding. If this is your birth date, you are an engaging and popular person with an interest in developing your physical abilities. Weightlifting or aerobics could be for you, but so could the more sedentary art of fiction writing. Keep your mind open to new opportunities, even if they seem a little daunting at first.

AFFIRMATION: The Sun enables me to meet challenges head on.

PLANETS: Mercury and Sun

KEYWORDS: Honest, genuine, attractive

31 JULY

People born on 31 July have real fondness for their fellow humans and will happily spend their whole lives studying others, whether from a university lecture hall, or a table in a busy café. They enjoy watching other people going about their day, and they love to sit and chat to strangers, collecting waifs and strays wherever they go. They are drawn towards inspirational or exceptional people, but enjoy the company of ordinary folk just as much. If you were born on this day, make sure people-watching doesn't mean you ignore your own life in favour of focusing on others. Get fully involved in things by revealing more about yourself.

AFFIRMATION: The Sun's light unveils the Moon and allows us to see her beauty.

PLANETS: Moon and Sun

KEYWORDS: Warm, caring, modest

1 AUGUST

If there is one word that perfectly describes a 1 August person, it is 'robust'. Their self-belief and strength of character is awe-inspiring, and their leadership qualities are among the most highly developed in the zodiac. They are extremely persuasive people and are very well suited to a high-pressure sales environment, but with the courage and strength of a lion comes a big heart. They can be very tender and will give themselves totally to a partner. If this is your birth date, people can mistake your self-confidence for arrogance. Make it clear to people that you don't take yourself too seriously by fooling about a bit more often. It will make you seem a little more approachable.

AFFIRMATION: Mars is strong and unyielding, but the Sun is warm and generous.

PLANETS: Mars and Sun

KEYWORDS: Vibrant, brave, popular

2 AUGUST

Venus's influence brings a love of beauty and heaps of charisma to 2 August natives. They are creative people, who like to put their own stamp on everything they do and who seek out stylish surroundings and glamorous partners wherever possible. If this is your birth date, you have been called unstoppable, because your energy and drive means you rarely let anything, or anyone, get in your way. You make a great interior designer, because you know what you like and have the tenacity required to get things done; but don't become a bulldozer, simply flattening every obstacle in your path without considering the consequences. Learn to listen to others more carefully and your life will be far more harmonious.

AFFIRMATION: Venus invites harmony into my life.

PLANETS: Venus and Sun

KEYWORDS: Artistic, determined, magnetic

3 AUGUST

If you were born on this day you have a positive and youthful outlook that people love. You are adventurous and enjoy trying anything new, from restaurants and holiday destinations to the latest technological gadgets. You are attracted to danger, and may choose to pursue a career that brings you into high-adrenalin situations. Failing that, you may enjoy skydiving, white-water rafting or any other extreme sport, especially those connected with fire. Walking on red-hot coals is the ideal charity event for a 3 August native; chances are you'll relish the challenge and enjoy raising money for a good cause.

AFFIRMATION: Mercury enables me to bring a message of positivity to others.

PLANETS: Mercury and Sun

KEYWORDS: Heroic, daring, fun-loving

4 AUGUST

Individuals born on 4 August have an air of authority about them that commands instant respect, but they also possess the rare skill to reach out to people of all kinds. They have real presence and the power to change things if they can shrug off undue criticism and concentrate on the job in hand. However, they can be easily distracted, and feel dejected when things don't go according to their master plan. If this is your birth date, learn to accept that you can't please all of the people all of the time, and focus on those that really matter. As time goes on you will learn to better handle that nagging rebellious streak, but don't deny it completely. A high-energy sport, like basketball, will help to ease some of that pressure.

AFFIRMATION: The Sun rises every day, no matter what. And so must I.

PLANETS: Moon and Sun

KEYWORDS: Proud, dignified, dependable

5 AUGUST

Those born on this day remain calm in any crisis, or at least they appear to. Underneath the surface, the picture is quite different. They may be bubbling over with feelings of anger, stress or resentment while wearing a mask of perfect serenity. Don't get angry with the 5 August native for hiding their true emotions – their success in life depends on it. Without the mask they feel vulnerable and exposed; their self-confidence falters and they are unable to achieve their goals. If this is your birth date, you need to find someone special with whom you can let down your guard. Failing that, write down your feelings in a letter and destroy it, preferably by burning. It will make you feel better instantaneously.

AFFIRMATION: The Sun's warmth permeates almost anything.

PLANETS: Sun and Sun

KEYWORDS: Generous, calm, warm

6 AUGUST

Do you fantasize about discovering some long-lost masterpiece in your attic, meeting your doppelganger, or seeing a ghost? People born on 6 August often do, because they are attracted to extraordinary and, even, impossible occurrences. So much so that they often send out psychic invitations, welcoming weird and wonderful influences into their lives without even knowing it. Consequently they are easily bored by anything mundane and commonplace, so if you are romantically involved with an August 6 person, you will need to work very hard to keep things interesting. If this is your birth date, you need to learn how to interact with real life, and accept all its boring bits.

AFFIRMATION: Mercury, the planet of reason, helps me accept the real world while keeping hold of my dreams.

PLANETS: Mercury and Sun

KEYWORDS: Creative, ethical, fun-loving

7 AUGUST

Those born on this day possess charm and grace, and cope well in all social situations. They are secretive types who are attracted to the idea of undercover missions and conduct their personal lives as if they were spies on a job. If you are romantically involved with a 7 August person, don't expect them to let you know where they are every minute of the day. It doesn't mean they're doing anything they shouldn't; they simply like to maintain an air of mystery. Think about making yourself slightly less available from time to time, they love the thrill of the chase.

If you were born on this day, you need to let your partner know you care – make a romantic gesture.

AFFIRMATION: Venus encourages me to welcome people in, not push them away.

PLANETS: Venus and Sun

KEYWORDS: Cool, intelligent, alluring

8 AUGUST

Those born on this day are multi-faceted and, a bit like their neighbours from 7 August, they like to play many different roles in life. They are attracted to danger, and need to keep the adrenalin pumping if they are to remain interested in a situation or a relationship. August 8 natives are challenge-oriented and welcome competition as it makes them feel alive. This means they are rarely settled or calm. They feel ill at ease with the idea of a 'quiet life' – 8 August people rarely retire until they are forced into it. If you were born on this day, it's good to remain flexible, as it allows you to roll with life's punches. Meditation can greatly benefit your well-being.

AFFIRMATION: Regenerative Pluto allows me to change and grow with time.

PLANETS: Pluto and Sun

KEYWORDS: Passionate, intriguing, active

9 AUGUST

The influence of Jupiter, the planet of adventure, means that 9 August natives like to get out and see the world. If this is your birthday you are always active, and tend to experience difficulties when the time comes to settle down. You struggle to believe that a conventional life can be a memorable one. You wish to leave a lasting legacy, and so shun anything that seems too ordinary, sometimes at the expense of your own lasting happiness. On the other hand, you are capable of making huge sacrifices for the greater good. You are a natural altruist, and easily combine your love of travel with the urge to help others. Natives of 9 August should always look to build a bit of voluntary work into their summer holiday, for extra satisfaction.

AFFIRMATION: I am happy to let Jupiter's spirit of adventure and the Sun's generosity shine for all to see.

PLANETS: Jupiter and Sun

KEYWORDS: Strong, intrepid, helpful

10 AUGUST

People born on 10 August are like really good books: stylish, lively, humorous and dependable without being overly predictable. They feel the need to be heard and so will often strike others as 'larger than life', but in fact, they know the value of privacy and will retreat into a world of their own once they have delivered their message. If this is your birth date, you make an excellent entertainer. Your company is often sought for this reason, but there is more to you than that, and you need people to recognize it. Try not to use self-deprecating humour or shrug off your real feelings quite so often; instead acknowledge your strengths and express the more serious side of your personality.

AFFIRMATION: Saturn challenges me to reveal the real me.

PLANETS: Saturn and Sun

KEYWORDS: Attractive, fun-loving, reliable

11 AUGUST

Those born on this day respect the truth above all else. Where something suspicious is going on, they'll stop at nothing to reveal it. For this reason they are often fascinated by the shadier side of life, and will seek out adventures that see them delving into it. If this is your birth date you would make a great law enforcer, as you're never scared to stand up for what you believe in. But, if your obsession with wrongdoing turns in on itself, you can come to represent the very thing you so detest. People born on 11 August tend to undergo a real journey during their lifetime, and can grow hugely as individuals given the right environment.

AFFIRMATION: Uranus, the planet of change, gives me the power to develop and grow.

PLANETS: Uranus and Sun

KEYWORDS: Original, honest, powerful

12 AUGUST

Natives of 12 August are highly respected in their chosen fields because they possess so much knowledge. They often concern themselves with keeping alive a dying tradition and make wonderful craftspeople and linguists, because they have an inbuilt love of history. Those born today know that knowledge is power and they will happily wield it over anyone they perceive as being less well-informed than them. For people who love studying the past, those born on this day live life at an incredible pace, rarely stopping to take stock. If this is your birth date, this may need to change. Set aside some reflection time each day.

AFFIRMATION: Neptune's psychic energy gives me the strength to pause and breathe.

PLANETS: Neptune and Sun

KEYWORDS: Clever, passionate, interesting

13 AUGUST

Those born on this day enjoy a challenge and are not satisfied when something appears to come to them too easily; they have to work and struggle in order to feel fulfilled. They greet every obstacle with a positive attitude and a generous portion of good cheer – a trait others find brilliant and baffling in equal measure. It therefore follows that 13 August people enjoy swimming against the tide; they naturally rebel against authority because they hate to simply fall into line with everyone else. If this is your birth date, you may need to manage your rebellious streak. A brisk walk in natural surroundings will help to calm you down and give you some thinking space.

AFFIRMATION: The Moon and the Sun find harmony in the heavens.

PLANETS: Moon and Sun

KEYWORDS: Dynamic, determined, friendly

14 AUGUST

The Sun's influence is strong on this day, and therefore 14 August people are usually warm, outgoing and magnanimous. They can often be found at the centre of a large circle of friends and family, or surrounded by work colleagues who look up to them. They tend to rise to positions of authority because they command immediate respect, but on the rare occasions that someone fails to give them the admiration they feel they're entitled to, they can be guilty of throwing the most outrageous temper tantrums. If 14 August is your birthday, allow others to bask in your warmth, whether or not they actually deserve it. Your capacity to rise above such petty squabbles proves your status in the universe.

AFFIRMATION: The Sun can't choose who he shines upon.

PLANETS: Sun and Sun

KEYWORDS: Friendly, authoritative, caring

15 AUGUST

Those born on this day have a regal air about them. They are natural leaders who will end up in a position of authority, whether or not they seek one out, because they radiate confidence. People born on 15 August are self-contained types who often choose to live alone, and appear somehow 'separate', even when they're surrounded by lots of people. This power to stand back from the crowd gives them great judgement, but they need to learn to muck in occasionally. On the other hand, 15 August natives are humorous and cheerful people and this balances out their inherent aloofness and renders them likeable, even loveable. They just need to remember to cooperate when it really counts.

AFFIRMATION: Mercury, the planet of communication, can help to build bridges.

PLANETS: Mercury and Sun

KEYWORDS: Independent, strong, funny

16 AUGUST

Natives of 16 August are power-hungry and will stop at almost nothing to achieve their goals. Their electric personalities mean they are capable of, and even delight in, shocking people, especially those of a nervous disposition. They don't take prisoners and have little or no patience with those they perceive as weak. They are highly sensual individuals, who see sexuality as an art form and regard themselves as master craftspeople. They have style and grace aplenty but may need to learn to moderate their behaviour in order to get on with people better. If you were born on this day, invest some energy in your spiritual self. A journey to a sacred place will help you reconnect.

AFFIRMATION: Venus, the planet of desire, can help me find harmony.

PLANETS: Venus and Sun

KEYWORDS: Courageous, dynamic, alluring

17 AUGUST

If you are a 17 August native, you have two clearly defined sides to your personality. Your public persona inspires awe. Your career is very important to you and you may well take up a position of power and responsibility. You are determined to succeed, and eventually you will. In private however, 17 August natives are quite different. An employee who bumps into his 17 August boss out of hours will be shocked to find a quiet, warm and relatively humble person in place of the fire-breathing dragon they're used to. You dislike mixing business and pleasure because it makes you feel exposed, but your colleagues would soon become your friends if they could see the generous and fun-loving nature you keep for weekends.

AFFIRMATION: The Sun gives me the determination to find balance.

PLANETS: Pluto and Sun

KEYWORDS: Tenacious, vital, versatile

18 AUGUST

Those born on this day value hard-earned success over instant gratification and this is just as well, because the latter is unlikely to come along frequently. They relish a challenge because it gives them an opportunity to show others what they're made of. They know that what doesn't kill them will eventually make them stronger and this mantra will help them to overcome almost any hurdle. If this is your birth date, you are an emotionally deep person who finds much of modern culture shallow. You tend to reject popular TV and magazines in favour of more 'worthwhile' pursuits, and will not be satisfied with a partner who likes nothing more than spending Saturday night in front of the box.

AFFIRMATION: Jupiter, the planet of adventure and optimism, brings me good fortune.

PLANETS: Jupiter and Sun

KEYWORDS: Resilient, patient, profound

19 AUGUST

Do friends complain that you never RSVP to their dinner invites, but set you a place anyway in case you turn up? Do you find it difficult to answer questions with a straight 'yes' or 'no'? Do you hate to be asked to order your meal in advance rather than choose from a menu at the time of eating? If you answered yes to these questions, you sound just like a typical 19 August person. Those born on this day hate to be pinned down, and prefer to see how they feel on the day rather than organize their social calendars long in advance. Others can find this trait very frustrating, but as you are cheerful, outgoing and loving you do make an excellent choice of friend.

AFFIRMATION: Saturn creates time for reflection.

PLANETS: Saturn and Sun

KEYWORDS: Friendly, spontaneous, enigmatic

20 AUGUST

Those born on this day often appear mysterious and thoughtful, even at times of great cheer and merriment. They are quiet and unassuming types who seem to have a slight air of melancholy about them, as if a past memory is casting a shadow over proceedings. They need to face up to their demons and deal with them in order to become the lively, imaginative and happy people they really are. Natives of 20 August have creative ability in abundance but they also have great financial sense and know-how to turn their dreams into a reality. If this is your birth date, you can be drawn towards extreme experiences. Try to set safe parameters within which to explore.

AFFIRMATION: Venus, the planet of love, allows me to make peace with my demons.

PLANETS: Venus and Sun

KEYWORDS: Multifaceted, adventurous, innovative

21 AUGUST

Natives of 21 August are curious about others, but dislike it when they, in turn, come in for scrutiny. They like to keep their private life private, but their public profile often makes this impossible. They would do well to accept their destiny and take up their rightful place in the universe, rather than worry about becoming susceptible to criticism. Those born on this day are people-oriented, and are regarded by relatives as the foundation stone on which their family is built. They are stable and unwavering in a crisis. If you were born on this day, it may be a good idea to allow some time for yourself. A night out with friends will blow away some of those cobwebs, and give you a chance to recharge your batteries ready for hectic family life.

AFFIRMATION: Mercury brings me out of the shadows.

PLANETS: Mercury and Sun

KEYWORDS: Modest, stable, loving

22 AUGUST

Those born on this day are happy to take their time building a bedrock of experience on which to base a career. They yearn for security and long-lasting success and have no time for gimmicks or quick fixes. They know that, eventually, they'll be able to look back and be proud of what they've achieved. Their family roots are important to them, and they see childhood as a springboard from which to launch. They are logical, loyal and resilient people who value others' opinion of them. If this is your birth date, it's important to express yourself wholly, but in doing so you can make yourself vulnerable. Be prepared for others to react to this behaviour in a wide variety of ways.

AFFIRMATION: The Moon gives me insight I can use for the greater good.

PLANETS: Moon and Sun

KEYWORDS: Honest, diligent, devoted

23 AUGUST

People born on 23 August have an amazing capacity for concentration. They can focus 100 per cent of their time and energy on a particular issue or problem, and make brilliant scientists and engineers because they are able to uncover how things work. Often the thing they care so much about is of little or no consequence to anyone else, but that doesn't mean it's not important or that their efforts are wasted. In the long run, 23 August people are often proved right, but at the time they may seem unnecessarily intense or even self-involved. If this is your birth date, don't feel you have to change to fit in with other people's priorities.

AFFIRMATION: Mercury can help me communicate more efficiently.

PLANETS: Mercury and Sun

KEYWORDS: Talented, logical, independent

Virgo

24 August–23 September

24 AUGUST

People born on 24 August are complex, and they are attracted to areas of life that are as unfathomable as they are. They enjoy games of all kinds, and can often be found tackling the most complicated crosswords or Sudoku puzzles. It follows that the partners they choose tend to be 'high maintenance' types, but this is how they like it. They enjoy the thrill of the chase, and the explosive chemistry that can result when two master game-players get together. Problems arise when the 24 August native becomes so tangled up in their own private affairs that they become blind to the plights of others. If this is your birth date, be mindful of this. A walk in the park on a bright, sunny day will open your eyes to the rest of the world.

AFFIRMATION: Mercury, the planet of communication, opens my eyes to the world around me.

PLANETS: Mercury and Mercury

KEYWORDS: Intelligent, dedicated, magnetic

25 AUGUST

Those born on this day know exactly which features to play up, and which to play down, in order to attract a partner, and once they've settled on who that will be, they'll go all out to get them. They have

highly active minds, but may not have pursued education quite as far as they would have liked, relying instead on their physicality and charm to get where they want in life. This may have given them a little bit of a complex around people who they feel are more educated than them. If the 25 August native can resist feeling jealous, they can achieve anything they put their minds to. If this is your birth date, why not enrol in an evening class so you can prove to yourself that you are not just a pretty face? You need to learn to love your whole self, not just the 'useful' bits.

AFFIRMATION: The power of Venus, the planet of love, and Mercury, the planet of intelligence, complete me.

PLANETS: Venus and Mercury

KEYWORDS: Outgoing, engaging, resourceful

26 AUGUST

If you were born on this day you are not afraid of delving into the darker side of life. You make an excellent friend because you are able to hold people's hands when they are going through the very toughest of times, long after most of their other friends have given up. This sense of loyalty runs like a vein through your life. You are a hardworking and meticulous employee who is valued by the rest of your team. When you do find yourself at the head of a project you tend to be controlling, because you aren't great at delegating, preferring to trust in yourself rather than others. Work on improving your faith in those around you and your professional life will proceed more smoothly.

AFFIRMATION: Pluto gives me the strength I need to accept change and trust others.

PLANETS: Pluto and Mercury

KEYWORDS: Dutiful, supportive, honest

27 AUGUST

Those born on this day are always seeking to improve the situations in which they find themselves and others. They are often involved in social reform and are capable of being extremely unselfish if it will help to get the job done. In setting extremely high standards for themselves and everyone around them, they leave themselves open to feelings of disappointment and disillusionment, and this can be harmful. If this is your birth date, you may do well to take some time out to question

♍ **VIRGO** 24 AUGUST–23 SEPTEMBER

why exactly it is you feel a need to put yourself last. If it is genuinely for the greater good, then so be it, but, if doing so gives you some kind of addictive buzz, you need to look more closely at your methods.

AFFIRMATION: Jupiter sends me on a mission of hope.

PLANETS: Jupiter and Mercury

KEYWORDS: Kind, selfless, charitable

28 AUGUST

People born on this day are capable of using any form of language, be it verbal, written, visual, symbolic, material or physical, to great effect. It is impossible to mistake what a 28 August person is trying to tell you, whether you want to hear it or not. If this is your birth date, people find you straightforward and down-to-earth, and so will gravitate to you when they need advice. This can be tiring, and, of course, if you are not in the mood to act as counsellor at that particular moment, it is written all over your face! You can't lie, so don't try to. Your friends respect your honesty and your ability to tell it like it is.

AFFIRMATION: Saturn's influence means I cannot deny my true nature.

PLANETS: Saturn and Mercury

KEYWORDS: Honest, direct, caring

29 AUGUST

Natives of 29 August are born people watchers. They love to observe the hustle and bustle of life because they find beauty in its peculiar patterns and rhythms. Those born on this day are extremely inventive in their approach to problem-solving and life in general, and others find them inspirational. They have progressive ideas and may feel drawn to an alternative lifestyle, such as communal living. They have plenty to offer the cause they believe in, and often take part in social work of one form or another. If this is your birth date you can strike people as somehow separate or superior, so practise 'joining in' by signing yourself up to a sports team. Mucking in with others shows them you aren't afraid to get involved.

AFFIRMATION: Uranus, the planet of individualism, means I can only be myself.

PLANETS: Uranus and Mercury

KEYWORDS: Liberal, innovative, unconventional

30 AUGUST

Those born on this day appreciate the simple things in life. They are light-hearted and humorous people who have usually got smiles on their faces because they simply refuse to take life too seriously. On the other hand, they tend to lose focus and give up on anything that begins to seem too much like hard work. They lack staying power, so if you are going to date a 30 August person it's worth taking this on board before getting involved. If this is your birth date you become quickly overwhelmed when your life or your surroundings begin to seem cluttered. Don't let it drain your energies – instead have a regular clear out and rid yourself of objects, activities and people that are bringing you down.

AFFIRMATION: Mercury, the planet of movement, makes me versatile.

PLANETS: Mercury and Mercury

KEYWORDS: Adaptable, caring, humorous

31 AUGUST

People born on 31 August are not extroverts – in fact they can be quite shy – but they nevertheless stand out from their peers whether they mean to or not. They are funny, entertaining people who know how to connect with those around them, so they are not seen as standoffish, but they have a certain separateness about them. In a classroom full of children wearing black socks, for example, they'll be the one wearing white ones. If 31 August is your birthday, you are a sensitive soul who doesn't enjoy feeling isolated from the pack. Don't be perturbed that people see you as different; instead learn to embrace it. Would you really like to be the same as everyone else?

AFFIRMATION: The Moon encourages me to nurture my differences, not deny them.

PLANETS: Moon and Mercury

KEYWORDS: Modest, humorous, fun-loving

1 SEPTEMBER

If you were born on this day you don't have patience with time-wasters or those who can't make up their minds. If you go out for a meal, you will already have gone online, read the menu and decided exactly what you are going to eat long before you arrive at the restaurant, so you are frustrated by those who like to ponder the menu for ages. You are the same at work: one step ahead of the game at all times, and this makes you difficult to compete with. You can be bullish, and those who come up against your steamrolling technique may feel like they're being bullied. Try to have more humility with your colleagues; they may not realize that you respect those who stand up to you.

AFFIRMATION: I may not always get what I want, but the power of Mars makes sure I get what I need.

PLANETS: Mars and Mercury

KEYWORDS: Direct, courageous, honest

2 SEPTEMBER

Natives of 2 September are not keen on fuss; they prefer to keep things low-key and can't bear histrionics of any kind. So, although they are creative and love art in all its forms, they can't be accused of possessing an artistic temperament. They have an affinity with nature and fall in love with the subtleties of each season as it morphs into the next. If you want to treat a 2 September partner, take them for a romantic walk in the woods on a cold day, before heading home for a steaming cup of cocoa. There are few things in life they'd enjoy more. If this is your birth date, you love routine and because of this your love life can become a bit stale. Break the mould every now and again and do something completely unexpected. This will keep your relationship feeling fresh.

AFFIRMATION: Venus invites variety into my life.

PLANETS: Venus and Mercury

KEYWORDS: Straightforward, honest, caring

3 SEPTEMBER

People born on 3 September are visionaries, who are often misunderstood because their spontaneous, playful sides overshadow the more serious aspects of their personalities. They are multi-talented but often one skill is focused on and the rest are ignored, and this can prove frustrating, especially when they want to change direction and find it difficult. Natives of 3 September are rebellious and can become cantankerous as time goes on. There is nothing really wrong with this but, if this is your birth date, make sure that the people you love know that it's just your idea of fun, and that you do, in fact, care about them. A meal with family and loved ones will bring you all closer together.

AFFIRMATION: Mercury expands my horizons.

PLANETS: Mercury and Mercury

KEYWORDS: Innovative, fun-loving, skilled

4 SEPTEMBER

People born on this day are good at bringing people together and building relationships, so they are great to have around on the first day of a project, when people are still getting to know one another. They tend to be good at seeing the bigger picture, so make excellent architects and construction workers. Some people will react negatively to being told what to do, and will dismiss these qualities as 'bossiness', but that is not the case. Natives of 4 September just know how to get the job done, and can usually see the quickest and most efficient route to the finish line. If this is your birth date, simply learn to ignore doubters and carry on with the job in hand.

AFFIRMATION: The Moon gives me insight I can use to build bridges.

PLANETS: Moon and Mercury

KEYWORDS: Capable, practical, comforting

5 SEPTEMBER

Those born on 5 September like to live the high life. If this is your birth date, you are the perfect person to celebrate with because you have a knack for throwing a party. The champagne is always flowing and the dance floor is always full, and this is just as well, because your active mind craves constant entertainment. When starved of the luxury and company you so crave, you can retreat into depression, so a partner that can handle the downs as well as the ups is of paramount importance. Friends and loved ones need to be available when you come down to earth with a bump, which is usually about the same time that your monthly credit card bill lands on the doormat. A little bit of harmless flirting keeps a twinkle in your eye.

AFFIRMATION: The Sun radiates warmth whatever the weather.

PLANETS: Sun and Mercury

KEYWORDS: Playful, romantic, sparkling

6 SEPTEMBER

Sometimes it is difficult being a 6 September person, because that critical eye sees imperfections everywhere and they can't help but nitpick at things others accept, and even treasure. This tendency is bound to frustrate those around them, so it might be a good idea for them to learn to bite their tongues when they think their criticisms might upset others. On the upside, 6 September people are conscientious, efficient and very caring. They make great friends because they are always honest, devoted and offer impartial advice, a rare trait that should be highly valued. If this is your birth date, an escapist's hobby like dancing might help you to forget yourself for a while, giving you a chance to unwind.

AFFIRMATION: Mercury helps me to accept reality and live with imperfections.

PLANETS: Mercury and Mercury

KEYWORDS: Tasteful, controlled, friendly

7 SEPTEMBER

People born on 7 September will pursue personal success to the ends of the earth, and will leap whatever hurdles they encounter on the way. If this is your birth date, it may take time for the world to sit up and take notice of you because your methods aren't especially new or attention-grabbing: it is your tenacity that makes you special. People who appreciate stamina and staying power will be drawn to you as a friend or lover. Not the type to engage in a light-hearted fling, once you are in a person's life, you are going nowhere. You love order; you have a place for everything and appreciate everything in its place. This can include colleagues, friends and family members. Try a new experience from time to time; it will help you to keep an open mind.

AFFIRMATION: Venus can help me to loosen up when the moment is right.

PLANETS: Venus and Mercury

KEYWORDS: Capable, efficient, loyal

8 SEPTEMBER

If you were born on this day you take the emotional side of life very seriously and often feel things more deeply than the average person. Your probing and analytical mind makes you curious about the darker aspects of existence. You are unshockable, so a career in the police force may beckon if you can find a way to settle your demons. Others find your independent attitude and charismatic personality sexually attractive, so you are rarely short of lovers. You just need to be careful when you meet 'the one' that you don't treasure your work more than you treasure them. A romantic evening under the stars with a bottle of something fizzy will help put jealousy to bed.

AFFIRMATION: Pluto, the planet of magnetism, draws people in.

PLANETS: Pluto and Mercury

KEYWORDS: Devoted, deep, sexy

9 SEPTEMBER

Natives of 9 September rarely shy away from a challenge, preferring to struggle through life towards a goal they perceive as worthwhile, rather than take the easy way out and live to regret never having pushed themselves harder. They are witty free spirits who will not listen to the advice of others, however well-meant it is. They're so determined to take their own path that they are more likely to do precisely whatever they are advised against doing than blindly follow orders. If you are a 9 September person reverse psychology works well on you, such is the contrariness implicit in your personality. You may benefit from learning that some fights are worth having and others are not.

AFFIRMATION: Even Jupiter, the planet of adventure, follows a pre-planned route.

PLANETS: Jupiter and Mercury

KEYWORDS: Strong-willed, independent, hard-working

10 SEPTEMBER

Anyone who is lucky enough to count a 10 September person among their friends knows they can be relied upon to be there, 100 per cent, no matter what happens. If this is your birthday, you are the person who will struggle into work even when it's blowing a Force 9 gale outside, and make everyone in the office a cup of coffee when you get there. This is what makes a 10 September person stand out. It might not be very glamorous, but 'stickability' is a very valuable quality, and one that can see you very far in life. You have what it takes to get to the very top in whatever profession takes your fancy, simply because you'll never give up. Saturn's influence often attracts you to older partners, who share your love of simple pleasures.

AFFIRMATION: Saturn will help me get to wherever I want in life.

PLANETS: Saturn and Mercury

KEYWORDS: Tenacious, sensible, trustworthy

11 SEPTEMBER

Natives of 11 September are wickedly amusing and draw people to them with their infectious humour and their ability to entertain a crowd. If you were born on this day, you love to collect things and can often be found trawling flea markets and antique fairs. Other people look up to you because your style choices are second to none. You seem to do things with an effortless charm that means people tend to overlook your faults, but you can be moody and when you are in a sulk, everyone in the immediate vicinity knows about it. You are incapable of hiding exactly what you are thinking. You don't know the meaning of the phrase 'poker face' and so should never engage in flattery; just temper your criticisms enough to make them bearable.

AFFIRMATION: Uranus, the planet of intuition, tells me when to speak up and when to keep silent.

PLANETS: Uranus and Mercury

KEYWORDS: Funny, dramatic, strong-willed

12 SEPTEMBER

Those born on 12 September make great politicians and team leaders. They have courage and stamina in bucket-loads, and are the perfect people to call upon when someone is needed to fulfil the role of 'reformer'. If you give them a job they will do it, no matter how difficult it is, and will always face up to their responsibilities. When something goes wrong, they will not make excuses but accept the criticism and learn from it. They enjoy speaking in front of an audience, not because they are egotistical, but because they are confident in their own abilities and know they can communicate well in all situations. If this is your birth date you can get so bogged-down with work that you forget to relax.

AFFIRMATION: Neptune, the planet of obligation, gives me a sense of duty that I can use to serve others.

PLANETS: Neptune and Mercury

KEYWORDS: Hard-working, honest, gracious

13 SEPTEMBER

If you want a job done well, particularly if it involves caring, ask a 13 September person. They are capable, dedicated and nurturing and can be relied upon to help out in any situation, however dire. They are excellent friends who deserve to be treasured by those around them,

and usually, they are. However, their inbuilt sense of loyalty means they are easily manipulated by the more unscrupulous people among us. They need to be aware of this fault so that they can combat those who would take advantage of their trusting natures. If this is your birth date, Mercury, the planet of reason, rules your sign. Burning an essential oil with a clean scent, like lavender, will help you to clear your mind and focus on the facts.

AFFIRMATION: Mercury can help me find the truth.

PLANETS: Mercury and Mercury

KEYWORDS: Devoted, kind, honest

14 SEPTEMBER

If you were born on this day, you cannot bear loose ends and as a consequence you often find yourself finishing what others started. You are the type of person who volunteers to make the tea if someone has boiled the kettle and forgotten about it, so you can either be seen as very helpful and conscientious, or as pushy and a bit rude, depending on the context. In your defence, this need for order and efficiency is compulsive – you can't help it – so if you do occasionally step on people's toes, it's not really your fault. You are an articulate perfectionist so your house is always immaculate and you love nothing better than to wax lyrical about your housekeeping methods. You are a fabulous host and should think seriously about entering the leisure and tourism industry, if you aren't already working in it.

AFFIRMATION: The Sun nurtures more than it burns.

PLANETS: Sun and Mercury

KEYWORDS: Useful, organized, intelligent

15 SEPTEMBER

There are plenty of people in the world who only ever do the minimum needed to 'get by' and never go beyond the call of duty in any task. People born on 15 September do not fall into this category; they are thorough, diligent and tenacious in everything they do and consequently they make brilliant parents, friends and professionals. Whether hosting an event or putting up shelves, they never give less than 100 per cent. They value practical skills over charm or charisma and are happiest to learn by doing, rather than by reading or observing. Children born on this day may benefit from extra attention at school; they tend to thrive in less conventional educational environments, as academia isn't usually their thing. If this is your birth date, never compromise on your beliefs – they are what make you, you.

AFFIRMATION: Mercury is the planet of communication. I communicate through deeds, not words.

PLANETS: Mercury and Mercury

KEYWORDS: Hardworking, principled, demonstrative

16 SEPTEMBER

Like their neighbours from 15 September, those born on this day like to exceed expectations, and love breaking personal records. In their dictionaries there is no such word as 'can't' and they'll take great pleasure in proving this to their doubters over and over again. Consequently, when things don't go according to plan, and something happens to stop them achieving their goals, they take the failure extremely hard and it can take a long time for them to bounce back. If this is your birth date, accept that there are some boundaries that just cannot be overcome, no matter how hard you try. Try not to push yourself so hard; direct your efforts towards supporting family members or colleagues and you will feel rewarded.

AFFIRMATION: Venus allows me to show my vulnerability.

PLANETS: Venus and Mercury

KEYWORDS: Honourable, brave, driven

17 SEPTEMBER

September 17 people never shy away from a challenge, and are able to overcome seemingly insurmountable odds in order to realize their dreams. They are unafraid of taking on any task and often end up tackling jobs that no one else will touch. They gravitate towards hobbies where the stakes are high, like extreme sports and rock climbing. Like a lot of other Virgos, they are extremely hardworking and will labour on for years without any recognition or gratitude. They don't much care for the opinions of others; what matters is getting to the finish line. If you were born on this date remember to make time for relaxing and having fun. Blood, sweat and tears are all very well, but laughter can sometimes do more good.

AFFIRMATION: Pluto gives me the stamina I need to try, try and try again.

PLANETS: Pluto and Mercury

KEYWORDS: Determined, honourable, brave

18 SEPTEMBER

People born on 18 September tend to see things as black or white, so will always side with one argument or another. They make extremely loyal friends and just as committed foes and cannot stand people who prefer to sit on the fence. Inaction is abhorrent to them. They are private individuals who prefer to work busily backstage rather than hog the limelight, although, rather strangely, they often inhabit positions in public life. If this is the case, they will work tirelessly to make sure that what they want to keep private (lovers, family, business interests) is kept out of the spotlight. If you are an 18 September native, you look at life as an amazing adventure, never to be repeated, so you'll strive to get the most out of it. An adventurous day out brings a smile when life seems to be becoming too serious.

AFFIRMATION: Jupiter inspires me with a love of the outdoors.

PLANETS: Jupiter and Mercury

KEYWORDS: Active, devoted, modest

19 SEPTEMBER

People born on this day have excellent taste and enjoy nothing more than expressing it in their immediate surroundings. Their homes are comfortable and beautiful and they enjoy spending time there. They quickly begin to feel frightened and out of their depth when faced with an unfamiliar environment and will rarely stray into an undesirable neighbourhood, preferring to stick to places they know and trust. Those born on 19 September can get carried away with their love of beauty, and may need to try harder to hold on to what's really important in life; friends, family and partners. If you were born on this day, a long walk by the sea, or in the countryside, will wake you up to the power of nature rather than material things.

AFFIRMATION: Saturn opens my eyes.

PLANETS: Saturn and Mercury

KEYWORDS: Immaculate, elegant, refined

20 SEPTEMBER

Capable, business-like and trustworthy are all words embodied by the 20 September native. They love to be useful, and appreciate this trait in others. Motivated by the common good, they'll rally whoever is about to work towards a group task, whether it's setting the table for dinner or drawing up a peace treaty at an international summit. Because of their ability to get the best out of others, 20 September people make great managers but they sometimes forget to take a step back and look at what they've helped to achieve. If this is your birth date, make sure you keep a daily diary so you can look at past entries and ascertain what worked, and what could be improved upon.

AFFIRMATION: Venus invites love into my life.

PLANETS: Venus and Mercury

KEYWORDS: Efficient, philanthropic, community-minded

21 SEPTEMBER

Mercury's influence means that 21 September people believe that life should be lived for kicks, not for profit, and this philosophy is evident in the choices they make. They are friendly and intelligent people who tend to do well in life but live for the present, and think little about the future. Preferring instant gratification, they often choose unconventional paths to success because traditional aspirations require too much planning. If this is your birth date, there is nothing wrong with appreciating today, but you need to keep one eye on tomorrow or your loved ones will have to make amends for your short-sightedness. List-making is a quick and easy way to begin organizing your day.

AFFIRMATION: Mercury, the planet of intelligence, helps me plan for the future.

PLANETS: Mercury and Mercury

KEYWORDS: Spontaneous, popular, enthusiastic

22 SEPTEMBER

Those born on this day are eternally young, and are great at using their positive attitude and zest for life to bring groups of people together. They love new beginnings, and throw themselves into each day with renewed energy and vigour, but they get quickly bored when expected to repeat the same tired routine over and over again. They speak their minds, because they believe this is the simplest, most honest way to live. Natives of 22 September have an affinity with animals, particularly dogs, because they admire their ability to heal emotional wounds with love and affection. If you were born on this day, why not get involved with your local animal rescue centre where your enthusiasm will be appreciated? Cooking for family helps to replenish you.

AFFIRMATION: The Moon's influence makes me nurturing and protective.

PLANETS: Moon and Mercury

KEYWORDS: Charismatic, fun-loving, influential

23 SEPTEMBER

People born on 23 September don't just do what is expected of them, they like to excel. They are exceptionally driven individuals who tend to devote much of their time to pushing forward into uncharted territories, and so their friends are sometimes more like followers, who can't wait to see what they'll get up to next. Part of the reason why 23 September people generate plenty of gossip is because they are attracted to material wealth and may be tempted to continue chasing it, even if it leads them down a dangerous path. If this is your birth date, remember to take time out to reassess what's really important. A small gesture of sacrifice may see you move up in the estimations of someone who is secretly very important to you.

AFFIRMATION: The Sun's energy inspires me to give.

PLANETS: Sun and Mercury

KEYWORDS: Intrepid, exciting, influential

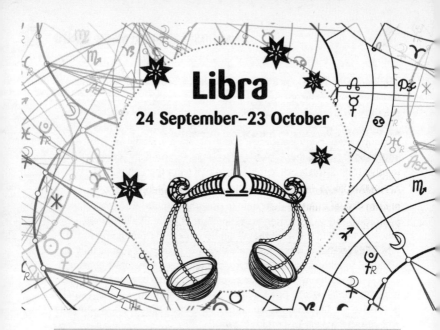

24 SEPTEMBER

With a slightly mischievous glint in their eye, those born on this day will appear youthful whatever their age. If this is your birth date, people will naturally gravitate towards you because of your easy-going ways, and yet you still have leadership qualities that are to be admired. Because you are able to balance pros and cons in a dispute, you are often called upon to act as mediator, bringing harmony to chaos. Despite your sunny disposition and charm, you tend to have a turbulent love life as you find it difficult to establish any hard rules, fearful that you might receive criticism. You have a great deal of creative talent and this may be reflected in your choice of career. You might make a great photographer, dancer or designer.

AFFIRMATION: Mercury teaches me to be diplomatic.

PLANETS: Mercury and Venus

KEYWORDS: Adolescent, cheeky, gifted

25 SEPTEMBER

If you were born on this day your goal is to find peace and harmony in all areas of your existence, as stress is your undoing. You have an inquisitive nature and like to delve into how things work. Sometimes a little too opinionated, you expect a great deal of yourself and have a tendency to brood if you do not manage to achieve what you want. You favour a small circle of select friends but your highly romantic nature can draw you into unsuitable relationships if the lure of excitement is too great. However, if the right union is formed, you will pull out all the stops to keep romance alive. You love candles, music and flowers. Your flair for languages draws you towards teaching and careers that involve travel. You work better as part of a team than on your own.

AFFIRMATION: Venus teaches me how to love wholeheartedly.

PLANETS: Venus and Venus

KEYWORDS: Questioning, peace-loving, romantic

26 SEPTEMBER

Natives of 26 September have style and panache, and they know it. If you were born on this day you know how to put people at ease but you do not feel complete unless you are one of a pair, as you need a direction in which to channel your warm, passionate and protective nature. You love to understand and appreciate the world around you and are extremely attracted to those who are successful and accomplished in their careers. Art holds a great attraction for you, and even if it is only a hobby, you can often be found with a paintbrush in your hands. Like your fellow Librans, you hate discord and will do anything to appease an un-harmonious situation. A visit to the theatre offers you a quick release from everyday tensions.

AFFIRMATION: Pluto teaches me how to be fair and just.

PLANETS: Pluto and Venus

KEYWORDS: Stylish, artistic, balanced

27 SEPTEMBER

Stamina and endurance are admirable qualities that belong to anyone born on this day. If that is you, you are popular because of your childlike outlook and can make any situation humorous if you feel it is getting too serious. You tend to be more energetic than many of your fellow Librans. You enjoy the chase and like to retain your independence when it comes to relationships, but can be cautious about settling down, making sure that the person you choose shares your optimism and enthusiasm. Because of your love of action, you often gravitate towards a career in the armed forces, which also satisfies your desire for order and discipline in your daily life.

AFFIRMATION: Jupiter helps me to see all sides to an issue.

PLANETS: Jupiter and Venus

KEYWORDS: Athletic, youthful, autonomous

28 SEPTEMBER

Because of their artistic natures, people born on 28 September can sometimes appear a little eccentric. They are kind-hearted and overly generous and will bend over backwards to help a friend in need. They are true humanitarians and as long as they feel they are helping those in need, they can achieve success in their chosen fields. If this is your birth date, you tend to choose a partner who has a passive nature and who can allow you periods of solitude. In return you will be loving, loyal and accommodating if that means that you can live in harmony. The downside to your character is that you find it hard to withstand disappointments. Learning that dreams don't always come true will help.

AFFIRMATION: Saturn helps to balance the scales and allows peace and harmony into my life.

PLANETS: Saturn and Venus

KEYWORDS: Talented, charitable, considerate

29 SEPTEMBER

A real Robin Hood character, benevolence seems to run in the veins of anyone born on this day. They are individuals with a cause and hate injustice of any kind, so will fight stoically to uphold their beliefs. They are extremely resourceful and often owe their success to the powerful influence of a mentor. Although they relate well on a one-to-one basis, these Librans sometimes lack the confidence to project themselves in a crowd, so they value the strength of good friends and colleagues around them. If you are a 29 September native, you have high expectations regarding romance which means you are often disappointed, but when the time is right you make a loyal and caring lover.

AFFIRMATION: Uranus can help me project and become more confident.

PLANETS: Uranus and Venus

KEYWORDS: Intellectual, altruistic, generous

30 SEPTEMBER

Perfectly groomed, good-humoured, generous and imaginative, those born on this day are basically romantics at heart. Like their neighbours, these individuals tend to avoid conflict and will back away from any difficult situations rather than have to face up to them. They tend to be a little too impulsive when it comes to romance, jumping in feet first before giving the relationship time to develop. What they do demand is loyalty at all costs and infidelity is a complete no-no. If you were born on this day, you work well in managerial positions as you have the ability to motivate others, but anyone who works for you needs to be prepared to put in a hard day's work.

AFFIRMATION: Mercury can help me achieve balance.

PLANETS: Mercury and Venus

KEYWORDS: Enterprising, humorous, administrative

1 OCTOBER

Constantly driven towards success, those born on 1 October are never happier than when chasing a dream or a goal. Although they do have the necessary people skills to be a team player, they thrive when working on their own, as their unwillingness to ask for help often pushes people away. They tend to have a wide circle of social contacts but very few close friends and they are fickle when it comes to romance as they are constantly falling in and out of love. Once married, however, these individuals will work very hard at making it work. Peace of mind is important to you if you were born on this day, and playing a competitive sport can help release some of your inner aggression.

AFFIRMATION: Mars can help me release a lot of pent-up energy.

PLANETS: Mars and Venus

KEYWORDS: Determined, industrious, energetic

2 OCTOBER

Relationships are the most important factors in the lives of 2 October people, and, if this is you, you probably need to be in love to be truly happy. Unfortunately, you tend to wear your heart on your sleeve and this often results in major disappointment. You are highly intellectual and can talk the hind legs off a donkey, but you need to make sure you don't steal anyone else's thunder. You love fashion and music and are usually wearing the latest labels as you tend to identify with the finer things in life. You have good business acumen but need to work in glamorous surroundings to bring out your best. You have a natural artistic talent, and a hobby can quickly blossom into something special.

AFFIRMATION: Venus teaches me diplomacy when it comes to matters of the heart.

PLANETS: Venus and Venus

KEYWORDS: Smart, debonair, creative

3 OCTOBER

If you are a 3 October person, you are a natural diplomat and you treat everyone as your equal. Others are drawn to your lighthearted and optimistic outlook and gain energy from the tremendous stamina that exudes from you. You strive for perfection, but are often disappointed in your search. However, you seem to bounce back from major life lessons without receiving too many battle scars. In love you have your fair share of ups and downs, but once you find someone who shares your high moral standards, you begin to think about marriage. Your powers of persuasion make you adept at selling and good at balancing the scales of justice as a lawyer or judge. Although you are as good at handling money as you are at making it, you are wise enough to know that money does not bring happiness.

AFFIRMATION: Mercury can help me balance my life.

PLANETS: Mercury and Venus

KEYWORDS: Prudent, effective, principled

4 OCTOBER

With many and varied interests, 4 October natives make great companions. If this is your birth date, your reputation is extremely important to you and you can be prone to exaggeration if you feel it puts you in a better light. You have a slow and steady approach to achieving your goals and, even if it takes many years, your steadfastness usually pays off. You are an extremely romantic individual who is prepared to go to great lengths to win the affection of the one you love. You have an acute sense of social awareness and are likely to pursue a career that brings you into contact with those less fortunate than yourself. You need to feel appreciated so a night in on the sofa with a loved one can provide that much-needed surge of contentment.

AFFIRMATION: The Moon creates a peaceful atmosphere.

PLANETS: Moon and Venus

KEYWORDS: Captivating, dedicated, romantic

5 OCTOBER

If you were born on 5 October, the Libran scales are slightly off balance and you can struggle to find a happy symmetry between the intellectual and spiritual aspects of your life. You are as good at listening as you are at talking and value friends who have similar interests to you. You are attracted to people who challenge you intellectually, and this often leads to stormy relationships so you often don't settle down until fairly late in life. Making a difference is very important to you and your work often controls your destiny as it usually involves moving to a new location. Meditation and yoga can be very beneficial for anyone born on this day.

AFFIRMATION: The Sun teaches me to stay calm in order to cope with the stresses of modern life.

PLANETS: Sun and Venus

KEYWORDS: Communicative, intelligent, benevolent

6 OCTOBER

People who are born on this day tend to find fantasy more interesting than reality. You love beauty in all forms and like to express yourself through your own imagination and creativity. Where friendship is concerned you prefer to have a few close friends than lots of acquaintances, but if you find the right partner you will be spoilt rotten. If you were born on this day you will prefer to work for yourself as an artist, a designer or anything that uses your creative skills. You love to try and make the world a better place and bring positive energy into anything you attempt. Surroundings are important to anyone born on this day. A week's break sees you redecorating your home in order to help bring inner harmony to your surroundings.

AFFIRMATION: Mercury can bring social harmony.

PLANETS: Mercury and Venus

KEYWORDS: Artistic, enthusiastic, observant

7 OCTOBER

With a rather dreamy outlook on life, you are always striving towards perfection and constantly looking for answers. You have a philosophical attitude and like to try to help others in whatever way you can, maybe by offering your services abroad after a major disaster.

You can be insecure about your own feelings so rarely open up fully to a partner unless you are sure you have found your ultimate soulmate, so it can take quite a long time for a relationship to reach total closeness. You are not particularly materialistic, preferring to use your skills and money to help others less fortunate than yourself. Running or jogging is your favourite pastime as it allows you time to think and keep fit simultaneously.

AFFIRMATION: Venus can help me to love and be loved.

PLANETS: Venus and Venus

KEYWORDS: Whimsical, charming, humanitarian

8 OCTOBER

The 8 October person is adept at the art of making others feel special and usually brings out the best in people. If this is your birth date, you tend to have a charming, quirky sense of humour and are usually at the top of the list when party invitations are handed out. You are creative, witty and more decisive than the typical Libra personality, so tend to find yourself in a managerial position where people warm to your subtle leadership skills. Those born on 8 October need the security of love and being part of a family and will very often marry their first partners. You do not cope well with the stress of a break-up and will very often stay on your own if things go wrong the first time round.

AFFIRMATION: Pluto encourages both diplomacy and harmony.

PLANETS: Pluto and Venus

KEYWORDS: Witty, lovable, influential

9 OCTOBER

Natives of 9 October are prone to mood swings. This can be frustrating for others, but these dramatic changes often bring out the best of their creativity. Acting may be the chosen career for the person born on this day and they may start showing signs of talent at a very early age. If this is your birthday, you possess a considerable strength of character and are intolerant of narrow-minded people. A loving relationship is extremely important to you but you have to be careful not to look for superficial attractiveness in preference to someone that suits you spiritually. Swimming or long walks gives the 9 October native time to think, as they love to daydream.

AFFIRMATION: Jupiter will help me to expand who, and what, I know.

PLANETS: Jupiter and Venus

KEYWORDS: Dramatic, distinctive, amorous

10 OCTOBER

The Libran born on this day is quite outspoken and always willing to put their view forward if they disagree with something. They are, however, charming and humorous which means they are usually quickly forgiven for their candour. If this is your birth date, you care a great deal about your appearance and reputation and will hardly ever be seen lounging around in a pair of old jeans and a T-shirt. You are relatively ambitious and usually take the initiative and go after exactly what you want. This applies to relationships too. Nothing will distract you from the object of your affection in the pursuit of love. Because you like to be in a position of power, you will often choose a career in management or politics.

AFFIRMATION: Saturn challenges me to face up to reality.

PLANETS: Saturn and Venus

KEYWORDS: Candid, smart, ambitious

11 OCTOBER

Typical of their sign, these individuals have the ability to make people feel at ease with their natural charm and enthusiasm. They want to live life to the full and tend to be drawn towards adventure and danger despite the fact that it takes them out of their comfort zone. These individuals can be vulnerable to emotional ups and downs but when they meet the right person their self-confidence and general well-being blossoms. If you are an 11 October native, you tend to express yourself artistically, so you need a job where you can use this talent to the full. You love playing sports, so any type of sporting activity can bring the release of energy you desperately need.

AFFIRMATION: Uranus teaches me to be cooperative, diplomatic and fair.

PLANETS: Uranus and Venus

KEYWORDS: Athletic, lively, creative

12 OCTOBER

Those born on this day need to keep a firm hold on the self-indulgent side of their natures, as they are not always fully in control of this. They are charming, likeable people who always have a full social calendar.

When it comes to romance they can be flirtatious and a little fickle, and even after settling down they are still likely to have a roving eye – that is, unless their partner has a knack for keeping them fully absorbed. If you were born on this day, your friends often turn to you for advice – you will always be asked to join a pub quiz team because of your vast knowledge on a wide range of subjects. Regular breaks from routine will help to recharge your batteries.

AFFIRMATION: Neptune can bring me the balance I desperately seek.

PLANETS: Neptune and Venus

KEYWORDS: Popular, sociable, intellectual

13 OCTOBER

Natives of 13 October appear quiet and thoughtful, but once you really get to know them they are pragmatic and full of common sense. They do not feel fulfilled unless they are in a meaningful relationship, but they can be emotionally weak so partners need to be prepared to support them. If this is your birthday, you are not afraid of hard work and, although you may not reach the top of your chosen career, you are usually successful for as long as you feel motivated. If you become bored you may lose the impetus to drive forward. Dancing is your favourite pastime because it offers you the chance to be creative.

AFFIRMATION: The Moon helps me define my emotional needs.

PLANETS: Moon and Venus

KEYWORDS: Realistic, hard-working, sensible

14 OCTOBER

Interior designer, architect, sculptor or artist: these are all careers that suit those born on 14 October as they have an amazing eye for form and structure. Despite being highly intelligent there is an almost child-like side to their character and they tend to look at the world through rose-tinted glasses. If you are a 14 October native, you appear lighthearted and warm but this is balanced by a serious core. You need to feel appreciated by loved ones so are not happy in relationships unless your partner is prepared to commit wholeheartedly. You are a conscientious worker and focus a lot of your energy into getting things right both in your personal and in your professional life.

AFFIRMATION: The Sun can help me see the world through another's eyes.

PLANETS: Sun and Venus

KEYWORDS: Analytical, animated, diligent

15 OCTOBER

With a powerful psychological aptitude, these individuals make good marriage counsellors but also excel in any areas involving the arts. They are strongly motivated by a desire for justice and need to create harmony in all areas of their life to feel completely happy. If you were born on this day you believe that love makes the world go round, so relationships are very important to you. You are fair-minded, forgiving and remain totally true once you make a commitment. You love luxurious surroundings and will work hard to earn them, although you do have a problem in coming to terms with your own inabilities. Indecision tends to be one of your weaknesses, so you need to think positively and learn from earlier mistakes.

AFFIRMATION: Mercury allows me to search for the truth.

PLANETS: Mercury and Venus

KEYWORDS: Romantic, tasteful, placatory

16 OCTOBER

The 16 October native is a master in the art of communication. Their love of words and language makes these individuals talented writers, and this ability is helped by their uncanny understanding of the subtleties of their fellow human beings. If this is your birth date, you value social contact more than most and, apart from when you are submerged in work, you like to be surrounded by people. In love, you tend to be drawn towards creative types as you like to share your love of beauty. You tend to be affected by your environment and to really relax you need to lie back and become absorbed in music.

AFFIRMATION: Sensual Venus teaches me to be generous with my affections.

PLANETS: Venus and Venus

KEYWORDS: Talkative, insightful, artistic

17 OCTOBER

People born on 17 October tend to surround themselves with friends because they have to feel needed in all areas of their lives. If you are a 17 October native, you can be lazy, so a partner that can push you brings out the best in a relationship. You are totally loyal and have a wonderful way with children. You do not like to live in cluttered surroundings so like to keep material possessions to a minimum. You would much rather pursue a career that channels your artistic talents than be unhappy in an administrative role, and for that reason you may change direction several times before settling. Your intentions are always good but it could be said that you do not always 'hit the nail on the head'.

AFFIRMATION: Pluto teaches me how to survive against all odds.

PLANETS: Pluto and Venus

KEYWORDS: Friendly, level-headed, dependable

18 OCTOBER

Anyone born on this day is a natural charmer, but they live at such an incredibly fast pace it is difficult for most people to keep up with them. They are visionary and have leadership qualities but tend to believe only what they want to believe, relying heavily on their own intuition. If this is your birthday, you tend to be driven by your strong sexual desires so need a partner that is prepared to keep up with you if the union is to survive. You are extremely ambitious and don't take to failure kindly, often pushing yourself too far to the detriment of your health. You sometimes struggle over making decisions as you can see both sides to any situation. You need to learn to take a deep breath before deciding which path to take.

AFFIRMATION: Jupiter can help me expand my knowledge.

PLANETS: Jupiter and Venus

KEYWORDS: Highly-motivated, sensual, intuitive

19 OCTOBER

With a fierce lust for knowledge and a curiosity about the past, people born on this date make great archaeologists and historians. They have outstanding memories and find fulfilment in discovering things about the world around them. They are charming but sometimes they will react badly if you push them in a direction in which they feel uncomfortable. If you are a 19 October native, you're an extremely focused individual who is constantly making and meeting goals. With your natural magnetism, friends and lovers come easily and you are quite happy to share your life as long as your partner allows you some time on your own. Taking a walk early in the morning, when the birds are singing their dawn chorus, will give you time to sort your thoughts out.

AFFIRMATION: Saturn allows me time to explore my personal boundaries.

PLANETS: Saturn and Venus

KEYWORDS: Inquisitive, knowledgeable, focused

20 OCTOBER

Anyone born on this day cannot fail to be moved by music and the written word. If this is you, you tend to choose your words carefully and allow your opponent to talk freely and give their point of view. You have an amazing sense of humour and seem to attract attention even in a large crowd of people. You can have an idealistic view of romance and are therefore often disappointed, but as long as your love is reciprocated you make a loyal and caring partner. You think very carefully before starting a family as you value your freedom, but you make a good parent and discipline comes high on your list of standards. You love the great outdoors and find relaxation in a challenging round of golf.

AFFIRMATION: Venus teaches me to delve deeply into my emotions.

PLANETS: Venus and Venus

KEYWORDS: Demonstrative, emotional, talkative

21 OCTOBER

Librans born on this day definitely need their space as, emotionally, they tend to pick up too many vibrations from people and things around them. This can make them feel overloaded and so they need to find their own ways of de-stressing. Allowed time to recover, these individuals quickly bounce back and are great fun to be with. If this is your birthday, loved ones and family are very important to you, and you like to keep a sense of adventure in a relationship to keep it alive. You are exuberant and engaging and make a wonderful teacher as you have a knack for passing your worldly knowledge on to others.

AFFIRMATION: Mercury helps me listen to what people are truly saying.

PLANETS: Mercury and Venus

KEYWORDS: Freedom-loving, resilient, informative

22 OCTOBER

People born on 22 October seem to draw strength from being on their own for quite long periods of time. Although they have a magnetic personality their manner can sometimes seem a little intimidating, so very close friends are few and far between. If this is your birth date, your main aim in life is to make your own mark on the world and you will strive to achieve this in whatever way you can. Despite enjoying your privacy, you can fall hook, line and sinker for a pretty face, making yourself vulnerable to a broken heart. Because of your creative streak, you tend to seek careers in the performing arts and find you can totally lose yourself in the characters you play.

AFFIRMATION: The Moon can help to improve my rapport with friends and lovers.

PLANETS: Moon and Venus

KEYWORDS: Independent, talented, ambitious

23 OCTOBER

Natives of 23 October are extremely observant and don't miss much of what is going on around them. There is a slightly mischievous streak in them and they can often be seen poking fun at more serious individuals. True romantics, they are idealistic about love and demand total loyalty, walking away if they get the slightest whiff of infidelity. They need a relationship that will allow them to express their singular personality, so finding a soulmate can be a little tricky. If you are a 23 October native, you not only think big, you act big too. Your goals may seem insurmountable to others, but you embrace them courageously. Boredom is your greatest enemy, so learning new skills can help to broaden your mind.

AFFIRMATION: Pluto teaches me the gift of compromise.

PLANETS: Pluto and Venus

KEYWORDS: Attentive, loyal, go-getter

Scorpio

24 October–22 November

24 OCTOBER

Although people born on 24 October do not do it intentionally, they seem to have a knack for seeing what makes other people tick. With an air of mystery, these individuals quickly pick up on emotions around them and this can affect their moods. They are intuitive and impulsive, but their dedication to the people they love is faultless. If you were born on this day, romance can be difficult for you as you are addicted to excitement and fuelled by a fiercely competitive streak. You enjoy jobs that involve a level of danger so enrolling in the police force, the army or becoming a firefighter gives you the thrill you're looking for. Reading a book gives you time to slow down and reflect on life.

AFFIRMATION: Mercury helps me to handle all situations logically.

PLANETS: Mercury and Pluto

KEYWORDS: Insightful, adventurous, competitive

25 OCTOBER

Like a good wine, 25 October natives seem to improve with age. As their experience and knowledge grows, so does their appetite for life. They are charismatic and intelligent and attract people like flies, although their sarcastic sense of humour is not to everyone's taste. They can dwell on the past, but are never afraid of a challenge and embrace them with enthusiasm. If you were born on this day, you are full of drive and imagination and are able to fully immerse yourself in a role, whether as an actor, a politician or a singer. You have a tendency to manipulate those closest to you, so you need to work to resist this temptation. Watching a good film is your favourite form of release.

AFFIRMATION: Venus helps me form an emotional union.

PLANETS: Venus and Pluto

KEYWORDS: Motivated, brave, intense

26 OCTOBER

People who are born on this day have a wonderful understanding of others and, with their analytical skills, make good doctors or psychologists. When they find true love, 26 October natives are extremely generous and exude great personal charm. If this is your birth date, you are a loyal friend and if you are told a secret it will go no further. If you have children, you form very close bonds with them that continue to grow with time. To keep fit you like outdoor forms of exercise such as hiking, cycling or horse riding rather than the restrictions of a gym. You have an affinity with animals, and a very good understanding of your own pets.

AFFIRMATION: Pluto helps to purify, allowing me to rise to higher levels of awareness.

PLANETS: Pluto and Pluto

KEYWORDS: Insightful, enquiring, loyal

27 OCTOBER

These individuals like to walk on the wild side, so don't let their quiet personalities fool you. They have many friends but very rarely allow people to see beyond their immaculate exteriors. When they fall in love, they give their heart and soul but they can show fits of jealousy which can lead to tempestuous relationships. If this is your birthday, you tend to have an inner restlessness and find it hard to settle, but, on the plus side, this can drive you to achieve great things. You would make a great teacher as you have a talent for captivating younger audiences. The secret is to learn how to harness your energy and use it to your advantage.

AFFIRMATION: Jupiter can help me expand my knowledge.

PLANETS: Jupiter and Pluto

KEYWORDS: Emotional, energetic, daring

28 OCTOBER

The strongest element of the 28 October native's character is their pioneering spirit. Never satisfied with what they have learned, they are always on the hunt for new discoveries. They are intriguing and make great inventors or scientists as they will always persevere until they come up with an answer to their question. With their love of precision, these individuals can quickly become disgruntled if they fail to live up to their own high standards. If you were born on this day, you are affectionate and value time with your family, preferring to keep your private life completely separate from your career. Try not to be too tough on yourself and take a trip to the theatre or the cinema to unwind.

AFFIRMATION: Saturn helps me control my emotions.

PLANETS: Saturn and Pluto

KEYWORDS: Inquisitive, tenacious, reliable

29 OCTOBER

People born on this day can live in a dream-world and are sometimes very excitable. They are always up for adventure and have a playful, spontaneous side to their natures. Their loyalty is very strong and they will do virtually anything to protect their loved ones. Being passionate about their own beliefs, these individuals love a good debate, and this can lead to misunderstandings if the other person does not know them well. There is an intense side to their natures which can make them very difficult to read. If you are a 29 October native, you tend to favour unusual careers and often end up working for yourself because you find routine too restrictive. Playing a musical instrument can be very rewarding for you.

AFFIRMATION: Uranus can help me to express myself more clearly to others.

PLANETS: Uranus and Pluto

KEYWORDS: Imaginative, mischievous, devoted

30 OCTOBER

These individuals can read between the lines of any given situation. They are intriguing and are able to make friends with virtually anyone as they are great fun to be around. They have the ability to build others' self-esteem and therefore make good mentors. As parents they are fun-loving and affectionate and find it very easy to get into a child's imaginary world. If this is your birthday, you have a strong sense of responsibility towards the environment and will fight to save the planet, perhaps by supporting green initiatives. You prefer careers that allow you to explore ideas, and although you are not academically inclined, you do love to learn from your experiences.

AFFIRMATION: Mercury's influence can help me see things more clearly.

PLANETS: Mercury and Pluto

KEYWORDS: Intuitive, sociable, youthful

31 OCTOBER

If you're looking for someone who will see a project through to the end, there is no one with more conviction than the person born on 31 October. They have a no-nonsense approach and tend to be very organized in both their personal and professional lives. They admire loyalty and truth in their colleagues and expect the same from their family. If this is your birth date, you will do almost anything to ensure that a romantic relationship is permanent but will not overlook infidelity. Because of your great physical and intellectual energy, you benefit from the Chinese exercise known as Qigong, which can help to control your emotional highs and lows.

AFFIRMATION: The Moon helps me to maintain a healthy perspective.

PLANETS: Moon and Pluto

KEYWORDS: Practical, determined, intellectual

1 NOVEMBER

Natives of 1 November are driven by the influence of Mars in their sign and so are full of boundless energy. They are passionate and crave activities that get them truly involved. They become absorbed in their careers, and to be completely satisfied they need to feel they are in control. November Scorpios tend to be more intense than their October siblings, and their passion for adventure drives them to try new and exciting things. If you were born on this day, you generate animal magnetism and have no problem meeting partners. However, you are not easy to tie down to a permanent relationship, often demanding more from a relationship than is possible.

AFFIRMATION: Mars helps me draw strength from my experiences.

PLANETS: Mars and Pluto

KEYWORDS: Dynamic, adventurous, magnetic

2 NOVEMBER

If you were born on 2 November, music plays an important role in your life. You may have a unique talent that showed itself at a very young age. Sometimes stubborn and emotional, those born on this day often appear quiet and introspective until something upsets their equilibrium. When something goes wrong they tend to over-dramatize the situation. They are very intuitive and their instincts usually prove to be right. If this is your birthday, you are very loyal to your friends and family and expect the same in return. Although very passionate, you show intense jealousy which can prove to be your downfall when it comes to finding a permanent relationship. The physical exertion of sports can help to soothe unnecessary anger and tension.

AFFIRMATION: Venus teaches me to be more trusting.

PLANETS: Venus and Pluto

KEYWORDS: Gifted, perceptive, passionate

3 NOVEMBER

With an innate ability to sense exactly what is going on around them, these individuals can usually make the best of any situation with their quick wit and sense of humour. They love to shock by making outrageous statements and are not scared to show that they are unique. Relationships are usually passionate and challenging and they demand loyalty at all times. To be completely happy with a loved one, 3 November people need to feel truly contented with themselves, which is not easy with their sensitive natures. If this is your birth date, you are very inventive and find it difficult to be tied to a desk, so a job that allows you freedom to stretch your abilities is essential. You can be a skilled investigator and love having a mystery to solve.

AFFIRMATION: Mercury helps me appreciate my own abilities.

PLANETS: Mercury and Pluto

KEYWORDS: Ingenious, ardent, innovative

4 NOVEMBER

Versatile and creative, those born on this day can show others how to succeed. However, beneath their cool exterior is a deep intensity which can get out of control. They search for meaningful relationships but are often disappointed on the journey. They are not interested in one-night stands – they want a passionate, committed partner for life.

If you are a 4 November native, you have a clever way with words and are likely to choose a career that showcases this talent as well as giving your outgoing personality a chance to shine. Although you are aware of your limitations, you will never stop dreaming what others might consider to be the 'impossible dream'.

AFFIRMATION: The Moon teaches me to let my feelings out.

PLANETS: Moon and Pluto

KEYWORDS: Talented, intense, demonstrative

5 NOVEMBER

Natives of 5 November have an aptitude for the written word and are never happier than when they are writing a masterpiece or have their heads buried in a book. They do not conform to established practices and tend to live life according to their own unique standards. Making friends comes easily to these individuals, but they do not like it if people probe too deeply, preferring to remain at a comfortable distance. Repressing their feelings is a downside to their nature, so if you were born on this day, try to let them out. Romantic liaisons can be exciting and passionate as long as your partner allows you to be who you want to be. Although not driven by conventional career success, you believe in living up to your potential.

AFFIRMATION: The Sun teaches me not to lose my patience.

PLANETS: Sun and Pluto

KEYWORDS: Eloquent, artistic, realistic

6 NOVEMBER

People born on this day have a charisma that sets them apart from everyone else. They have an inquisitive mind and are constantly searching for the key to life's secrets. They are always ready to lend a helping hand, but would expect colleagues to reciprocate if the occasion arose. They have executive qualities and recognize the value of teamwork, and tend to be persuasive rather than pushy in motivating people. Be cautious though, the 6 November native can have a sharp tongue. If this is your birthday, you are both romantic and passionate and will continue to search for your dream partner, overcoming heartache on the way. A day of pampering at a spa can help soothe away life's irritating little problems.

AFFIRMATION: Mercury teaches me to think before I speak.

PLANETS: Mercury and Pluto

KEYWORDS: Charming, curious, organized

7 NOVEMBER

There are not many people who have as much love to give as the 7 November native. They are full of compassion and take friendship seriously. Being a friend and a mentor comes as second nature to them. They do not commit themselves lightly and have a powerful sense of their mission in life. They have a positive attitude and rely on meditation to keep themselves in balance. They are totally loyal to their family and will put them first above all else. If you were born on this day you tend to steer towards jobs that involve helping others, dedicating most of your life to doing good. You become very sensitive if you feel an injustice has been done and, on a personal level, you hate to feel misunderstood.

AFFIRMATION: Venus can help me to focus my passion in the right direction.

PLANETS: Venus and Pluto

KEYWORDS: Caring, committed, attentive

8 NOVEMBER

The 8 November person does not act impulsively; they like to work a problem out logically before taking action. They can be set in their ways and this can make them difficult to live with, but if you can get past the secretive side of their nature you will find an extremely sensual and romantic spirit. If this is your birthday, you tend to do things in your own way and are better suited to self-employment as you find it difficult to conform to someone else's regime. You are more willing to dish out advice than take it. Persistence and hard work are your finest traits and, if channelled in the right direction, can prove to be very fruitful. A trip to the opera is your idea of the perfect night out.

AFFIRMATION: Pluto knows how to bring things that are hidden out into the light.

PLANETS: Pluto and Pluto

KEYWORDS: Rational, determined, deep

9 NOVEMBER

The 9 November native can be described as a 'Jack of all trades, master of none'. With their adventurous spirits they flit from one situation to another, absorbing a lot of diverse information but rarely using it to their best advantage. If this is your birth date, you live life on your own terms, learning from your mistakes on the way, never quite satisfying your profound curiosity. In relationships you tend to make all the moves and are constantly searching for true love. If you can manage to stand still for long enough, you make a great partner and will do everything you can to make a relationship last. You tend to change career several times, eager to expand your horizons and take in life's enriching experiences.

AFFIRMATION: Jupiter helps me see the reality in a situation.

PLANETS: Jupiter and Pluto

KEYWORDS: Inquisitive, intuitive, imaginative

10 NOVEMBER

The hardest thing for a 10 November person to do is to remain focused, as they have so many different interests that they are easily distracted from their original goals. Their enthusiasm is strong, but they get bored quite quickly. A partner who can keep their feet on the ground is a great asset. Romantic love is probably the most profound experience these individuals will have and they will settle for nothing less than their ultimate soulmate. If you are a 10 November native, you have a profound interest in philosophy and science and need to be involved in work that challenges you intellectually. You are extremely generous and occasionally spend money foolishly, so you need to think carefully before going out on a shopping spree.

AFFIRMATION: Saturn teaches me to face my fears.

PLANETS: Saturn and Pluto

KEYWORDS: Well-rounded, romantic, benevolent

11 NOVEMBER

The 11 November native might raise a few eyebrows along the way, but they were born to lead and quickly earn the respect of their colleagues. If this is your birth date, you have a blend of sensitivity and integrity which gives you an almost magnetic quality, attracting many friends as you go about your daily life. You are creative and have mastered the art of good storytelling, able to keep your audience captivated from start to finish. When you fall in love you tend to give your whole self and, while this can produce an amazing union with the right person, it can also lead to complications of its own. As money has no strong hold on you, you often struggle to choose a career.

AFFIRMATION: Uranus teaches me to be an original thinker.

PLANETS: Uranus and Pluto

KEYWORDS: Commanding, perceptive, loving

12 NOVEMBER

The determination of the 12 November native is so overpowering that it can sometimes lead them down the wrong path. However, if it is channelled in the right direction they can achieve anything they set their heart on. With a keen eye for style and design, working in the fashion business uses this natural talent, although they prefer to work in the background than in the public eye. If this is your birth date, you are capable of arousing strong feelings, some good and some bad, and you have problems with placing trust in others. You sometimes have difficulty in showing emotion, but if you meet the right person you can be a loving and tactile partner.

AFFIRMATION: Neptune helps me deal with inner issues.

PLANETS: Neptune and Pluto

KEYWORDS: Purposeful, creative, influential

13 NOVEMBER

If you were born on this day you are wise beyond your years. Your personality is split down the middle – on one hand you are strong and determined, but on the other you are rather emotional and sensitive soul. Inclined to daydream rather than take action, success can sometimes elude you, so learning to stay focused is very important. Exercise and meditation can help you channel your energies in the right direction. You have a tendency to choose partners who come from a completely different background, so getting the balance right can be a struggle. Be careful that you are not lured into a career that leaves you feeling unsettled; make sure it involves using your astute mathematical brain.

AFFIRMATION: The Moon gives me strength, beauty, grace and the power to create.

PLANETS: Moon and Pluto

KEYWORDS: Discerning, curious, analytical

14 NOVEMBER

Natives of 14 November find it difficult to maintain equilibrium and need stability in their lives. Because of their perceptiveness they are good at giving advice, but when it comes to romance they need to seek the advice of others. They are highly passionate and tend to have rather dramatic love affairs which often end in heartbreak. If this is your birthday, you should pursue a career that allows you to be inventive. Being tied down to regular office hours leaves you feeling restrained. You are so gifted you can find fulfilment in any form of employment, but often find you are most comfortable in an academic situation. You feel a close kinship with nature, so you should learn to switch off by spending as much time as possible outdoors.

AFFIRMATION: The Sun helps me recognize the strength within myself.

PLANETS: Sun and Pluto

KEYWORDS: Insightful, brilliant, inventive

15 NOVEMBER

People born on this day are fun-loving and like to be the centre of attention, but like their fellow Scorpios, they have a restless side to their nature. They are very astute and talented and can usually choose from a variety of careers, although many gravitate towards fashion, art or film. Relationships can be a little challenging as they often choose opposites in character, but they are sensual and loving and can make rewarding partners. If you are a 15 November native, you tend to fall in love at first sight. You are not very materialistic and would rather be free than feel bogged down with possessions. Time spent in a quiet place in the countryside brings out the best in you.

AFFIRMATION: Mercury teaches me to take a rest from time to time.

PLANETS: Mercury and Pluto

KEYWORDS: Convivial, artistic, sensual

16 NOVEMBER

Do you think that life is meant to be lived to the full or not at all? Then the chances are you were born on 16 November. You have so much energy and self-confidence that you generally excel at whatever task you undertake. Although you can be rather demanding of others, you would never dream of asking anyone to do something you would not attempt yourself. You can become so totally focused that you work until you drop, so you can be your own worst enemy, and need to remember to allow yourself some time to relax. You have an immense sense of pride. You find it hard to forgive and, once wronged, can simmer for a long time.

AFFIRMATION: Venus helps me reveal myself to those closest to me.

PLANETS: Venus and Pluto

KEYWORDS: Hard-working, enthusiastic, attentive

17 NOVEMBER

Those born on 17 November have a natural talent for communication but they are by no means an open book. They tend to get noticed wherever they go because they seem to have such vibrant personalities, but underneath this exterior is the less outgoing personality of most Scorpios. If you were born on this day your life would make an excellent book, as you tend to attract change and even crisis, but you have the strength of character to overcome even the biggest obstacles. You carry yourself with great personal dignity and make very close friends and companions. You are desperate to have your love reciprocated and need to find your soulmate in order to be truly happy.

AFFIRMATION: Pluto allows me to destroy the old and build the new.

PLANETS: Pluto and Pluto

KEYWORDS: Animated, resilient, committed

18 NOVEMBER

People born on this day are very perceptive and quickly pick up on the atmosphere surrounding them. They have a fiery temperament and it is nearly always impossible to win an argument against them, but they do make interesting opponents. Because of this trait, these individuals sometimes struggle to make close friends and they tend to look for someone who has a similar temperament. If this is your birth date, you are so physical that desk jobs do not suit you, so you need to find a career that allows you freedom and a way of releasing some of your pent-up energy. You are very goal-oriented and will endure much hardship to reach your target. A fast game of squash or tennis can help use up some of that spare energy.

AFFIRMATION: Jupiter teaches me not to tread on other people's toes.

PLANETS: Jupiter and Pluto

KEYWORDS: Energetic, insightful, irrepressible

19 NOVEMBER

Scorpios born on this day do not tend to go with the flow. They stand out from a crowd, not in a flashy or ostentatious way, but because of their tremendous strength of character. As natural humanitarians, they like to feel that they are helping others, and they need to take a leading role in order to feel satisfied. If this is your birthday, you tend to guard your emotions and are therefore cautious about letting people get too close to you – whether they are just a friend or a lover. You are, however, never short of admirers as you exude charm. You need to realize that achievements are much better when shared between friends.

AFFIRMATION: Saturn teaches me to share with others.

PLANETS: Saturn and Pluto

KEYWORDS: Distinguished, fashionable, benevolent

20 NOVEMBER

Natives of 20 November let very little get in their way and tend to seek others' approval by striving towards career success. They are family oriented and make wonderful partners as long as they are allowed a certain amount of freedom. If this is your birth date you are a loyal and totally devoted partner. You tend to live in one place for a long time because you loathe change and upheaval. When choosing a career you will gravitate towards a position that is related to environmental concerns, and will fight tirelessly to help make the world a better place. Any activity that involves spending time with your family will keep you feeling contented.

AFFIRMATION: Venus helps me listen to my heart.

PLANETS: Venus and Pluto

KEYWORDS: Goal-oriented, dependable, loving

21 NOVEMBER

Although 21 November people are prepared to graft until the job is done, they want to have fun while doing it. They have a unique combination of passion and playfulness which means they light up a room as soon as they enter it. They are determined to experience life on all levels but need to be careful not to act impulsively as this can get them into trouble. If you were born on this day you believe in your own abilities and you often attempt projects that would intimidate

others. Your tenacity means you usually succeed. A sunny individual, you prefer to be married than have numerous flings and, once settled, you make a wonderful partner and parent, making sure everyone has a good time.

AFFIRMATION: Mercury helps me to use my depth of wisdom wisely.

PLANETS: Mercury and Pluto

KEYWORDS: Fun-loving, adventurous, dependable

22 NOVEMBER

The 22 November native will put themselves on the line for the people they love and the causes they value and this endears them to everyone they meet. They are exceptionally active and hate to feel caged in, so anyone embarking on a relationship with these individuals will need to remember they require a lot of freedom. In return they will give a lot of love and passion. If you were born on this day, you love to travel and friends made overseas will remain lifelong buddies. Health is important to you. You constantly watch your diet and weight and like to participate in sports on a regular basis. You love to read and appreciate the value of learning, so a career that gives you the chance to pass this passion on to others is important to you.

AFFIRMATION: The Moon helps me to live with more integrity.

PLANETS: Moon and Pluto

KEYWORDS: Supportive, energetic, daring

Sagittarius
23 November–21 December

23 NOVEMBER

The 23 November native enjoys having freedom of thought and seeks diversity in everyday experiences. They have a keen intellect and use travel to further their knowledge of the world. Their multiple interests encourage them to branch out in many directions, but they need to be careful not to overtax themselves and put their health at risk. If this is your birth date, you can be impulsive, but this can be used to your advantage as it gives you the courage to do things you wouldn't normally do. You love the passion attached to new romances, but are wary about settling down. Sports such as golf, tennis or squash can help relieve tension and build self-esteem.

AFFIRMATION: The Sun helps me make the most of my vast knowledge.

PLANETS: Sun and Jupiter

KEYWORDS: Inquisitive, knowledgeable, free-spirited

24 NOVEMBER

Natives of 24 November have strong opinions about everything and it is important for them to be able to debate and discuss their ideas. People born on this day make great teachers as they love to share their vast knowledge with others. They have magnetic personalities which attract others to them like moths to a flame. They are active, alert and charming and have the ability to make people feel young in their company. If you were born on this day, you are both emotionally and spiritually strong and show compassion to loved ones. You are also generous with your time and do not shy away from commitment. Your ability to laugh is one of your greatest traits. A perfect night out is a trip to the theatre or a comedy club.

AFFIRMATION: Mercury offers me freedom of thought.

PLANETS: Mercury and Jupiter

KEYWORDS: Altruistic, funny, seductive

25 NOVEMBER

People born on 25 November ooze charm. They are easy to be with and extremely popular because of their fun-loving ways. Their adventurous natures mean they like to travel and to form friendships all over the world, and their social calendar is always full. To bond totally with a partner they will need to share their love of play, travel and discussing world cultures and they need to be prepared for an active social life as this person does not like to sit still for too long. If you are a 25 November native, you tend to gravitate towards vocations that allow you to come into contact with people, and your caring side makes you an excellent counsellor. Try relaxing by cooking a gourmet dinner for your loved one.

AFFIRMATION: Venus opens doors and allows me to get to know people.

PLANETS: Venus and Jupiter

KEYWORDS: Alluring, communicative, active

26 NOVEMBER

People born on this day are not afraid to take a gamble as they strive to shape their destiny. Emotionally they have highs and lows – but until you get to know them well this may not be obvious. They tend to be practical and committed in romantic affairs and are not happy playing the field. Unlike most of their Sagittarian neighbours they are likely to actively seek the chance to settle down and start a family. If this is your birth date you love to achieve and need to find a career in which you are allowed and even encouraged to take risks. You appreciate the need for regular exercise to stay healthy and happy. Practising yoga can help you relax.

AFFIRMATION: Pluto gives me the strength to regenerate my body and soul.

PLANETS: Pluto and Jupiter

KEYWORDS: Energetic, hard-working, committed

27 NOVEMBER

If you were born on this day you earn respect from your friends and colleagues because of your ability to come up with new ideas. Although you are warm and friendly, you still have the adventurous and independent streak of your Sagittarian neighbours, and this can sometimes make you hard to read. You like to be the centre of attention and, with your clever way with words, you tend to head for jobs in which you are in charge. You are a notorious practical joker which often gets you in trouble, but you can bring out the best in people when you are on top form. Just remember to balance work, play and down-time to avoid exhaustion – your friends will still be there tomorrow.

AFFIRMATION: Jupiter helps me fully appreciate new experiences.

PLANETS: Jupiter and Jupiter

KEYWORDS: Diligent, unconstrained, candid

28 NOVEMBER

It has often been said that a person born on 28 November can be their own best friend or their worst enemy. They will do almost anything to seek attention and their infectious smile usually means they have their audience's full concentration. Although they struggle with mood swings, these people love to have fun and make compassionate partners. Because they can sometimes struggle to understand themselves, 28 November natives often rely on friends and partners to help them through difficult times. If this is your birthday you can be rather erratic and sometimes make unusual career choices. You have a close affiliation with animals so working at an animal rescue centre or zoo avoids the boredom of a regular nine-to-five job.

AFFIRMATION: Saturn teaches me to tread carefully and become more tolerant.

PLANETS: Saturn and Jupiter

KEYWORDS: Emotional, adventurous, hard-working

29 NOVEMBER

Natives of 29 November get most satisfaction from the love of others. They are charismatic, warm and intuitive and love to make people laugh – which means they usually have a large circle of friends. They have a strong sense of responsibility which can make them worry about the future, so partners need to remain upbeat. They like to be kept informed and learning new things is one of their life's main objectives. If you were born on this day you tend to be vulnerable when it comes to romance, because your own insecurities often lead to mistrust. Self-doubt can also inhibit your ability to set firm goals. Learn to trust in yourself and your own decisions and your life will take a turn for the better: meditation can help in this.

AFFIRMATION: Uranus teaches me that no one has all the answers.

PLANETS: Uranus and Jupiter

KEYWORDS: Articulate, informative, responsible

30 NOVEMBER

If heads turn whenever you walk into a room, then the chances are you were born on 30 November. You are easy to be with and attract people wherever you go. You live life flamboyantly and yet beneath the sharp wit and enormous personality, you enjoy your own company. Because you are so popular, romantic partners may find it hard to share you with others, so mutual respect is essential for a harmonious relationship. Shrewd and determined, you have a flair for journalism as this allows you to express yourself in words rather than actions. You particularly enjoy difficult assignments overseas. A quiz night allows you to use your vast general knowledge and helps you to relax.

AFFIRMATION: Mercury helps me expand my mental horizons.

PLANETS: Mercury and Jupiter

KEYWORDS: Talented, eyecatching, perceptive

1 DECEMBER

An adventurous spirit and sunny personality are characteristics of the native of 1 December. They crave variety and their artistic streak means they often become artists or designers so that they are constantly doing something different. Sometimes they lose the ability to focus so it is important for them to work on their self-discipline to feel really happy. If this is your birthday you use your bubbly personality to hide inner insecurities and your love life can be turbulent. Money does not seem to have an important bearing on your life and it tends to be a case of 'easy come, easy go'. Try to find money-making ways to harness your skills and bring out the best in your character.

AFFIRMATION: Mars brings out the sense of adventure in me.

PLANETS: Mars and Jupiter

KEYWORDS: Daring, sensitive, artistic

2 DECEMBER

People born on 2 December can be described as mysterious. They are private individuals and like to stay out of the limelight. Like their neighbours from 1 December, they tend to channel their energy towards the arts, but they will stay firmly backstage wherever possible. They may choose a partner unwisely, but, if the union is right, they will love on a grand scale. If this is your birthday, your sincerity is your greatest strength. As a parent you tend to take a less assertive role, allowing your partner to lead in matters of discipline while encouraging your children to explore their creative flair. Meditation and exercise help to dispel any negative feelings and help you to focus on your goals.

AFFIRMATION: Venus can help me find harmony in my relationships.

PLANETS: Venus and Jupiter

KEYWORDS: Enigmatic, inspired, nurturing

3 DECEMBER

Natives of 3 December know how to stand up for themselves and are willing to enter into fervent debate to make their point. They tend to be restless due to their over-inquisitive nature, and yet they are also dependable and value permanence. They are adventurous lovers, although they sometimes lose interest once the chase is over, so they will need a partner who can stimulate their sharp mind and allow them the freedom they crave. If you were born on this day you are never short of friends and, although you are unlikely to explore the quieter side of your nature, you make a great companion and love to party. With your love of communication, you would make an excellent writer or journalist.

AFFIRMATION: Mercury can help satisfy my thirst for knowledge.

PLANETS: Mercury and Jupiter

KEYWORDS: Self-assured, dependable, fun-loving

4 DECEMBER

Are you attracted to a challenge? Do you like taking risks? Do you stand by your beliefs? If you answered yes to all of these questions then the chances are you are a 4 December native. You are an enthusiastic person who is afraid of very little in life, and you take the same attitude in love. You tend to dive in head first and pay for the consequences of your passionate nature later on. You are a revolutionary trendsetter and although you can be a little difficult at times, people tend to follow your example. You have holistic beliefs and interests, tending to draw your strengths from the world around you and your own experiences, rather than from established institutions.

AFFIRMATION: The Moon helps bring me back down to Earth.

PLANETS: Moon and Jupiter

KEYWORDS: Open-hearted, impulsive, eccentric

5 DECEMBER

The 5 December native is a true visionary with the necessary skills to back it up. If you want a job done properly then ask a 5 December person, as they are very resourceful and quick to respond. Like their neighbours, people born on this day are freedom-loving. They tend to fall in love very easily but beware, they can change their feelings at a moment's notice. If this is your birthday your sociable and outgoing nature tends to draw people to you, and your incredible verbal skills often guide you in your choice of career. You are attracted to science and physics, and have the potential to be very inventive. You probably always dream the impossible dream, but try to set yourself achievable goals.

AFFIRMATION: The Sun stops me from getting bogged down by emotional complexities.

PLANETS: Sun and Jupiter

KEYWORDS: Articulate, footloose, ingenious

6 DECEMBER

Their thirst for knowledge and constant search for the truth makes 6 December natives restless individuals. Their brains are like sponges, absorbing every piece of new information they can glean. To stay interested in a relationship they need constant intellectual stimulation.

Should they be lucky enough to find their equals, these individuals will quite happily make a lifelong commitment. If this is your birthday you have a genuine love for and understanding of people. You tend to put your points of view over in a quiet, yet persuasive manner. By keeping your body in good condition you are able to achieve your goals on many levels. A brisk walk in the hills can be extremely invigorating.

AFFIRMATION: Mercury helps me find a connection between dreams and reality.

PLANETS: Mercury and Jupiter

KEYWORDS: Intellectual, harmonious, understanding

7 DECEMBER

Just a little mischievous, the person born on this day doesn't know what it is to grow old. They are great thinkers, and their ability to learn is second to none. They make wonderful teachers as they love to share their knowledge with others and will take great care to make sure that no one gets left behind. Romance is a serious business for these individuals, and they tend to be drawn to someone who can teach them life's important lessons. With a fascination for the stars, they may gravitate towards astrology to satisfy their psychic abilities. They can be excellent parents as they understand the needs of youngsters and usually form a relationship that remains strong into adulthood.

AFFIRMATION: Venus helps me search for love beyond the city walls.

PLANETS: Venus and Jupiter

KEYWORDS: Impish, informative, spiritual

8 DECEMBER

Natives of 8 December can be a little headstrong. They are deep thinkers who stand up for what they believe in and can often be found at the head of a demonstrating crowd. They tend to act impulsively and sometimes regret an action later on, but Pluto is there to help them learn some vital lessons. If you were born on this day you fall in love easily, but long-term commitment can be a problem. With your sharp brain and skilled hands you might make a great doctor or surgeon. You are very generous and have a wide circle of friends, but beware that they may be a bit confused by your constant personality changes and mood swings. Try to make more effort to explain your actions.

AFFIRMATION: Pluto helps me ride the crest of shifting waves.

PLANETS: Pluto and Jupiter

KEYWORDS: Idealistic, spontaneous, skilled

9 DECEMBER

Although 9 December natives have dreams and aspirations, they may not pursue them with quite the same vigour as their neighbours. They know how to have a good time and if they are lucky enough to be successful that is an added bonus. They are the envy of their friends because they always seem to be having fun, but underneath is a sensitive, soft-hearted person hiding away. If you were born on this day you have a reputation for being fickle and may not settle down until much later in life. A partner with the ability to make you laugh has the best chance of capturing your heart. You are very confident and talkative with a good sense of humour. Watching a funny film is the best form of medicine for anyone born on this day.

AFFIRMATION: Jupiter helps me stay calm.

PLANETS: Jupiter and Jupiter

KEYWORDS: Optimistic, resilient, fun-loving

10 DECEMBER

People born on this day can handle most situations thrown at them, with the exception of emotional crises. Although they may appear invincible, they have a fear of being hurt and therefore build an invisible barrier around themselves. They have sunny dispositions, good humour and an enthusiasm that rubs off on those closest to them. However, if anyone dares get too close, they will back away rapidly. If you were born on this day you are capable of deep love as long as your partner is not too demanding. You love to solve problems and are prepared to work hard, so any job that uses your analytical brain will suit you down to the ground. Use jogging to blow away some of the cobwebs of daily routine.

AFFIRMATION: Saturn helps me banish negative thoughts.

PLANETS: Saturn and Jupiter

KEYWORDS: Cheerful, energetic, logical

11 DECEMBER

Those born on this day want to make a difference in the world and often enter politics for that very reason. They are highly ambitious and sometimes appear intense, working tirelessly until they get the job done, especially if the problem concerns the environment. They are usually the centre of attention as people are attracted to them for their huge amount of confidence. If this is your birth date, you treasure your freedom but also crave security, so these factors can sometimes lead to conflict in your life. If you are able to really connect with someone, you are capable of a loving and lasting relationship, and you will probably amaze yourself with the power of your commitment.

AFFIRMATION: Uranus helps me keep abreast of the latest discoveries.

PLANETS: Uranus and Jupiter

KEYWORDS: Zealous, conscientious, self-assured

12 DECEMBER

Those born on 12 December long for experiences that will expand their horizons. They love to travel, are fascinated by philosophy and sometimes use religion as a basis for their lives. They tend to have a dual personality – on the one hand they are tolerant, on the other hand they can be blinded by their own ideals. Despite their free spirits, these individuals are capable of deep love and like to shower their friends and partners with gifts. If this is your birthday, you have a strong competitive spirit that shows in all areas of your life. You love words, have a witty sense of humour and make a great dinner guest.

AFFIRMATION: Neptune gives me the ability to overcome challenges.

PLANETS: Neptune and Jupiter

KEYWORDS: Adventurous, free-spirited, garrulous

13 DECEMBER

Natives of 13 December are naturally athletic and love to be outdoors. If you were born on this day, you tend to choose a career that is physically demanding as you find a regular desk job too claustrophobic. You will do anything to escape routine, and if things get really tough you won't be seen for dust. If you are given the freedom you yearn for, you are a happy-go-lucky individual who is great fun to be around. When it comes to relationships you tend to be a little impatient, not taking the time to really get to know someone. This leaves you vulnerable to being hurt. You are highly driven and, as long as you remain active, the restless side of your nature will stay under control.

AFFIRMATION: The Moon teaches me to think before I act.

PLANETS: Moon and Jupiter

KEYWORDS: Energetic, competitive, liberated

14 DECEMBER

People born on 14 December require their own space and their love of adventure and travel means they find it hard to stay in one place. Constantly on the move, it is difficult for them to find love unless they meet their equal – someone who sees each day as a new adventure. They also need intellectual stimulation and spend any leisure time with their nose buried in books. If this is your birthday, you are self-confident, positive and enthusiastic. You are not known for your diplomacy, and are prone to using harsh words when you are in an argumentative mood. Office jobs are not for you, so working for an airline or travel company can seem particularly attractive. To relax, horse riding is ideal as you have a natural affinity with animals.

AFFIRMATION: The Sun will help me keep my temper under control.

PLANETS: Sun and Jupiter

KEYWORDS: Explorative, studious, uninhibited

15 DECEMBER

Those born on this day are witty and versatile. They become bored easily and so need new challenges to satisfy their restlessness. They are truly empathetic and if you ever need a helping hand these individuals will be there for you. The emotional side of their character is a little more complex; romance can be complicated but that doesn't stop them from trying to make it work. If this is your birthday you are a good salesperson and are brilliant at telling stories, so a career in writing might help you to put your thoughts down in black and white. It is important to remember not to be discouraged by disappointments – treat them as a lesson well learned and move on.

AFFIRMATION: Mercury teaches me to focus my mind.

PLANETS: Mercury and Jupiter

KEYWORDS: Adaptable, jocular, quick-thinking

16 DECEMBER

People born on this day are affectionate, friendly and demonstrative. However, they do not like to plan ahead and tend to live from day to day, meeting each new challenge as and when it arises. Their intuition usually means they make a success of whatever they do, and their power of observation is superb, which means they make natural psychologists. If you were born on this day you can be difficult to live with because your strong sense of independence means you refuse to accept conventional codes of behaviour. You prefer to let a relationship build over time rather than rush into anything permanent, but you will make a lifelong commitment if everything seems to be going in your favour.

AFFIRMATION: Venus teaches me to express myself through love.

PLANETS: Venus and Jupiter

KEYWORDS: Warm-hearted, amicable, outgoing

17 DECEMBER

If you were born on this day you are a natural leader. Your unique insight, wisdom and organizational skills mean that people from all walks of life turn to you for advice. You greatly admire anyone who has a strong work ethic and, if you are the boss, expect the best from your employees. Although usually disciplined, you occasionally like to break the rules, which shows that your armour can be penetrated. You prefer to be part of a couple and you will do your utmost to keep romance alive. You love to succeed, and success can cure any doubts you have about your own abilities. Regular exercise is essential to keep you in tip-top condition.

AFFIRMATION: Pluto helps me examine the depths of my beliefs.

PLANETS: Pluto and Jupiter

KEYWORDS: Commanding, wise, romantic

18 DECEMBER

Anyone born on 18 December is a go-getter by nature, but in the nicest possible sense. They are open and generous and have an amazing sense of humour, which makes them very popular. They have many close friends to whom they show a great amount of loyalty and, because they hate to be alone, are usually surrounded by people. If this is your birthday you are attracted to success, and hard work comes naturally to you. You are a sentimental person who works hard in relationships, trying constantly to balance your commitment with the freedom you so enjoy. You like to maintain a good standard of living but you need to be careful not to push yourself in too many directions at once. Remember that moderation is key.

AFFIRMATION: Jupiter helps me find contentment and joy.

PLANETS: Jupiter and Jupiter

KEYWORDS: Dynamic, appreciative, soft-hearted

19 DECEMBER

Powerfully magnetic characters, 19 December natives lean towards drama, so directing or acting in films brings this natural talent to the fore. Very determined individuals, they will put their heart and soul into whatever they do and their fearlessness will take them to the top of whichever career path they choose. They tend to have a reputation for being great lovers, but they need to make compromises if they want a long-term relationship. If you were born on this day you tend to gravitate towards glamorous partners because you have an acute sense of outward beauty, but this often means you walk an emotional tightrope. True love can be found if you learn to look beyond mere appearances.

AFFIRMATION: Saturn helps me stop my ambition from getting in the way.

PLANETS: Saturn and Jupiter

KEYWORDS: Charismatic, steadfast, demonstrative

20 DECEMBER

As a 20 December native you are outgoing, confident and attractive to others. However you can view love relationships as something of a challenge because you see your main priority as having a good time. You tend to be flirtatious which can lead to jealous outbursts from partners, so if you want a long-term relationship you may need to lose a little of your carefree manner. If life starts to get tough you find it hard to fight the urge to walk away, so it is important that you learn to face up to your responsibilities. With a desire to remain forever young, you tend to watch your diet carefully, but the odd splurge on something delicious can do wonders to lift your spirits. Treat yourself occasionally.

AFFIRMATION: Venus guides me in my relationships.

PLANETS: Venus and Jupiter

KEYWORDS: Sociable, enticing, youthful

21 DECEMBER

There is no one more capable of turning dreams into reality than the person born on this day. When an idea grabs them they will go all out to make it materialize and luck is usually on their side. They love to be the centre of attention and their charisma is clear for all to see. Acting or teaching are great choices of career, as 21 December natives have incredible memories and a wonderful ability to inspire others. If you were born on this day you shy away from romantic involvement, but if you do decide to commit you make a wonderfully honest and trustworthy partner. You are fiercely motivated and this is mirrored in your fitness regime, so you need to be careful that this side of your character does not make you become fanatical.

AFFIRMATION: Mercury values mental freedom.

PLANETS: Mercury and Jupiter

KEYWORDS: Ambitious, charismatic, ingenuous

Capricorn
22 December–20 January

22 DECEMBER

Beneath that carefully constructed mask of indifference, the native of 22 December is both giving and supportive, sometimes to the point of self-sacrifice. They make wonderful counsellors, and great friends because they always take the time to listen. Humanitarian work abroad is a sure way to express this caring side of their natures. However, when it comes to personal relationships they are emotionally vulnerable and they find it difficult to let others see this side of them. If you were born on this day you are very intelligent but you tend to concentrate on your limitations rather than your qualities. You are prone to working too hard, so take extra care not to neglect family life.

AFFIRMATION: The Moon helps me keep my feet on solid ground.

PLANETS: Moon and Saturn

KEYWORDS: Benevolent, discerning, hard-working

23 DECEMBER

Those born on this day exude an air of authority. They sometimes use their status and power for personal gain, but in general they are admired for their achievements. Natives of 23 December are born with a definite sense of purpose and they make the most of their creative talents to reach the top. Once in a position of authority they tend to relax and radiate a warmth that brings out the best in those around them. Because of their ability to motivate others, they make good mentors or even teachers, keeping their students captivated with their wit and intelligence. If you are a 23 December native, you value stability in relationships and will not separate unless there is no alternative. Allow your creativity to come to the fore by discovering a new craft or hobby.

AFFIRMATION: The Sun reminds me of my purpose in life.

PLANETS: Sun and Saturn

KEYWORDS: Steadfast, commanding, funny

24 DECEMBER

If you are a 24 December native you tend to hide your emotions and so others find you difficult to read. If you find someone willing to get to know you properly, you will be an extremely caring and patient partner. Appearance is important to you, and this often involves a strict diet and exercise routine, but you need to remember that people love you for who you are and not how you look. You sometimes find it hard to differentiate between a simple fascination and genuine love, so learn to tell one from the other in order to avoid breaking hearts. You have a great respect for history and anything that has stood the test of time, and so taking part in an archaeological dig is a great way for you to unwind.

AFFIRMATION: Mercury gives me the patience to see a project through to the end.

PLANETS: Mercury and Saturn

KEYWORDS: Self-disciplined, congenial, inquisitive

25 DECEMBER

Highly intuitive and yet grounded, if you were born on this day, you could be described as 'psychic' and 'earthy'. You have strong powers of perception but you usually prefer to keep your insights to yourself, fearing that you may not be taken seriously. Although you take a while to open up to people, once settled you reveal an enduring sensuality that keeps your relationships strong. In turbulent times you will often try to help others as it helps put your problems into perspective. Your old-fashioned side gives you a desire to settle down. Time spent gardening helps you to reconnect with nature.

AFFIRMATION: Venus teaches me maturity.

PLANETS: Venus and Saturn

KEYWORDS: Eccentric, sensual, insightful

26 DECEMBER

If you were born on this day you are extremely determined and ambitious and others look up to you. Like many of your fellow Capricorns you exude an air of respectability and authority. People often turn to you for practical advice, and for some you embody a kind of mother or father figure. The downside of your character is that you are also restless and competitive. If you don't have something definite to focus on you will seek excitement and adventure in any form, and this can mean that you stray into dangerous territory. You love to take part in high impact sports. Racket sports like squash or tennis can relieve stress and help to keep you on the straight and narrow.

AFFIRMATION: Pluto shows me the light at the end of the tunnel.

PLANETS: Pluto and Saturn

KEYWORDS: Wise, practical, ambitious

27 DECEMBER

If you were born on this day you have a heart of gold. You truly value family and friends and always have their best interests at heart. You are benevolent and are quite happy to make personal sacrifices if it will help those who you perceive are in need. In your working life you can be quite demanding as you tend to have a perfectionist streak, sometimes appearing intolerant of others' weaknesses. You are practical and your authoritarian nature means you are adept at handling other people. You make an excellent partner although you tend to be more sexually motivated than romantic. However, your loyalty and willingness to help at all times makes up for this. Days out with the family bring 27 December natives fulfilment.

AFFIRMATION: Jupiter shows me how to act with integrity.

PLANETS: Jupiter and Saturn

KEYWORDS: Dependable, charitable, disciplined

28 DECEMBER

Natives of 28 December have an intriguing and charming way of expressing themselves. They have an inquisitive nature and like to find out about what makes people tick. They make good counsellors as they seem to have an intuitive understanding of what makes relationships work. They do have a dominating side but they are basically peace-loving and make very considerate partners. If you were born on 28 December, you have brilliant people skills and are good at making people feel relaxed in your company. You take pride in everything you do, even in the smallest tasks, and have a very optimistic outlook on life. You are probably a talented cook and find relaxation in experimenting with new recipes.

AFFIRMATION: Saturn helps me find joy in accomplishment.

PLANETS: Saturn and Saturn

KEYWORDS: Beguiling, perceptive, convivial

29 DECEMBER

People born on 29 December know how to use their intellect to the full. They have perfect people skills which makes them popular party guests, taking a genuine interest in others. They are drawn to close relationships and are constantly on the lookout for their ideal partner. Unlike the majority of Capricorns, people born on this day enjoy taking risks and travel is usually to exotic and far-flung places. They make good parents as they remember what it was like to be a child, and will often indulge their children's fantasies. If you were born on this day you need to learn that to make relationships work you must relax and not be burdened by the mistakes of the past.

AFFIRMATION: Uranus helps me understand the nature of patience.

PLANETS: Uranus and Saturn

KEYWORDS: Communicative, understanding, clever

30 DECEMBER

People who were born on this day tend to feel lost without a goal to strive for. Nervous energy seems to be their driving force and they like to live their lives on a 'work hard, play hard' schedule. To achieve complete satisfaction, the 30 December native needs to find stability in their family life and will make sacrifices to create the necessary harmony. They have great leadership qualities and with their good entrepreneurial skills they tend to do well in their own business ventures rather than working for someone else. If you were born on this day, making money is quite high on your list of priorities as you are a born provider. You have the knack of balancing both your personal and professional lives successfully. The best way for you to relax is to go to a concert.

AFFIRMATION: Mercury shows me how to listen.

PLANETS: Mercury and Saturn

KEYWORDS: Ambitious, caring, enterprising

31 DECEMBER

If you were born on this day you put organization and order at the top of your agenda. You find it impossible to settle if your daily life is in a mess and you will go out of your way to keep things on an even keel. You love to be surrounded by groups of friends, but when it comes to personal relationships you often experience a great deal of heartbreak before settling down. Many 31 December natives suffer from sleep disorders due to stress; meditation, yoga or any form of gentle exercise can have a calming effect. It is not uncommon for them to change jobs a number of times before they find their true vocation as they need to feel truly appreciated. Managerial positions offer them an ideal opportunity to use their organizational skills.

AFFIRMATION: The Moon teaches me not to be stubborn.

PLANETS: Moon and Saturn

KEYWORDS: Authoritative, enthusiastic, outgoing

1 JANUARY

Although highly independent, the person born on 1 January needs people around them to feel totally secure. They are achievers because of their enormous amount of willpower. They will not give up until the job is finished. Fear of failure can be a drawback, as they expect a lot of themselves and always strive to live up to their own high standards. Because they set the bar so high it is sometimes difficult for them to find true romance, but if they do meet the right partner they are loyal and eager to settle down. If this is your birthday, you need to be careful not to expect too much of your children as you tend to see them as a chip off the old block. Brisk walks are essential to keep you in good health as you do tend to over-indulge.

AFFIRMATION: Mars gives me the drive to succeed.

PLANETS: Mars and Saturn

KEYWORDS: Unconstrained, supportive, dynamic

2 JANUARY

Underneath the thick skin of the 2 January native is a loving, animated and happy person waiting to be released. They tend to keep their true feelings hidden because they have a fear of being judged by others, so only reveal their more sensitive sides to those closest to them. They value personal relationships highly and when the right partner comes along their caring, protective natures shine through. If this is your birth date you love the adrenalin rush that exercise provides, and you generally keep a careful eye on your diet. A financial career suits you as you have a very good head for figures. Learning to be flexible is your greatest challenge.

AFFIRMATION: Venus teaches me how to respect others.

PLANETS: Venus and Saturn

KEYWORDS: Energetic, protective, tender

3 JANUARY

People born on 3 January simply refuse to grow old. They have a wonderful, quirky sense of humour and love to be the centre of attention. Good things seem to come their way without the need to exert too much effort, but they do have problems letting go of their romantic inhibitions. If this is your birth date you are an independent person who has difficulty in expressing your true feelings, but if you let someone see behind the mask they will find a true romantic. You tend to thrive under pressure and can succeed in a variety of professional positions, from minister to lecturer. You have endless aspirations and usually achieve what you set out to do. Learning new skills will help keep your intelligent brain active.

AFFIRMATION: Mercury helps lift me to higher levels of consciousness.

PLANETS: Mercury and Saturn

KEYWORDS: Bright, humorous, ambitious

4 JANUARY

Natives of 4 January have a pioneering spirit. Humanitarian work is ideal for these people because they love to get involved and get their hands dirty. Once they have set their heart on a goal, they let very little get in their way and their determination nearly always wins through. They make caring partners as long as you are prepared to always hear the truth; they are not ones to mince their words. With their

adventurous spirits you might find they are away from home for long spells at a time. If you were born on this day, settling down might not be on the cards if you are not allowed to enjoy your freedom. You want to experience life to the full and find it hard to concentrate on the more mundane aspects of life. Writing can help you live out some of your more far-fetched dreams.

AFFIRMATION: The Moon helps me fulfil a dream.

PLANETS: Moon and Saturn

KEYWORDS: Kindhearted, daring, pioneering

5 JANUARY

These brilliant individuals always appear to be in a hurry, but they love to communicate so if you can catch them they make great companions. They are clever, imaginative and compassionate but it is important for them to find a direction in which to channel these traits. If you were born on this day, you quickly become bored so need to constantly find new ways of releasing your energy. Unable to stand in one spot for very long, you rely on exercise to keep and maintain equilibrium between your physical and intellectual selves. You strive to learn more about the world so working in a job that involves travel can be beneficial and fulfilling.

AFFIRMATION: The Sun helps me unlock my potential.

PLANETS: Sun and Saturn

KEYWORDS: Tenacious, friendly, inquisitive

6 JANUARY

Capricorns born on this day are not as inhibited as their neighbours. They are exceptionally hard-working and are only truly happy in an organizational role. They are at their best when chasing after an elusive dream and tend to be perfectionists in all that they do. They are peace-loving but do not like to be bound by conventional rules. If this is your birth date, you love having fun and are loathe to give up your independence unless the right person manages to catch your eye. You are charming and life with you will never be dull, but your partner will need to remember that you cannot be tied to their apron strings. Reading helps give you a rare chance to turn off from reality.

AFFIRMATION: Mercury helps me turn ideas into reality.

PLANETS: Mercury and Saturn

KEYWORDS: Adventurous, purposeful, captivating

7 JANUARY

Those born on 7 January possess a deep awareness and understanding, and it is important for these individuals to choose a career that allows them to use these talents. The creative worlds of fashion and architecture hold a fascination for them and they can easily get lost while putting their ideas down on paper. If you are a 7 January native, you have a sensitive, slightly vulnerable quality that endears you to others but you occasionally have problems accepting what society expects of you. You like the security of a large circle of friends but have a rather idealistic view of romance. You act on impulse and love to whisk your partner off to romantic places, but remember to find a place in your life for reality as well as fantasy.

AFFIRMATION: Venus helps me overcome disappointments in love.

PLANETS: Venus and Saturn

KEYWORDS: Appreciative, creative, motivated

8 JANUARY

People born on this day have a very strong sense of purpose, and can rise to meet most challenges. These individuals sometimes have difficulty in expressing themselves vocally, and prefer to use the written word to get across their points of view. They are creatively gifted people and yet they are full of self-doubt so need to be encouraged by friends to bring out the best in themselves. If you were born on this day you demand total loyalty and devotion from loved ones but you give a lot in return. You appreciate financial security but at the same time you are very generous with your money. Discovering exactly what you want out of life is probably your greatest challenge.

AFFIRMATION: Pluto forces me to release my hidden feelings.

PLANETS: Pluto and Saturn

KEYWORDS: Resolute, gifted, truehearted

9 JANUARY

Like many of their Capricorn neighbours, people born on this day can appear to be complicated and constantly at war with themselves. They are dependable and extremely committed to finishing whatever they start, but at times they can seem exceptionally restless and distant. They have brilliant minds and constantly strive for perfection, but they need to learn that it is not always important to have the approval of others. If you are a 9 January native you will be quite happy to settle down when you find someone who can challenge you intellectually. You will only ever open yourself emotionally to those closest to you. A fast game of squash or badminton can help satisfy the competitive side of your nature.

AFFIRMATION: Jupiter helps me make the best of a difficult situation.

PLANETS: Jupiter and Saturn

KEYWORDS: Trustworthy, intelligent, determined

10 JANUARY

People born on this day have a forthright approach to life and sometimes this can make them appear a little abrupt. They are highly intelligent, organized and deal with business matters in a direct and honest manner. Despite this slightly hard exterior, they are really friendly and gain a lot of respect and admiration from their friends and work colleagues. Their manners are impeccable and they make the perfect dinner guest with their witty remarks and charm. If you were born on this day you love anything connected to fine art, antiques or exquisite food so anyone lucky enough to capture your heart will only be treated to the best. You need to learn to have a really good laugh in order to release inner tensions.

AFFIRMATION: Saturn offers me opportunity.

PLANETS: Saturn and Saturn

KEYWORDS: Stylish, intellectual, amiable

11 JANUARY

Ambitious, enterprising, responsible – these are all characteristics of people born on 11 January. They handle power with ease and their original business ideas, especially in the electrical or aeronautical fields, can bring them both fame and fortune. They like their lives to feel structured and can be perfectionists, but the calming aura they exude makes them wonderful friends and companions. If you were born on this day your romantic and sensual nature is highly charged and you are never short of dates. Before you settle down you need a partner that shows you respect and allows you to be just a little controlling. Plenty of fresh air can help to keep you feeling fit and relaxed.

AFFIRMATION: Uranus helps me accomplish great things.

PLANETS: Uranus and Saturn

KEYWORDS: Resourceful, romantic, talented

12 JANUARY

Natives of 12 January are charming and slightly intriguing. They have an air of mystery surrounding them. People born on this day tend to be adventurous, always looking for the next new and exciting thing to do. They are very partnership oriented and love to do everything as part of a pair, even the most simple of activities. If this is your birth date you love good company and entertaining, and with your amazing sense of humour you make a brilliant host. Working in films, theatre or in television can help you live out some of your fantasies, but before you can be truly successful you need to fully recognize your talents. Learning to play a musical instrument can open the door to a more fulfilling existence.

AFFIRMATION: Neptune can help me realize my dreams.

PLANETS: Neptune and Saturn

KEYWORDS: Imaginative, beguiling, committed

13 JANUARY

If you were born on 13 January then you are eager to meet life's challenges, even if it means upheaval. You are extremely driven and always ready for change, so tend to deal with any problems without delay. Although you may slip up on the way, you are able to laugh at your own mistakes and can see the funny side to most situations. You are hard-working and enterprising and have extremely good managerial skills. Partnerships are very important and you may choose to marry young. You will be an excellent parent because you are able to use your own life experiences to guide your offspring in the right directions. Meditation can help you stay focused long enough to bring your goals to fruition.

AFFIRMATION: The Moon can help me learn self respect.

PLANETS: Moon and Saturn

KEYWORDS: Adaptable, daring, inspirational

14 JANUARY

People born on 14 January stand out from the crowd, but they need to be careful not to intimidate others with their strong personalities. They are ambitious and only really happy when they are juggling a variety of responsibilities. Rather than delegate, they like to do a job themselves, and for that reason can sometimes appear as if they are pushing people away. If this is your birthday you need your own space and do not thrive in conventional relationships. If you do choose to settle in a long-term partnership you will make a wonderful parent as you can give your children a sense of adventure. If you can learn to lower your expectations a little you will learn to appreciate the simple things in life.

AFFIRMATION: The Sun keeps my feet on the ground.

PLANETS: Sun and Saturn

KEYWORDS: Tenacious, disciplined, prudent

15 JANUARY

Although extremely creative, the person born on this day is also very practical – a rare combination. With many hobbies and interests, it is sometimes hard for them to work out exactly where to channel their talents and for that reason they may try several jobs before finding the right one. If you were born on this day you enjoy the good things in life and never lose sight of your goals. Although you tend to be a loner at heart, you have a certain magnetism that draws people to you. You will only give your heart once, so you expect a lot from a relationship, but with your sensitive nature your partner will not go short of romantic gestures. Painting or writing can help you find happiness and leave something by which you can be remembered.

AFFIRMATION: Mercury can teach me patience.

PLANETS: Mercury and Saturn

KEYWORDS: Tasteful, charismatic, sensual

16 JANUARY

If you still enjoy reading comics or watching the occasional cartoon, then the chances are you were born on this day. Not wanting to grow old, people born on 16 January tend to use fantasy to escape reality and they never lose the ability to play. Although they are ambitious it is not an overpowering trait, for the entertainer in them keeps them drifting between work and play. They thrive in the entertainment business but they do not handle mundanity well. If you were born on this day your inner energy makes you irresistible to others. You tend to go for partners who have a similar sense of fun and adventure but can stay in tune with your spiritual side. You shy away from serious responsibility as you are scared of losing your freedom and individuality.

CAPRICORN 22 DECEMBER–20 JANUARY

AFFIRMATION: Venus helps make me more determined to succeed in love.

PLANETS: Venus and Saturn

KEYWORDS: Youthful, exuberant, entertaining

17 JANUARY

The person born on 17 January may have the sense that a guardian angel is guiding them through life. They love nothing better than to sit down and read a good mystery because they love problem-solving. If you are in a relationship with a 17 January native, you can be certain that life will not be boring, but they can sometimes be a little too demanding of their partners. They are ambitious and goal-oriented and, with Pluto behind them, you can be sure they will make a success of whatever they do. If this is your birth date, you love to learn and are constantly seeking ways of broadening your mind, using your intuition as a guide. You like to stay in peak condition and tend to watch your diet carefully. A weekend away can help relieve stress.

AFFIRMATION: Pluto teaches me to be socially responsible.

PLANETS: Pluto and Saturn

KEYWORDS: Intuitive, inquisitive, goal-oriented

18 JANUARY

The aim of people born on this day is to achieve and, once they have reached one goal, they search for the next one. They are appealing and charismatic which means they can charm almost anyone – friends and colleagues alike – but they need to be careful not to use this gift in a manipulative way. If you are an 18 January native, you are forthright and totally honest with loved ones, but constantly craving excitement can make you wary of commitment. Your love of the high life can lead to financial problems. It is important for you to find balance in your professional and your personal life in order to feel fulfilled.

AFFIRMATION: Jupiter helps me conduct myself with integrity.

PLANETS: Jupiter and Saturn

KEYWORDS: Ambitious, fascinating, sociable

19 JANUARY

People born on this day have powerful emotions and a wonderful sense of humour. Once they have their minds set on a goal it is hard to steer them from their chosen path because success is very important to them. Once they have learned to let down their guard, they are kind and protective and make good partners. If this is your birth date, you like to listen to the advice of close friends and colleagues and are always there to return the favour. You have a talent for numbers so banking or accountancy positions are good options for you. Try to remember that regular exercise can help stave off any negative feelings about yourself and that good friends are always there to help boost you.

AFFIRMATION: Saturn has the power to guide me to the top of my chosen field.

PLANETS: Saturn and Saturn

KEYWORDS: Demonstrative, receptive, challenging

20 JANUARY

If you were born on this day you have boundless physical energy and would make the perfect trainer or sports coach. Your appearance is important to you and with your creative flair you are quickly able to adapt an outfit for any occasion. You are reliable, broad-minded and intuitive which makes you a perfect role model, although you do have a tendency to be rather strict with your own children. You may find it hard to give up your freedom and consequently settle down later in life, because your curiosity keeps you searching for adventure. Like your Capricorn neighbours, you have a determination to succeed, but it is important for you to learn from any mistakes you make on the way. Swimming is a good way for you to unwind.

AFFIRMATION: Venus helps me share my love.

PLANETS: Venus and Saturn

KEYWORDS: Determined, questioning, active

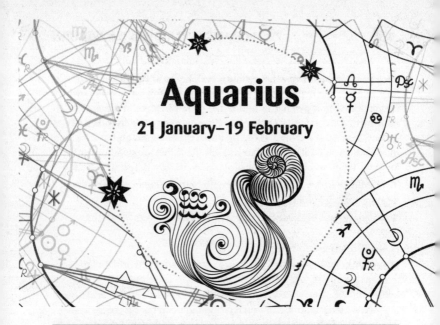

Aquarius
21 January–19 February

21 JANUARY

People born on 21 January are bright, intuitive and have an innate ability to understand unconventional ideas and concepts. If you were born on this day you will not jump into anything with both feet: careful consideration is always required before you make your final decision. You are appreciated for your fairness and friends feel happy that they can count on you for an objective opinion. You are charming and talented and a little moody, but your ability to laugh at your own mistakes makes up for the temperamental side of your character. Your fun-loving and generous nature makes you an ideal partner, but you need small and regular goals to aim for or you'll lose your motivation.

AFFIRMATION: Mercury in Aquarius can help me to be receptive to new ideas.

PLANETS: Mercury and Uranus

KEYWORDS: Inventive, humorous, open-minded

22 JANUARY

Aquarians born on 22 January need freedom. They value their independence highly and this can keep them from forming ties that feel limiting in any way. They are highly intelligent, but others don't always understand their more advanced ideas, so they need to find a way to communicate them in an accessible way. They require a demanding job with plenty of challenges because they are easily bored and quickly distracted. If you were born on this day you are drawn to glamorous partners and this doesn't always reap the necessary rewards. You need to look beyond the outer packaging in order to find fulfilment. You make a loyal friend and companion, but time spent alone with your own thoughts can be beneficial.

AFFIRMATION: The Moon in my sign can help me connect with others.

PLANETS: Moon and Uranus

KEYWORDS: Independent, talented, thoughtful

23 JANUARY

Anyone born on this date is determined to make the world a better place. They are strong individuals who like to take control of all aspects of their lives. They have excellent organizational skills, but sometimes people have difficulty in understanding their complex systems. If this is your birth date you are inclined to be hard-headed and realistic – the strong and silent type. You are resilient, tough and appear to be able to cope with anything life throws at you, but underneath that outer shell is a softer, more vulnerable individual who makes a gentle, caring lover. It is important that you don't try to be something you are not. Allow your true character to come to the fore.

AFFIRMATION: The Sun can help me accept changes and achieve personal stability.

PLANETS: Sun and Uranus

KEYWORDS: Humanitarian, organized, resilient

24 JANUARY

These multi-talented people avoid routine because they need constant stimulation in their day-to-day lives. They can appear sophisticated and even aloof but this is just a protective barrier to keep others at a distance. Beneath the surface they have a genuine love for others and will open up to the right soulmate. If you are a 24 January native, friends may not come easily because your competitive streak can blind you to social possibilities, but once a friendship is formed you are dependable and true. You tend to feel like you need validation from others in order to believe in yourself but sometimes this is just not forthcoming. Learn to accept this and believe in yourself regardless of the opinions of others.

AFFIRMATION: Mercury can help me see another person's point of view.

PLANETS: Mercury and Uranus

KEYWORDS: Dependable, active, ambitious

25 JANUARY

Although others find them a little mysterious, people born on this day have an amazing insight into the characters of others. They tend to go through life feeling a little misunderstood and form a protective barrier around themselves. If this is your birth date you feel more comfortable in a large crowd than when spending time alone with your partner. However, if you can find someone who can match your intellect and intuition, sparks will begin to fly and romantic (and creative) liaisons will be powerful. You are magnetic, charming and have a profound sense of your own destiny, but do not suffer fools gladly. Meditation or Pilates can help to ground you.

AFFIRMATION: Venus will help me find the freedom I crave.

PLANETS: Venus and Uranus

KEYWORDS: Knowledgeable, passionate, reserved

26 JANUARY

People born on this day tend to have strong philosophical leanings and love to learn. They are always willing to share their knowledge with others and are never happier than when guiding the conversation in a direction of their choosing. They are often drawn to professions that allow them to exert authority, so you may find them on the board of directors of a firm or organization. If this is your birth date your strength of character gives you a unique persona that others admire and your innate financial and people skills make success in business likely. You believe that age has nothing to do with romantic happiness and so may well choose a partner who is either much older or younger than yourself.

AFFIRMATION: Pluto can bring about dramatic change in me.

PLANETS: Pluto and Uranus

KEYWORDS: Progressive, communicative, alluring

27 JANUARY

With their magnetic personalities and astute minds, people born on this day make wonderful teachers. They have analytical brains and are creative in a variety of ways. They are great at motivating and encouraging people to push themselves to get results, but like other Aquarians they don't accept restrictions easily. If this is your birthday you have a wide circle of friends and tend to suffer from wanderlust when it comes to personal relationships. Although your heart remains true, your spirit is always looking for excitement. You can be eccentric and unconventional, and are often extremely difficult to tie down but, for a patient partner, the effort will be rewarded.

AFFIRMATION: Jupiter is larger than life, optimistic, loves adventure and risk.

PLANETS: Jupiter and Uranus

KEYWORDS: Gracious, intelligent, dramatic

28 JANUARY

With a strong competitive spirit and more than a modicum of perfectionism, the person born on this day can sometimes overtax themselves. Their powerful character can have a negative effect on personal relationships, but if their partner is willing to accept, and learn to work with their flair for the dramatic, they will find a loving and lasting union. If you were born on this day you have an analytical mind and a love of mathematics, science and music. You may find a rewarding career in any of these fields. Remember that exercise is important to keep the body and mind in balance. An aerobics class sees you discovering a side of yourself that you didn't know existed.

AFFIRMATION: Saturn encourages openness and fairness in all things.

PLANETS: Saturn and Uranus

KEYWORDS: Strong-willed, analytical, emotional

29 JANUARY

People born on this day are extremely likeable. They have a youthful quality that stays with them throughout their lives and their gentle, caring nature draws plenty of people into their company. They have a brilliant mind and a love of a good debate, and this leads to lots of stimulating conversation. If this is your birthday you are a true crusader who will lay your reputation on the line if you feel it might bring about a necessary change. You might choose to launch a political career in order to help make the world a better place. You tend to shy away from romance because you feel it represents loss of independence, but if you are prepared to let go, you are capable of finding a profound, spiritual love.

AFFIRMATION: Uranus allows time for discovery and exploration.

PLANETS: Uranus and Uranus

KEYWORDS: Caring, idealistic, revolutionary

30 JANUARY

Aquarians born on 30 January are capable of practically anything they set their mind to. The hardest part is finding something worthwhile to focus on, as they need a mammoth project to reap any satisfaction. They absolutely hate to feel caged in, so anyone embarking on a relationship with a 30 January native needs to be aware they have to allow them a lot of freedom. If this is your birthday you have an extremely intelligent and astute mind, which makes it difficult for you to turn off; this can, in the long run, lead to health problems. Finding ways to relax and refocus is very important and time spent on your own, whether walking, reading or resting, is essential to your well-being.

AFFIRMATION: Mercury helps me take great mental leaps forward.

PLANETS: Mercury and Uranus

KEYWORDS: Clever, thoughtful, generous

31 JANUARY

If you are born on this date, your charm and charisma will have you constantly surrounded by fans. You were literally born to be a lover and have an uncanny knack for bringing out the best in your partners. You seem to attract friends like flies and will form many close friendships throughout your life. You are a well-organized, hard-working and robust person who likes to lead a healthy lifestyle. You are aware of keeping your body in harmony with your spiritual side and often use meditation to relax. You have a brilliant mind but this can be overshadowed by foolish choices so you need to learn to think carefully before you act.

AFFIRMATION: The Moon in Aquarius makes me sympathetic without being sentimental.

PLANETS: Moon and Uranus

KEYWORDS: Passionate, spiritual, magnetic

1 FEBRUARY

Natives of 1 February typically surround themselves with many friends, but do not allow many of them to get close. They treat lovers in the same way and usually try to keep them at a distance. If you were born on this day you are strong-minded and can be quite stubborn when putting over your points of view. You can be a little impulsive, starting lots of new hobbies and projects but very rarely seeing them through to the end. You are never short of new ideas, so if you can keep your focus on one specific area, you can be extremely creative. There is an inquisitive side to your nature which tends to attract danger.

AFFIRMATION: Mars makes me proud of my independence.

PLANETS: Mars and Uranus

KEYWORDS: Confident, inquisitive, friendly

2 FEBRUARY

People born on 2 February are driven equally by career and relationships. If you were born on this day you are a genuine achiever who has strong willpower as well as a powerful intuition. Your spirit is there for all to see and your strong character makes people stand up and take notice. You have a modern outlook on life and a youthful attitude that never fades. Like most Aquarians, you have a tendency to hold back a little bit of yourself which can make lovers a little wary of commitment. You don't like to be accountable to anyone and will do anything to retain your individualism. Try opening up to your friends or your partner over a convivial dinner.

AFFIRMATION: Venus helps promote harmony.

PLANETS: Venus and Uranus

KEYWORDS: Motivated, youthful, individual

3 FEBRUARY

Never ones to sing their own praises, Aquarians born on 3 February are talented and modest. They believe that hard work pays off and embrace their chosen careers wholeheartedly. They thrive in the worlds of journalism or advertising, as they love communicating with people from all walks of life. If you were born on this day you do not play emotional games; once you are interested in someone you make your intentions clear. You are a humanitarian and are always happy to contribute to causes you believe in, but you need to be careful not to take on more than you can handle. Helping with local charitable events can help to satisfy the benevolent side of your nature without pushing you too hard.

AFFIRMATION: Mercury leans towards communication and learning.

PLANETS: Mercury and Uranus

KEYWORDS: Altruistic, enterprising, communicative

4 FEBRUARY

This is one of the most hard-working and productive of Aquarian birthdays. The people born on this day are full of sound advice and their ability to prioritize and organize are second to none. They are inspired by what can be achieved by hard work and rarely ask for help. They enjoy the sense of power in keeping themselves fit, so they tend to have a regimented workout schedule. If you are a 4 February native, you thrive on strong friendships – although you tend to connect more on an intellectual than emotional level which makes you less successful in romantic relationships. Humanitarian and social issues are very important to you, but you need to learn that it is not always possible to make your dreams come true.

AFFIRMATION: The Moon has access to the mysteries of the universe.

PLANETS: Moon and Uranus

KEYWORDS: Organized, robust, giving

5 FEBRUARY

People born on 5 February tend to go about their lives with a far-away look in their eyes, but these inspiring individuals are probably just wondering which brilliant project to embark upon next. Their minds have a tendency to wander and for this reason people born on this date make great pioneers in the fields of science and technology. If you are born on this day you like to follow your own instincts and are frequently inspired to make changes in your life. You regard personal relationships as sacrosanct but can struggle with the decision to make a total commitment because you fear getting hurt. A venture into the arts may help you to explore possibilities unavailable to you in your day-to-day life.

AFFIRMATION: The Sun has the ability to heal inner wounds.

PLANETS: Sun and Uranus

KEYWORDS: Artistic, innovative, emotional

6 FEBRUARY

Those born on this day possess a strong sense of personal integrity.
They are often called upon to act as mediators in disputes and have the
potential to become well-known because of their powerful personas as
well as their tendency to use their abilities to embrace humanity and
help others. If this is your birthday you have a natural gift for forming
enduring friendships and when you eventually fall in love it is likely
to last forever. Although you cannot be classed as sentimental, you will
open your heart to the right partner. You possess plenty of common
sense but tend to have very high ideals and so may find it difficult to
live up to your own expectations.

AFFIRMATION: Mercury allows me to break a few rules.

PLANETS: Mercury and Uranus

KEYWORDS: Dependable, peace-loving, businesslike

7 FEBRUARY

The Aquarian born on 7 February is a true people person, but likes
to balance this with time on their own. They can be obstinate which
makes it difficult to push them into doing anything they don't want to
do. They love to travel and learn about foreign cultures and are always
searching for new experiences to provide answers to their questions.
If you were born on this day you have a secretive side which you are
unwilling to share with anyone other than those closest to you. You are
often slow to commit to love but once you do it is usually a powerful
and binding relationship. You will only take a career path that you
consider to be valuable to humanity, and you tend to take a rather
relaxed attitude towards finance.

AFFIRMATION: Venus is freethinking and gives me my own style.

PLANETS: Venus and Uranus

KEYWORDS: Adventurous, sociable, loyal

8 FEBRUARY

There is nothing modest about the person born on 8 February. They
thrive on hard work and take a dim view of anyone they consider
not to be pulling their weight. They have the drive and spirit to be
successful and their confident attitude instils enthusiasm in people
that they deal with on a day-to-day basis. Friendships are important to
these individuals, but they need to trust a friend implicitly before they

will embark on any long-term emotional relationship. If you were born on this day, you are a creature of extremes, so you need to be cautious when it comes to your health. You often struggle to find the right career that can offer you the freedom you yearn, so you need to learn to be a little more realistic in your dreams.

AFFIRMATION: Pluto helps steady an erratic nature.

PLANETS: Pluto and Uranus

KEYWORDS: Nonconformist, confident, imaginative

9 FEBRUARY

Those born on 9 February could be described as intense and may suffer from nerves if their energy is not channelled in the right direction. They tend to be extremely creative, so they are likely to pursue a career in the arts in order to truly fulfil their passions. If you were born on this day you are a very caring individual but you may choose not to show it because you find it difficult to trust others. If you can overcome a few of your inhibitions you will reap the rewards in the form of a loving and lasting relationship. Taking time out in wild open spaces will help to release some of the pressures of daily life.

AFFIRMATION: Jupiter encourages optimism and adventure.

LANETS: Jupiter and Uranus

KEYWORDS: Impassioned, free-spirited, creative

10 FEBRUARY

The life and soul of the party, 10 February people are very popular and make extremely good friends because they are full of boundless social energy. They do have an independent streak but they also value personal relationships and will take a long time to get to know someone. Generous with their time as well as their cash, they are able to see beyond their own concerns, and find it easy to put themselves in other people's shoes. If you were born on this day you are passionate about everything you do and believe wholeheartedly in your ability to achieve greatness. You sometimes struggle to make time for yourself, but need to remember that time spent alone is very valuable.

AFFIRMATION: Saturn is out to teach me mastery over my life.

PLANETS: Saturn and Uranus

KEYWORDS: Energetic, romantic, generous

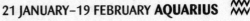

11 FEBRUARY

Very little can stop the 11 February native from achieving their dreams. They are robust, successful and possess a tremendous appeal that has the power to inspire and influence others. They are often tempted to take risks and will turn unexpected corners in order to better themselves. If this is your birthday, you are creatively strong and may well pursue a career in fashion in order to leave your mark. You have a sunny disposition and often enjoy a colourful and varied love life. People born on this date are some of the most goal-oriented of all Aquarians and once they have reached one goal target, they will set themselves even tougher ones. Sometimes they need to learn to be able to walk away from a challenge.

AFFIRMATION: The powerful influence of Uranus means I am ahead of my time.

PLANETS: Uranus and Uranus

KEYWORDS: Ambitious, fashionable, cheerful

12 FEBRUARY

People born on 12 February are usually strong-minded, but need to bear in mind that words can have a powerful effect on others. Success is important to them and with diligence they usually achieve what they set out to do. Impatience is the negative side to this character, but this usually improves with age. If you were born on this day, your charismatic nature draws others to you but you find it very hard to make close friends. Career choices are difficult for 12 February people as they tend to be driven by their spiritual needs. Keeping fit is very important to them and they enjoy an active lifestyle. These people need to learn to balance the positive and negative aspects of their personality.

AFFIRMATION: Illusion, fantasy and dreams are the strengths of Neptune.

PLANETS: Neptune and Uranus

KEYWORDS: Inventive, determined, fascinating

13 FEBRUARY

If you were born on this day you are a go-getter. Overcoming difficulties is something you thrive on and this makes you determined, hard-working and extremely energetic. Although you appreciate what you have, you worry that it might be gone tomorrow, so tend to go through life with a feeling of nervous apprehension. You love to party, spending time with people you like, but you sometimes enjoy the single life a little too much and shy away from commitment. As long as you find your job stimulating, you work with determination and focus. Be careful not to fall victim to addictions in order to help you keep up with your active lifestyle.

AFFIRMATION: The Moon helps to reveal the part of me that is kept hidden.

PLANETS: Moon and Uranus

KEYWORDS: Fun-loving, tireless, diligent

14 FEBRUARY

A natural-born entrepreneur, the person born on 14 February seems to have an unlimited supply of new ideas. These individuals refuse to grow old and stay spirited and playful into old age. They have acquired the gift of the gab and can talk their way into, and out of, most situations. Friendships come easily to them and they have a tendency to fall passionately in love. If you were born on this day you are prone to worry and it is easy for you to use stress to your advantage as it becomes a driving force to meet deadlines. You prefer to go for careers that aren't too demanding, but creating something new is important to you. You are forever optimistic and will constantly strive to fulfil your dreams.

AFFIRMATION: The Sun sheds light on inner traits.

PLANETS: Sun and Uranus

KEYWORDS: Hopeful, animated, resourceful

15 FEBRUARY

Full of personal magnetism, people born on this day have a singular view of the world and love to share this with others. They are able to accept people at face value and therefore have a natural flair for forming close friendships. They let go of all their inhibitions when they fall in love, but partners need to be aware they can have a sarcastic side to their nature. As parents they have the ability to bring out the best in their children's imaginations. If this is your birthday you are clever with words and may well choose a career that involves writing.

However, you are renowned for leaving projects incomplete, so you need a driving force to keep you motivated. Learn to use your skills to your full potential and not rely on loved ones to do all the pushing.

AFFIRMATION: Mercury inspires ideas.

PLANETS: Mercury and Uranus

KEYWORDS: Captivating, generous, artistic

16 FEBRUARY

Easy-going and popular, people born on 16 February are very generous, especially when giving their time to others. When inspired, these individuals work very hard, but they have to be careful that their perfectionism doesn't spoil their experience. They are able to win someone's respect and affection with ease and do not make emotional demands on romantic partners. They allow the relationship to run freely and do not show jealousy or allow petty arguments to get in the way. If you are a 16 February native, you have a laid-back nature until it comes to sports and then your competitive streak comes to the fore. You are committed to getting the most out of life but your true beauty lies in the fact that you don't forget your friends on the way.

AFFIRMATION: Venus represents the qualities of love, romance and sensuality.

PLANETS: Venus and Uranus

KEYWORDS: Amenable, unflappable, caring

17 FEBRUARY

If you want someone with stamina and staying power then look no further than a 17 February person. Their professional life is very important to them but they need to take care that their ambition does not get in the way of their personal relationships. If you were born on this day, you have a cool and collected approach to the world, but your lack of openness sometimes leaves you feeling alone and unloved. You always keep your emotions in check because you are worried about the intensity of your feelings. If you can learn to let go of these inhibitions you have a lot to offer; showing the compassionate side of your nature just doesn't come easily to you.

AFFIRMATION: Pluto will help me to let go of unwanted memories.

PLANETS: Pluto and Uranus

KEYWORDS: Intense, self-possessed, tenacious

18 FEBRUARY

Dedicated to the pursuit of perfection, Aquarians born on 18 February are no strangers to hard work and perseverence. They have a true appreciation of both beauty and harmony and will search unreservedly for the ultimate soulmate. If you were born on this day, your generosity means you are popular as long as your acquaintances don't mind the occasional criticism. You tend to be quiet and introspective and enjoy your own company. You do not rush quickly into career decisions and often know from a very young age exactly what you want to do. You need to learn not to be so tough on yourself and perhaps let a few more people into your inner circle.

AFFIRMATION: The Moon can help me to get through hardships.

PLANETS: Moon and Uranus

KEYWORDS: Diligent, generous, focused

19 FEBRUARY

People born on this date have a thirst for knowledge and frequently set high standards for themselves. They are very independent and time on their own is important if they want to run at full capacity. Although at times they can appear moody, they have enough personal charisma to overcome this trait but, as they are always seeking love and approval, their personal lives can be turbulent. If you are a 19 February native, you may well choose a career in the arts because you enjoy exchanging ideas. If you can overcome your insecurities you can become a sensitive and imaginative lover with a lot to offer your partner. An evening course in a new language will give you confidence and indulge your love of learning.

AFFIRMATION: Saturn reminds me how important it is that I mature and grow.

PLANETS: Saturn and Uranus

KEYWORDS: Enquiring, independent, imaginative

Pisces
20 February–20 March

20 FEBRUARY

Those born on 20 February work hard to be taken seriously and for that reason can be seen as overly forceful or even aggressive in nature. They are competitive and need to try not to trample on other people in their attempts to win, but they do have a well-developed softer side. They are very artistic and, with their vivid imaginations, are suited to the art and design sectors. If this is your birthday you need to learn to balance your outwardly assertive character with your inner vulnerabilities so as not to lurch from one extreme to the other. Make the most of Venus's influence in your chart and use it to find balance and, ultimately, love. Meditative exercise such as yoga can help you to achieve this equilibrium.

AFFIRMATION: The magnetism of Venus can bring out the strengths in my character.

PLANETS: Venus and Neptune

KEYWORDS: Perceptive, creative, unforgettable

21 FEBRUARY

People born on this day are very popular and can be an inspiration to others – both at work and in social circles. Those close to them know they can rely on the 21 February native for help and advice, as they embrace responsibility wholeheartedly. If you were born on this day, you are fun-loving with a bright and intuitive mind. You like to be in the limelight and will be the one still talking at the end of a party when others are flagging. One of your greatest assets is your fine sense of humour, but on the flip side you can be moody and frequently experience restlessness on an emotional level. It is essential you are on the same wavelength as your partner to bring out your full potential.

AFFIRMATION: Mercury helps me to love myself and others.

PLANETS: Mercury and Neptune

KEYWORDS: Loving, energetic, humorous

22 FEBRUARY

People born on 22 February stand out from a crowd and yet can still be sensitive and concerned about the welfare of others. Sometimes too emotional, they can be swept along by what other people are thinking and feeling, but this caring side is an asset to those who choose counselling as a career. If you were born on this day you love to share new ideas with others and can be very persuasive in your attempts to communicate concepts. You make a great parent as you are totally in tune with your family's needs. Water has an enormous influence, so living close to the sea has a profound and calming effect on you. If this is not possible, a water feature in the garden can be extremely beneficial.

AFFIRMATION: Neptune helps to turn dreams into reality.

PLANETS: Sun and Neptune

KEYWORDS: Intriguing, compassionate, sensitive

23 FEBRUARY

Once you have found your true path in life, you will show considerable determination and passion. Your love of variety, however, can mean that you will quickly become bored, so interests outside of the workplace are very important. With a very playful and lively nature, you will have many followers as you can bring out the best in others. You do exceptionally well in the entertainment world, but need applause and compliments to attain your goals. Idealistic in relationships, you need to avoid the trap of expecting too much from your partner. Exercise in the fresh air can help you de-stress.

AFFIRMATION: The Sun brings out my individuality.

PLANETS: Sun and Neptune

KEYWORDS: Focused, loving, talented

24 FEBRUARY

A person born on 24 February has charm and dynamism that sets them apart from their fellow Pisceans. Although they have good business sense it can take them a long time to choose the right career, but with their people-skills a position in the medical profession could be fulfilling. If this is your birth date you will collect friends from all backgrounds, as an interesting social life is very important to you. You can be extremely romantic, but occasionally fall in love rather too rapidly. A vivid imagination and a tendency to fantasize may leave you struggling to focus, so this needs to be balanced against your spiritual requirements with regular walks in the open air.

AFFIRMATION: Neptune allows me to translate my dreams into reality.

PLANETS: Mercury and Neptune

KEYWORDS: Imaginative, emotional, magnetic

25 FEBRUARY

Natives of 25 February are considered deep thinkers and may appear to be in a world of their own. They respect honesty, loyalty and diplomacy and, with the right partner, can have a fulfilling relationship which becomes an integral part of their life. If this is your birth date, you prefer a small number of acquaintances to large social gatherings and are at your most powerful when you set your mind to helping others. You have a tendency to be drawn towards the supernatural due to an amazing psychic sensitivity, which means you sometimes find it hard to balance your physical and spiritual sides. Experimenting with some different foods can help to satisfy some of your more exotic tastes.

AFFIRMATION: Neptune emphasizes my natural psychic and mystic capacities.

PLANETS: Venus and Neptune

KEYWORDS: Open-minded, mystical, intuitive

26 FEBRUARY

If you were born on this date you have an exceptionally romantic nature, but sometimes this intensity of emotion can get you into deep waters. Time on your own is very important as you need the room to sort out your feelings without outside intervention. You are intuitive and are quick to size up a person you have only just met. Although prone to day-dreaming, 26 February people work hard to achieve goals, even to the extent of letting their personal lives take a back seat for a while. Partners of people born on this day should be prepared for a roller coaster ride, although their relationship could never be called boring. A night at the opera can help relieve many day-to-day pressures.

AFFIRMATION: Pluto allows me to break down my psychological walls.

PLANETS: Pluto and Neptune

KEYWORDS: Energetic, perceptive, supportive

27 FEBRUARY

People born on 27 February are full of compassion and love giving to others. Like their neighbours from 26 February, these people need 'alone time' to recharge their batteries. They have a mysterious charm that draws others to them like moths to a flame, but they can be moody, which can have a negative effect on anyone who is in their company at the time. They are very protective of those they love and tend to be a little controlling which can lead to disappointments. If this is your birth date, finding a happy medium can take a while to master, but with your analytical mind, you usually find your soulmate after some searching. Being involved with a charitable organization can be rewarding.

AFFIRMATION: Jupiter brings out my sense of adventure.

PLANETS: Jupiter and Neptune

KEYWORDS: Intelligent, caring, giving

28 FEBRUARY

People born on 28 February have an amazing zest for life but they need to be careful not to get carried away. They are always hungry for knowledge and have an independent streak that can sometimes get in the way of a fulfilling relationship. They tend to dream on a rather grand scale, which can lead them towards more romantic vocations such as film or theatre, hopefully rewarding them with the fast-paced lifestyle they thrive on. If this is your birthday, you are exceptionally loyal and will always stand by your friend, even through the darkest of times. Harmonious surroundings are important as you can quickly become negative if you do not like where you live. Decorating your home allows you to create your ideal environment.

AFFIRMATION: I accept Saturn's gifts with gratitude.

PLANETS: Saturn and Neptune

KEYWORDS: Talented, loving, loyal

29 FEBRUARY

Because 29 February is such a unique day in our calendar, it is only natural that the person born on this day should have quite distinct talents and personality. People born on 29 February remain young at heart, are good-natured and always appear optimistic. Although they can appear emotionally reserved, underneath their cool exterior they are warm and caring people who know when to combine sensitivity with a sense of responsibility. If this is your birth date you have strong views on political matters, and would be the ideal campaign aide. You like to see the positive side of any problem and, although you could never be called naive, you still retain a certain child-like quality. You love to be part of a team so any kind of sport will give you the camaraderie you seek.

AFFIRMATION: Uranus gives me my individualism.

PLANETS: Uranus and Neptune

KEYWORDS: Optimistic, enthusiastic, animated

1 MARCH

Natives of 1 March are very good at picking themselves up and dusting themselves off after a fall, even if it means making life-altering decisions. They want to change the world, but should try to err on the cautious side rather than jumping in with both feet. If this is your birthday you are very persuasive, but you are also able to show an enormous amount of compassion when necessary. Your friends are a vital part of your life, as you not only require emotional support, but also feel a need to give the same in return. You take parenthood seriously, often blaming yourself when your children stray from the straight and narrow. Guilt is not a constructive emotion, you need to learn to forgive yourself and move on.

AFFIRMATION: Mars offers stamina and survival in difficult times.

PLANETS: Mars and Neptune

KEYWORDS: Pioneering, ambitious, resilient

2 MARCH

People born on 2 March are full of love and compassion and they are always looking for new ways to express this. Anyone who is lucky enough to have won the heart of a 2 March native will feel safe and nurtured at all times. If this is your birthday you lack self-confidence and need a boost from friends and loved ones from time to time in order to allow your creativity to flourish. You thrive away from the hustle and bustle of city life and enjoy outdoor pursuits such as gardening and rambling in the countryside. A career as a chef in a rural restaurant would allow you to fulfil many of your creative aspirations. Cooking a meal for a loved one brings out the very best in you.

AFFIRMATION: Venus influences my decisions.

PLANETS: Venus and Neptune

KEYWORDS: Creative, affectionate, kind-hearted

3 MARCH

The key word for anyone born on this day is 'determined', as they know exactly what they want and they strive to attain it. They do not concern themselves with monetary gain, but rather the challenges that are involved in achieving their goals. They are amusing, have a great sense of humour and a delightful way with words, making them great companions whatever the occasion. If you were born on this day you sometimes have problems getting to grips with a loving relationship, because you can quickly feel stifled and yearn to break free. When you do find a meaningful relationship you tend to rely on your partner for emotional support, but you give back in abundance.

AFFIRMATION: Mercury enhances gentle communication.

PLANETS: Mercury and Neptune

KEYWORDS: Down-to-earth, versatile, intriguing

4 MARCH

The Piscean born on 4 March chooses to spend much of their time alone, not because they don't like being around other people, but because they want to fulfil their creative goals and others tend to get in the way. Painting and photography appeal to 4 March natives and their pictures can be really powerful. If you were born on this day, you are generally orderly and organized and find it difficult to live among clutter. You suffer from an excess of nervous energy and are rarely comfortable in a job where your creativity is suppressed. You are attracted to people who share your spontaneity and artistic flair, but your partner needs to accept that sometimes you will want to be on your own with your art.

AFFIRMATION: The Moon gives me room to be alone with myself.

PLANETS: Moon and Neptune

KEYWORDS: Artistic, energetic, solitary

5 MARCH

People born on this day are restless and always looking for the next big adventure. Routine bores them and nine-to-five jobs tend to stifle their ability to progress. They need to choose a career that allows them the freedom to grow and learn from experience. If you were born on this day you are humorous and can talk quite confidently among a group of strangers. You are intelligent and look for a certain uniqueness in others. You need a partner who is able to share your love of travel and is impulsive enough to whisk you away for a surprise romantic break. With your love of language you would make a great journalist or travel writer, but you do tend to suffer from a lack of confidence when it comes to financial affairs.

AFFIRMATION: The Sun makes me receptive and open-minded.

PLANETS: Sun and Neptune

KEYWORDS: Adventurous, intellectual, communicative

6 MARCH

The saying 'hard work never hurt anyone' is one rule that the 6 March native lives by. They are dedicated, hardworking individuals and will strive tirelessly to achieve their goals. If this is your birth date you are a free spirit who, although not extremely rebellious, does not like to conform. You can't resist beauty in any form, and are drawn towards the arts where your natural musical talent is most appreciated. You have a tough time finding love, as you tend to be a perfectionist, always on the hunt for that flawless masterpiece. Accept that your soulmate may come in a less than perfect package and you won't have to look far to find someone you can be happy with forever.

AFFIRMATION: Mercury helps me search out an appreciative audience.

PLANETS: Mercury and Neptune

KEYWORDS: Curious, dedicated, perfectionist

7 MARCH

People born on 7 March could be described as mysterious. It can be hard to penetrate their tough exterior and get a glimpse of what's beneath, but those that are privileged enough to do so will find a true visionary and humanitarian who likes to feel connected to a meaningful purpose in life. With a love of elegance and beauty they often choose to work in the fashion world, but they don't embrace its glamorous party scene, preferring to lead highly private lives away from work. If you were born on this day you like to avoid conflict in any form and tend to back away from an argument before it has even begun. Exercise that involves graceful movements, such as Thai-chi, can help relieve stress.

AFFIRMATION: Venus gives me a sense of direction.

PLANETS: Venus and Neptune

KEYWORDS: Ethical, idealistic, sensitive

8 MARCH

The Piscean born on 8 March can sometimes be at odds with the status quo. They have few close friends, but those dear to them are totally devoted and find their intense nature fascinating. They can be distrusting, but if they allow their heart to rule their head they will give themselves totally to a loving relationship. If you are an 8 March native, you are a hard-working, responsible employee who is extremely ambitious and who will work steadfastly until you reach your goal. Although you will strive for perfection in all you do, you are usually fairly popular within the working environment. You need excitement and passion to satisfy the wilder side of your nature, so an adventurous holiday once in a while helps to maintain balance.

AFFIRMATION: Pluto allows me to accept radical change.

PLANETS: Pluto and Neptune

KEYWORDS: Intuitive, individual, enterprising

9 MARCH

People born on 9 March are adventurers who tend to rely on their own instincts to get them through life. Since they are not able to settle into routine easily, these people tend to be explorers or philosophers and keep their extremely active minds fed with new and exciting information. They are strong and determined but have a sensitive side to them which can work well in a relationship as long as their partner is aware of their need for freedom. They may experience a conflict between the two sides of their nature – wanting to nurture and care for the family but being torn by the desire to travel and escape routine. Long, strenuous hikes across unusual terrains could help to keep that wanderlust under control.

AFFIRMATION: Jupiter strengthens my ability to make my dreams a reality.

PLANETS: Jupiter and Neptune

KEYWORDS: Passionate, adventurous, impulsive

10 MARCH

This day is a powerful birthday and many rulers and leaders have been born on 10 March. Both charming and attractive, these people demand attention and nearly always get it. They are self-reliant and like to be in a vocation where they set the pace. If you were born on this day you will need to learn the art of perseverence, which can be particularly hard if the only praise you receive is from yourself. You are flattered by attention, but sometimes find it hard to see who your true friends are. This is reflected in your romantic relationships as well. To fully realize your potential, you need to feel what you are doing is vital to others: open up to them about your goals and you will feel galvanized.

AFFIRMATION: Saturn teaches me the art of perseverance.

PLANETS: Saturn and Neptune

KEYWORDS: Strong, charming, determined

11 MARCH

Intuition is a key quality for anyone born on this day. Emotional ups and downs can upset their natural balance, so learning to focus their energies is of paramount importance. If you were born on this day you have an artistic temperament, and need to choose your career path carefully to allow you to express this creativity. Among friends and family, make sure you allow your loving and caring side to show through. An intellectual mind is essential for anyone who wants to capture the heart of an 11 March person. They possess a deep respect for family values so make good parents. Meditation can help them retain their emotional and physical equilibrium.

AFFIRMATION: Uranus gives me the ability to be compassionate.

PLANETS: Uranus and Neptune

KEYWORDS: Intuitive, imaginative, tasteful

12 MARCH

People born on 12 March refuse to grow old and very often remain youthful in appearance and mentality. With a vivid imagination they make excellent writers and are always ones to come forward with a new idea. Full of romantic whims and dreams, they have difficulty in maintaining any kind of permanence in relationships, so they need someone that can bring them back down to earth from time to time. If you are a 12 March native, you have a magical, spiritual intelligence and you are always willing to lend a hand or lift other people's spirits with words of encouragement. It is important for you to achieve an equal balance between reality and fantasy and you often need a lot of time on your own to recharge your emotional and spiritual batteries.

AFFIRMATION: Neptune brings an enhanced state of consciousness.

PLANETS: Neptune and Neptune

KEYWORDS: Sensitive, youthful, mystical

13 MARCH

The sign for Pisces shows two fish swimming in opposite directions and this is symbolic of the Piscean nature. Those born on this day tend to be talented, yet erratic, showing a tendency to be highly-strung. They are generous to a fault and show an unusually strong awareness and compassion for the suffering of others. They are extremely independent and will work tirelessly to surround themselves with the security they desire. If this is your birth date, you tend to have your own way of working things out and will rarely take the conventional approach. You have a quiet charm which can be very alluring, but capturing your full attention is difficult. Spend some time learning not to take yourself so seriously.

AFFIRMATION: The Moon–Neptune connection brings out my calm and sensitive side.

PLANETS: Moon and Neptune

KEYWORDS: Gifted, compassionate, captivating

14 MARCH

People born on this day are receptive to all forms of energy, both good and bad, and for that reason they can differ greatly from one moment to the next. If you were born on this day you are multi-talented, ambitious and very strong-minded, but you still have the ability to give yourself freely to someone you care about. You have a sexual magnetism which can captivate, and your air of mystery makes you even more appealing. The stage has a powerful draw for you as you can become whoever you want through the art of role play. You also have the ability to create illusion through poetic verse. You need to choose carefully where you live, as you are very sensitive to your surroundings.

AFFIRMATION: The Sun allows me to pick up good vibrations from the world around me.

PLANETS: Sun and Neptune

KEYWORDS: Tenacious, gifted, mysterious

15 MARCH

Natives of 15 March are strong-minded and find it hard to accept other people's points of view. If you were born on this day you do not respond well to negativity and like to see the positive side of everything. You have a personal magnetism and inner strength and are totally sincere in your friendships. Success is achieved through hard work and mutual respect and your persuasive nature makes you a popular colleague. Your ability to laugh at yourself takes the edge off the more serious side of your personality but loved ones need to be able to accept that your mood can change from day to day. Trying a little Reiki will help to soothe your soul.

AFFIRMATION: Mercury makes me highly responsive.

PLANETS: Mercury and Neptune

KEYWORDS: Positive, persuasive, charming

16 MARCH

People born on this day are self-motivated and perceptive. They find it hard to accept things at face value and are constantly searching to understand exactly how things work. Poised and charming, these Pisceans have an ability to empathize with other people and therefore make great healers or therapists, although they may have a hard time choosing which career to follow. If you were born on this day you need to feel constantly attractive so appearance is very important to you. You are a loyal and dependable partner, but it may take you a considerable time before you make the decision to settle down. Any outdoor activity from camping to rock climbing can give you a break from normality.

AFFIRMATION: Venus teaches me to be less dependent on others.

PLANETS: Venus and Neptune

KEYWORDS: Motivated, sympathetic, dependable

17 MARCH

People born on 17 March often find themselves haunted by a feeling of restlessness, especially during their youth, but with a bit of focus and self-discipline they will keep themselves on the right path. As an adult their main priority is usually finding a loyal and loving partner and their career may go on the back burner in the process. If this is your birthday you tend to concentrate on the practical side of life but need to be careful not to ignore your spiritual side as well. Do not walk away if things become complicated or difficult, as there is a lot to learn in sticking it out and fighting for what you want. Making time for a daily physical release like swimming can be very therapeutic.

AFFIRMATION: Pluto can guide us over the hurdles of daily life and relationships.

PLANETS: Pluto and Neptune

KEYWORDS: Purposeful, romantic, receptive

18 MARCH

People born on 18 March are dependent on psychic awareness to guide their actions. Although sometimes hard to read, they relate well to people from all walks of life and make lively and interesting conversationalists. They are exceptionally intuitive and require an intellectual partner to keep the relationship on track. If you were born on this day you are not afraid to face challenges and have a constant desire for stimulation and change in your day-to-day activities. Physical activity is very important to you and unless this is controlled you can become obsessive about daily workouts at the gym. Because you are not afraid to explore unknown territories, you are likely to achieve greatness.

AFFIRMATION: Jupiter brings out the inner mystic in me.

PLANETS: Jupiter and Neptune

KEYWORDS: Sensual, fearless, pragmatic

19 MARCH

Those born on this day have a sunny disposition and a resolutely positive outlook on life. They have a quirky sense of humour, are highly creative and adept at translating their imaginings into reality, whether through art, writing or conversation. Their caring and compassionate natures endear them to others. If this is your birthday, your idealistic attitude can make you vulnerable to disappointment and this provokes feelings of protectiveness from loved ones. You are well aware of your many strengths and weaknesses and are likely to choose a career that encourages you to overcome some of your inhibitions. Destiny sees you trying something that takes you completely out of your comfort zone.

AFFIRMATION: Saturn turns sensitivity into a positive emotion.

PLANETS: Saturn and Neptune

KEYWORDS: Goal-oriented, humorous, appreciative

20 MARCH

If you think you truly know a person born on 20 March, then think again; they never really come out from behind their masks. They are extremely creative, charismatic, warm and enterprising, but the need for constant variety in their lives makes them rather unpredictable. If this is your birth date you have an innocent charm, but the insensitive side of your nature makes for stormy relationships. You love everything to do with beauty and grace so you do best in a career where creativity is involved. Easily distracted, you need to learn to focus on one task at a time and see it through to the end. Designing a garden can help satisfy your creative side if your professional life does not.

AFFIRMATION: Venus stops me being tossed about on a sea of emotion.

PLANETS: Venus and Neptune

KEYWORDS: Imaginative, resourceful, charismatic

Further Reading

The following titles are a small selection of books that are available on the subject of astrology. Many of these are classic texts and may be of interest to those who are taking their first steps in the study of astrology.

Arroyo, Stephen, *Chart Interpretation Handbook: Guidelines for Understanding the Essentials of the Birth Chart* (CRCS Publications, 1990).

Arroyo, Stephen, *Astrology, Psychology and the Four Elements* (CRCS Publications, 1984).

Clifford, Frank, *British Entertainers: The Astrological Profiles*, Third Edition (Flare, 2003).

Cunningham, Donna, *An Astrological Guide to Self-Awareness* (CRCS Publications, 1978).

Greene, Liz, *Astrology for Lovers* (Weiser, 2009).

Greene, Liz, *Relating: An Astrological Guide to Living with Others*, Revised Edition (Weiser, 2009).

Hone, Margaret, *The Modern Text-Book of Astrology*, Revised Edition (Astrology Classics, 2010).

Huber, Bruno, *Astrological Psychosynthesis: Astrology as a Pathway to Growth*, Reprinted Edition (Hopewell, 2006).

Marks, Tracy, *The Art of Chart Interpretation: A Step-by-Step Method of Analyzing, Synthesizing & Understanding the Birth Chart*, Reprinted

Edition (Ibis Press, 2008).

Martin, Clare, *Mapping the Psyche*, Volumes 1, 2 & 3 (CPA Press, 2005, 2007 and forthcoming).

Oken, Alan, *Complete Astrology: The Classic Guide to Modern Astrology*, Reprinted Edition (Hays Nicolas Limited, 2007).

Parker, Julia and Derek, *Parkers' Astrology: The Definitive Guide to Using Astrology in Every Aspect of Your Life*, Revised Version (Dorling Kindersley, 2009).

Parker, Julia and Derek, *Parkers' Encyclopedia of Astrology* (Watkins, 2009).

Quigley, Joan, *What Does Joan Say? My Seven Years as White House Astrologer to Nancy and Ronald Reagan* (Birch Lane Press, 1991).

Sasportas, Howard, *The Twelve Houses*, Reprinted Edition (Flare, 2007).

Spencer, Neil, *True as the Stars Above: Adventures in Modern Astrology* (Orion, 2001).

Tompkins, Sue, *Aspects in Astrology* (Rider, 2001).

Tompkins, Sue, *The Contemporary Astrologer's Handbook: An In-Depth Guide to Interpreting Your Horoscope* (Flare, 2007).